Samuel Boyse, William Cooke

The Pantheon

Fabulous history of the heathen gods, goddesses, heroes

Samuel Boyse, William Cooke

The Pantheon
Fabulous history of the heathen gods, goddesses, heroes

ISBN/EAN: 9783337196714

Printed in Europe, USA, Canada, Australia, Japan

Cover: Foto ©Lupo / pixelio.de

More available books at **www.hansebooks.com**

THE
PANTHEON:
OR,
FABULOUS HISTORY
OF THE
HEATHEN GODS,
GODDESSES, HEROES, &c.

Explained in a Manner entirely new;
And rendered much more useful than any hitherto published.

ADORNED WITH
FIGURES from ancient PAINTINGS, MEDALS, and GEMS,
for the USE of those who would understand HISTORY,
POETRY, PAINTING, STATUARY, COINS, MEDALS, &c.

WITH
A DISSERTATION on the THEOLOGY and MYTHOLOGY of
the HEATHENS, from the WRITINGS of MOSES, the
ÆGYPTIAN, GRÆCIAN, ROMAN, and EASTERN
HISTORIANS, PHILOSOPHERS, POETS, &c.

BY SAMUEL BOYSE, A.M.

WITH
AN APPENDIX,
Treating of their ASTROLOGY, PRODIGIES, AUGURIES,
AUSPICES, ORACLES, &c. in which the Origin of each
is pointed out; and an HISTORICAL ACCOUNT of
the Rise of ALTARS, SACRED GROVES,
PRIESTS, and TEMPLES.

BY WILLIAM COOKE, A.M.
Late Rector of Oldbury, Vicar of Enford, Chaplain to the
Earl of Suffolk, and Author of the Medallic History
of Imperial Rome, 2 vols. in 4to.

THE SEVENTH EDITION.

TO WHICH IS NOW FIRST ADDED,
A further ILLUSTRATION of the DII MAJORES of the
ROMANS, particularly adapted to the CLASSICS.

DUBLIN:
PRINTED FOR J. JONES, No. 111, GRAFTON-STREET.
M.DCC.XCII.

TO HIS GRACE

HENRY,

DUKE OF BEAUFORT.

MAY IT PLEASE YOUR GRACE,

It has been long objected to the modern method of education, that so great and valuable a part of youth is spent amidst the ruins of Idolatry; whence an early taint and corruption (hard to be got over) both in principles and morals, has sometimes ensued. Indeed the Heathen Theology is so interwoven with the writings of the ancients, and makes so large a part of classical learning especially, as to be utterly inseparable from it. He, therefore, who shall effectually divest it of the marvellous, leaving it rational and accountable, and,

at

at the same time, make the whole subservient to the cause of virtue and true religion, will be allowed to have rendered an acceptable service to mankind.

Such was the attempt of the ingenious author of this work. It must be admitted, that he has in great part succeeded. Had he lived to revise it carefully, and to prepare it for another edition, all foreign assistance had probably been needless. As it is, what seemed wanting, or the effect of inadvertency and error, I have endeavoured to supply and amend.

Having thus done what I could for this adopted offspring, it is time that I recommend it to a better and more able benefactor, whose further support may be of use towards its settlement in the world. And my acquaintance with the goodness of your GRACE's spirit on

many

DEDICATION.

many occasions, leaves me no room to doubt, that you will take this orphan also into your protection.

Indebted to your GRACE's illustrious house for all that I am, thither every grateful consideration is wont to direct my views and affections. An apprehension which then struck me, that such a performance might be particularly serviceable to your GRACE, first inclined me to listen to the overtures which were made for preparing another and more complete edition of this work; against which my little leisure, from other important avocations, had else determined me. When, therefore, I sat down to examine the contents of it, and saw evidently the general usefulness of the design, I could with-hold no longer the little assistance which I was capable of giving. Your GRACE's name will bring it to the public test. If then it shall appear in some sort to answer the intent, and be poffeffed of intrinfic worth enough to fave it, I fhall find my great and leading expectation anfwered in the fame degree; which was, that it might be improved into fomething agreeable and ufeful to your GRACE; an end, which will ever principally command the attention of

 May it pleafe your GRACE,

  Your GRACE's moft dutiful,

   And devoted humble Servant,

    WILLIAM COOKE.

THE

PREFACE.

WE have here no design to raise the reputation of this work, by depreciating the many others that have already been published on this subject; it is sufficient for us to say, that we have followed a plan entirely new, and, at the same time, such an one as appeared to us much more useful, more rational, and less dry than any that has gone before it.

As all works of this kind must necessarily consist of materials collected from other authors, no expence, no labour has been spared; the most celebrated works on this subject have been consulted and compared with each other, and it has frequently happened, that scattered hints, widely dispersed, have served to clear up the most difficult and intricate meanings, to a degree of demonstration; but amongst all the authors to which we have had recourse, we must here particularly acknowledge the great advantage we have received from that ingenious gentleman, the Abbe Pluche, in his history of the heavens.

But

But as that learned and valuable writer seems now and then to have carried matters a little too far, the reader will find less use made of him than in the first edition. We have been careful to allow all things to evidence and reason; but as little as might be to conjecture. We have also received some useful hints from the Abbe Banier's mythology. But it behoves us especially, to acknowledge the great service which we have received from the writings of the learned Bochart, Pignorius, Casalius, Kircher, Lipsius, Montfaucon, and others, who have professed to treat of the Phœnician, Egyptian, Greek, a Roman antiquities.

Some acquaintance with the heathen gods and the ancient fables, is a necessary branch of polite learning, as without this it is impossible to obtain a competent knowledge of the Classics; impossible to form a judgment of antique medals, statues, or paintings; or even to understand the performances of the moderns in these polite arts.

Hence these studies have been generally esteemed necessary for the improvement of youth; but in works of this kind, sufficient care has not been taken to unfold the origin of the heathen gods, which has generally been mistaken. Some imagining that they had been kings and princes; others, that they were the various parts of nature; and others, that they were the patriarchs and heroes of the Jewish nation. But each of these have been found equally contrary to truth, when applied to the pagan theology, though some of their fables have been embellished with many circumstances related in the Mosaic history. In

works

works of this kind, no care has hitherto been taken to give the least intimation of abundance of circumstances necessary to be known; and a person reads the history of the gods without finding any thing added, that can help him to unravel the mysteries he meets with in every page, or to entertain the least idea of the religion of their worshippers.

The Greeks were entirely ignorant as to the origin of their gods, and incapable of transmitting their history to posterity. Herodotus informs us, that the gods of the Greeks were originally brought from Egypt and Phœnicia, where they had been the objects of religious worship before any colonies from these countries settled in Greece. We ought then to search in Egypt and Phœnicia for the origin of the gods; for the gods whose worship was chiefly promoted by the Egyptians, and carried by the Phœnicians over all the coasts of the world then known. The first Egyptians, unacquainted with letters, gave all the informations to the people, all the rules of their conduct, by erecting figures, easily understood, and which served as rules and orders necessary to regulate their behaviour, and as advertisements to provide for their own safety. A very few figures diversified by what they held in their hands, or carried on their heads, were sufficient for this purpose. These were ingenious contrivances, and, such as were absolutely necessary in a country, were the least mistake in point of time was sufficient to ruin all their affairs.

But

But these Egyptian symbols, giving way to the easy method of reaping instruction from the use of letters, which were afterwards introduced, soon became obsolete, and the memory of some particular virtues still remaining, they were revered as the images or representations of superior and friendly beings, who had frequently delivered them from impending dangers, and soon were worshipped as the gods of their fathers. Their histories were wrote in verse, and embellished with fictions founded on ancient traditions. The priests of different countries increased the delusion; they had read the Mosaic history, or at least, had heard that the sons of God had conversation with the daughters of men, and from hence, influenced by lust or avarice, cloaked their own debaucheries, and sometimes those of princes and great men, under those of a god; and the poets, whenever a princess failed in point of modesty, had recourse to the same method, in order to shelter her reputation from vulgar censure. By this means the deities in after times were said to live in various countries, and even in far distant ages. Thus there became three hundred Jupiters, an opinion derived from there being a number of places in which, in different ages, Jupiter was said to have lived, reigned, and performed some extraordinary actions, which ancient fables, the fictions of the poets, and the artifices of the priests had rendered famous. But notwithstanding all these fables, Jupiter was always acknowledged by the wisest heathens to be impeccable, immortal, the author of life, the universal creator, and the fountain of goodness.

This

PREFACE. xi

This scheme is here carried on and explained with respect to each heathen deity, and added to the common histories and fables of the gods and goddesses.

In the short Dissertation on the Theology of the Ancients, we have shewn the rise of idolatry, and its connection with the ancient symbols. We have there exhibited the sentiments of the Pagans with regard to the unity of the deity, and the perfections they ascribe to him, from the concurrent testimony of the philosophers in various ages, amongst the Egyptians, Greeks and Romans. And the whole is concluded with a short account of the progress of idolatry.

In the Dissertation on the Mythology of the Ancients, we have endeavoured to account for the rise of a variety of fables from the licence of poetry, embellishing the common incidents of life, by personating inanimate beings, introducing fictitious characters, and supernatural agents. We have given the history of the creation of the world, the state of innocence, the fall of man, the universal deluge, &c. according to the traditions of different nations, and the opinions of the poets and most eminent philosophers, and compared them with the account given by Moses. In short, we have here given a view of their religious, as well as moral sentiments.

To the whole is added, by way of Appendix, a rational account of the various superstitious observances of astrology, and the manner by which influences and powers became ascribed to the signs and planets; of prodigies, auguries, the auspices and oracles; of altars, sacred groves, and sacrifices; of priests and temples, &c. In which the origin of each is pointed out, and the whole interspersed with such moral reflections, as have a tendency to preserve the minds of youth from the infection of superstitious follies, and to give them such fundamental principles, as may be of the greatest service in helping them to form just ideas of the manners, principles, and conduct of the heathen nations.

THE THEOLOGY AND HISTORY OF THE HEATHENS,

EXPLAINED AND ILLUSTRATED.

CHAP. I.

OF CHAOS.

HESIOD, the firſt author of the fabulous ſyſtem of the creation, begins his genealogy of the gods with chaos. Incapable of conceiving how ſomething could be produced from nothing, he aſſerted the eternity of matter, and imagined to himſelf a confuſed maſs lying in the womb of nature, which contained the principles of all beings, and which afterwards riſing by degrees into order and harmony, at length produced the univerſe. Thus the Heathen poets endeavoured to account for the origin of the world; of which they knew ſo little, that it is no wonder they diſguiſed rather than illuſtrated the ſubject in their writings. We find Virgil repreſenting Chaos as one of the infernal deities, and Ovid, at his firſt ſetting out in the Metamorphoſis, or transformation of the Gods, giving a very poetical picture of that diſorderly ſtate in which all the elements lay blended without order or diſtinction. It is eaſy to ſee, under all this confuſion and perplexity, the remains of truth; the ancient tradition of the creation being obscured with a multiplicity of images and allegories, became an inexhaustible fund for fiction to improve upon, and swelled the heathen theology into an unmeasurable compass: so that, in this sense, Chaos may indeed be properly stiled the father of the Gods.

Though it does not seem easy to give a picture, or graphical representation of Chaos, a modern painter (1) has been so bold to attempt it. Beyond the clouds, which compose the body of his piece, he has represented an immense abyss of darkness, and in the clouds an odd medly of water, earth, fire, smoke, winds, &c. But he has unluckily thrown the signs of the Zodiac into his work, and thereby spoiled his whole design.

Our great Milton in a noble and masterly manner has painted the state in which matter lay before the creation.

> *On heaven'ly ground they stood, and from the shore*
> *They view'd the vast unmeasurable abyss*
> *Outrageous as a sea, dark, wasteful, wild,*
> *Up from the bottom turn'd by furious winds*
> *And surging waves, as mountains, to assault*
> *Heaven's height, and with the centre mix the pole.*
>
> Book VII. l. 215.

CHAP II.

OF CÆLUS AND TERRA.

CÆLUS, or Uranus, as he was called by the Greeks, is said to be the offspring of Gaia or Terra. This goddess had given him birth, that she might be surrounded

---

(1) The painter's name was Abraham Diepenbeke. He was born at Bois le Duc, and for some time studied under Peter Paul Rubens. M. Meysens, in his book entitled *Des Images des Peintres*, gives him the character of a great artist, especially in painting on glass. The piece above mentioned has been considered by most people as a very ingenious jumble, and 'tis plain the painter himself was fond of it; for he wrote his name in the mass to complete the confusion.

rounded and covered by him, and that he might afford a manfion for the gods. She next bore Ourea, or the mountains, the refidence of the wood nymphs; and, laftly, fhe became the mother of Pelagus, or the ocean. After this fhe married her fon Uranus, and had by him a numerous offspring, among whom were Oceanus, Cæus, Creus, Hyperion, Japhet, Theia, Rhea, Themis, Mnemofyne, Phœbe, Tethys, Saturn, the three cyclops, viz. Brontes, Steropes, and Arges; and the giants Cottes, Gyges, and Briareus. Terra, however, was not fo ftrictly bound by her conjugal vow, for by Tartarus fhe had Typhæus, or Typhon, the great enemy of Jupiter. Cælus having, for fome offence, imprifoned the cyclops, his wife, to revenge herfelf, incited her fon Saturn, who by her affiftance took the opportunity to caftrate his father with an inftrument fhe furnifhed him with. The blood of the wound produced the three furies, the giants and the wood nymphs. The genital parts, which fell into the fea, impregnating the waters, formed Venus, the moft potent and charming of the goddeffes.

According to Lactantius, Cælus was an ambitious and mighty prince, who, affecting grandeur, called himfelf the *fon of the fky*; which title his fon Saturn alfo affumed in his turn. But Diodorus makes Uranus the firft monarch of the Atlantides, a nation inhabiting the the weftern coaft of Africa, and famous for commerce and hofpitality. From his fkill in aftronomy, the *ftarry heavens* were called by his name, and for his equity and beneficence he was denominated *king of the univerfe*. Nor was his queen Titea lefs efteemed for her wifdom and goodnefs, which after her death procured her the honour of being deified by the name of Terra. She is reprefented in the fame manner as Vefta, of whom we fhall have occafion to fpeak more particularly.

CHAP. III.

OF HYPERION AND THEIA.

THEIA, or Bafilea, fucceeded her parents, Cælus and Terra, in the throne: fhe was remarkable for her modesty and chastity; but being desirous of heirs, she married Hyperion her brother, to whom she bore Helios and Selene (the sun and moon), as also a second daughter, called Aurora (or the morning); but the brothers of Theia conspiring against her husband, caused him to be assassinated, and drowned her son Helios in the river Eridanus (2). Selene, who was extremely fond of her brother, on hearing his fate, precipitated herself from a high tower. They were both raised to the skies, and Theia, after wandering distracted, at last disappeared in a storm of thunder and lightning. After her death the conspirators divided the kingdom.

Historians say, that Hyperion was a famous astronomer, who, on account of his discovering the motions of the celestial bodies, and particularly the two great luminaries of heaven, was called the father of those planets.

CHAP. IV.

OF OCEANUS AND TETHYS.

THIS deity was one of the eldest sons of Cælus and Terra, and married his sister Tethys, besides whom he had several other wives. Each of them possessed an hundred woods and as many rivers. By Tethys he had Ephyre, who was matched to Epimetheus, and Pleione the wife of Atlas. He had several other daughters and sons, whose names it would be endless to enumerate, and indeed they are only those of the principal rivers of the world.

Two of the wives of Oceanus were Pamphyloge and Parthenope. By the first he had two daughters' Asia and Lybia; and by the last, two more called Europa and Thracia, who gave their names to the countries so denominated. He had also a daughter, called Cephyra, who educated Neptune, and three sons, viz. Triptolemus, the favourite of Ceres, Nereus, who presided over salt waters, and Achelous, the deity of fountains and rivers.

The

(2) This seems copied from the story of Phaeton.

The ancients, regarded Oceanus as the father of gods and men, on account of the ocean's encompaſſing the earth with its waves, and becauſe he was the principle of that radical moiſture diffuſed through univerſal matter, without which, according to Thales, nothing could either be produced or ſubſiſt.

Homer makes Juno viſit him at the remoteſt limits of the earth, and acknowledge him and Tethys as the parents of the gods, adding that ſhe herſelf had been brought up under their tuition.

Oceanus was depicted with a bull's head, to repreſent the rage and bellowing of the ocean when agitated by ſtorms.

CHAP. V.

OF AURORA AND TITHONUS.

WE have already obſerved, that this goddeſs was the youngeſt daughter of Hyperion and Theia.—By the Greeks ſhe was ſtyled ἠώς; and by the Latins Aurora, on account of her bright or golden colour, and the dew which attends her. Orpheus calls her the harbinger of Titan, becauſe the dawn beſpeaks the approach of the Sun; others make her the daughter of Titan and the earth. She fell in love with a beautiful youth named Cephalus, (whom ſome ſuppoſe to be the ſame with the ſun) by whom ſhe had Phaeton. She had alſo an amour with Orion, whom ſhe firſt ſaw a hunting in the woods, and carried him with her to Delos. By Aſtreas her huſband one of the Titans, ſhe had the ſtars, and the four winds, Argeſtus, Zephyrus, Boreas, and Notus. But her greateſt favourite was Tithonus, to whom ſhe bore Æmathion and Memnon. This young Prince ſhe tranſported to Delos, thence to Æthiopia, and laſt into Heaven, where ſhe obtained for him, from the deſtinies, the gift of immortality; but at the ſame time forgot to add youth, which alone could render the preſent valuable. Tithonus grew old, and ſo decrepid as to be rocked to ſleep like an infant. His miſtreſs, not being able to procure death, to end his

miſery

misery changed him into a grass hopper; an insect which by casting its skin renews its youth, and in its chirping still retains the loquacity of old age.

The historians say, that Tithonus was a great improver of astronomy, and used to ride before morning to make his observations. They add, that his vigilance and temperance were rewarded with a long life; but when the infirmities of old age came on at last, Aurora, by the help of oriental drugs, restored him to health and vigour. Thus have they done justice to the salubrity of the morning. This prince is said to have reigned in Media, where he founded the city of Susa on the river Choaspes, which became afterwards the seat of the Persian Empire.

The story of Cephalus is related differently. He was the nephew of Æolus, and had married Procris, daughter of Erichtheus, king of Athens. Aurora seeing him often early in the woods, intent on his sport, conceived a violent passion for him, and carried him with her to Heaven, where she in vain used all her arts to engage him to violate his conjugal vow. The prince, as fond of his wife as the goddess was of him, remained inexorably faithful. Aurora therefore, to undeceive him, sent him to Procris in the disguise of a merchant, to tempt her constancy by large presents: this artifice succeeded, and just when his spouse was on the point of yielding, the unhappy husband discovered himself, and Procris fled to the woods to hide her shame. But being afterwards reconciled, she made Cephalus a present of an unerring dart. A present like this increased his inclination to hunting, and proved doubly fatal to the donor. It happened the young prince, one day, wearied with his toil, sat down in the woods, and called for Aurora, or the gentle breeze, to cool him (3): this being overheard, was carried to Procris, who, though inconstant, was woman enough to be jealous: influenced by this passion, she followed her husband, and concealed herself in a thicket, where she could observe his motions. Unluckily the noise she made alarmed her husband, who thinking some wild beast
lay

(3) In a capital picture, near the Hague, this goddess is represented in a golden chariot drawn by white horses winged, on her head is the morning star, and she is attended by Phœbus and the dawn.

lay concealed, discharged the infallible arrow, and pierced her to the heart.

Mr. Pope, in some lines upon a lady's fan of his own design, painted with this story, has with his wonted delicacy and judgment applied it.

Come, gentle air! th' Æolian shepherd said,
While Procris panted in the secret shade;
Come, gentle air, the fairer Delia cries,
While at her feet her swain expiring lies.
Lo the glad gales oe'r all her beauties stray,
Breathe on her lips, and in her bosom play!
In Delia's hand this toy is fatal found,
Nor could that fabled dart more surely wound,
Both gifts destructive to the givers prove;
Alike both lovers fall by those they love.
Yet guiltless too this bright destroyer lives,
At random wounds, nor knows the wound she gives;
She views the story with attentive eyes,
And pities Procris while her lover dies.

There is no goddess of whom we have so many beautiful descriptions in the poets as Aurora. Indeed it is no wonder they are luxuriant on this subject, as there is perhaps no theme in nature which affords such an extensive field for poetry or painting as the varied beauties of the morning, whose approach seems to exhilirate and enliven the whole animal creation.

CHAP. VI.

OF ATLAS.

ATLAS was the son of Japetus and Clymene, and the brother of Prometheus. In the division of his father's dominions, Mauritania fell to his share, where he gave his own name to that mountain, which still bears it. As he was greatly skilled in Astronomy, he became the first inventor of the sphere, which gave rise to the fable, of his supporting the heavens on his shoulders. He had many children. Of his sons the most famous was Hesperus, (Tooke calls him his brother,

ther, p. 325) who reigned some time in Italy, which from him was called Hesperia. It is said, this prince being on mount Atlas to observe the motion of the stars, was carried away by a tempest, and, in honour to his memory, the morning star was afterwards called by his name. He left three daughters, Ægle, Arethusa, and Hesperithusa, who went by the general appellation of Hesperides, and were possessed of those famous gardens which bore golden fruit, and were guarded by the vigilance of a formidable dragon.

Atlas had seven daughters, called after his own name Atlantides, viz. Maia, Electra, Taygete, Asterope, Merope, Alcyone, and Celæno. All these were matched either to gods or heroes, by whom they left a numerous posterity. These from their mother Pleione, were also stiled Pleiades (4). Busiris, king of Egypt, carried them off by violence; but Hercules, travelling through Africa, conquered him, and delivering the Princesses, restored them to their father, who to requite his kindness taught him astronomy, whence arose the fable, of that hero's supporting the heavens for a day to ease Atlas of his toil. The Pleiades, however, endured a new persecution from Orion who pursued them five years, till Jove, prevailed on by their prayers, took them up into the heavens, where they form the constellation, which bears their name.

By Æthra, Atlas was the father of seven daughters, called Ambrosia, Eudora, Pasithoe, Coronis, Plexaris, Pytho, and Tyche, who bore one common appellation of the Hyades (5). These virgins grieved so immoderately for the death of their brother Hyas, devoured by a lion, that Jupiter, out of compassion, changed them into stars, and placed them in the head of Taurus, where they still retain their grief, their rising and setting being attended with extraordinary rain. Others make these last the daughters of Lycurges, born in the isle of Naxos, and translated to the skies, for their care in the education of Bacchus, probably because these showers are of great benefit in forwarding the vintage.

According

(4) So call'd from a Greek word, which signifies sailing; because they were reckoned favourable to navigation.

(5) From the Greek verb to rain, the Latins called them Suculæ, from the Greek της, or swine, because they seemed to delight in wet and dirty weather.

According to Hyginus, Atlas having affifted the giants in their war againft Jupiter, was by the victorious god doomed, as a punifhment, to fuftain the weight of the heavens.

Ovid gives a very different account of Atlas, who, as he fays, was the fon of Japetus and Afia. He reprefents him as a powerful and wealthy monarch, proprietor of the gardens which bore golden fruit; but tells us, that being warned by the oracle of Themis, that he fhould fuffer fome great injury from a fon of Jupiter, he ftrictly forbad all foreigners accefs to his court or prefence. Perfeus, however, had the courage to appear before him, but was ordered to retire, with ftrong menaces in cafe of difobedience. But the hero prefenting his fhield with the dreadful head of Medufa to him, turned him into the mountain which ftills bears his name.

The Abbe La Pluche has given a very clear and ingenious explication of this fable. Of all nations the Egyptians had, with the greateft affiduity, cultivated aftronomy. To point out the difficulties which attend the ftudy of this fcience, they reprefented it by an image, bearing a globe or fphere on its back, and which they called Atlas, a word fignifying (6) *great toil or labour*. But the word alfo fignifying *fupport* (7), the Phænicians, led by the reprefentation, took it in this laft fenfe; and in their voyages to Mauritania, feeing the high mountains of that country covered with fnow, and lofing their tops in the clouds, gave them the name of Atlas, and fo produced the fable, by which the fymbol of aftronomy ufed among the Egyptians, became a Mauritanian king, transformed into a mountain, whofe head fupports the heavens.

The reft of the fable is equally eafy to account for. The annual inundations of the Nile obliged that people to be very exact in obferving the motions of the heavenly bodies. The Hyades or Huades, took their name from the figure V which they form in

(6) From Talaah, to ftrive, comes Atlah, toil; whence the Greeks derived their αυτλος or labour, and the Romans *exantio*, to furmount great difficulties.

(7) From Telah, to fufpend, is derived Atlah, fupport, whence the Greek word Ετηλ, for column or pillar.

the head of Taurus. The Pleiades were a remarkable constellation, and of great use to the Egyptians in regulating the seasons. Hence they became the daughters of Atlas; and Orion, who rises just as they set, was called their lover. By the golden apples that grew in the garden of the Hesperides, the Phænicians expressed the rich and beneficial commerce they had in the Mediterranean; which being carried on during three months of the year only, gave rise to the fable of the Hesperian sisters (8).

CHAP. VII.

Of JAPETUS, and his sons EPIMETHEUS and PROMETHEUS; of PANDORA's Box, and the Story of DEUCALION and PYRRHA.

JAPETUS was the offspring of Cælus, and Terra, and one of the giants who revolted against Jupiter. He was a powerful and haughty prince, who lived so long that his age became a proverb. Before the war he had a daughter, called Anchiale, who founded a city of her own name in Cilicia. He had several sons, the chief of whom were Atlas, (mentioned in the preceding chapter) Buphagus, Prometheus (9), and Epimetheus. Of these, Prometheus became remarkable, by being the object of Jupiter's resentment. The occasion is related thus: having sacrificed two bulls to that deity, he put all the flesh of both in one skin, and the bones in the other, and gave the god his choice, whose wisdom for once failed him so, that he pitched upon the worst lot. Jupiter, incensed at the trick put upon him, took away fire from the earth, 'till Prometheus, by the assistance of Minerva, stole into heaven, and lighting a stick at the chariot of the sun, recovered the blessing, and brought it down again to mankind. Others say the cause of Jupiter's anger was different. Prometheus being a great artist, had formed a man of clay of such exquisite workmanship, that
Pallas,

(8) From Esper, the good share or best lot.

(9) So called from της προμιθιας, or providence, that is his skill in divination.

Pallas, charmed with his ingenuity, offered him whatever in heaven could contribute to finish his design: for this end she took him up with her to the celestial mansions, where, in a ferula, he hid some of the fire of the sun's chariot wheel, and used it to animate his image (1). Jupiter, either to revenge his theft, or the former affront, commanded Vulcan to make a woman, which, when he had done, she was introduced into the assembly of the gods, each of whom bestowed on her some additional charm of perfection. Venus gave her beauty, Pallas wisdom, Juno riches, Mercury taught her eloquence and Apollo music: from all these accomplishments, she was stiled Pandora (2) and was the first of her sex. Jupiter, to complete his designs, presented her a box, in which he had enclosed *age, diseases, war, famine, pestilence, discord, envy, calumny*, and in short, all the evils and vices which he intended to afflict the world with. Thus equipped, she was sent down to Prometheus, who wisely was on his guard against the mischief designed him. Epimetheus his brother, though forwarned of the danger, had less resolution; for enamoured with the beauty of Pandora (3), he married her, and opened the fatal box, the contents of which soon overspread the world. Hope alone rested at the bottom. But Jupiter, not yet satisfied, dispatched Mercury and Vulcan to seize Prometheus, whom they carried to mount Caucasus, where they chained him to a rock, and an eagle or vulture was commissioned to prey on his liver, which every night was renewed in proportion as it was consumed by day. But Hercules soon after killed the vulture and delivered him. Others say, Jupiter restored him his freedom for discovering his father Saturn's conspiracy (4), and dissuading his intended marriage

(1) Some say his crime was not the enlivening a man of clay; but the formation of woman.

(2) So called from παν δωρον, i. e. loaded with gifts or accomplishments. Hesiod has given a fine description of her in his Theogony, Cook, p. 770.

(3) Others say Pandora only gave to the box the wife of Epimetheus, who opened it from a curiosity natural to her sex.

(4) Lucian has a very fine Dialogue between Prometheus and Jupiter upon this subject.

marriage with Thetis. Nicander, to this fable of Prometheus, lends an additional circumstance. He tells us some ungrateful men discovered the theft of Prometheus first to Jupiter, who rewarded them with *perpetual youth*. This present they loaded on the back of an ass, who stopping at a fountain to quench his thirst, was hindered by a water snake, who would not let him drink till he gave him the burthen he carried. Hence the Serpent renews his youth upon changing his skin.

Prometheus had an altar in the academy at Athens, in common with Vulcan and Pallas. His statues are represented with a scepter in the hand.

There is a very ingenious explanation of this fable; it is said Prometheus was a wise Prince, who reclaiming his subjects from a savage to a social life, was said to have animated men out of clay: he first instituted sacrifices (according to (5) Pliny) which gave rise to the story of the two oxen. Being expelled his dominions, by Jupiter, he fled to Scythia, where he retired to mount Caucasus, either to make astronomical observations, or to indulge his melancholy for the loss of his dominions. This occasioned the fable of the vulture feeding upon his liver. As he was also the first inventor of forging metals by fire, he was said to have stole the element from heaven. In short, as the first knowledge of agriculture, and even navigation, is ascribed to him, it is no wonder if he was celebrated for forming a living man from an inanimated substance.

Some authors imagine Prometheus to be the same with Noah. The learned Bochart imagines him to be Magog. Each opinion is supported by arguments, which do not want a shew of probability.

The story of Pandora affords very distinct traces of the tradition of the fall of our first parents, and the seduction of Adam by his wife Eve.

CHAP.

(5) Pliny, Book. 7, cap. 56.

CHAP. VIII.

OF DEUCALION AND PYRRHA.

Deucalion was the son of Prometheus, and had married his cousin-german Pyrrha, the daughter of Epimetheus, who bore him a son, called Helenes, who gave his name to Greece. Deucalion reigned in Thessaly (6), which he governed with equity and justice; but his country, for the wickedness of the inhabitants, being destroyed by a flood, he and his queen only escaped by saving themselves on mount Parnassus. After the decrease of the waters, this illustrious pair consulted the oracle of Themis in their distress. The answer was in these terms, *Depart the temple, veil your heads and faces, unloose your girdles, and throw behind your backs the bones of your grandmother.* Pyrrha was shocked at an advice, which her piety made her regard with horror: but Deucalion penetrated the mystical sense, revived her, by telling her the earth was their grandmother, and that the bones were only stones. They immediately obey the oracle, and behold its effect: the stones which Deucalion threw, became living men; those cast by Pyrrha rose into women. With these, returning into Thessaly, that prince repeopled his kingdom, and was honoured as the restorer of mankind.

To explain this fable it is necessary to observe, there were five deluges, of which the one in question was the fourth, in order of time, and lasted, according to Aristotle's account, the whole winter. It is therefore needless to waste time in drawing a parallel between this story and the Mosaic flood. The circumstance of the stones (7) seems occasioned by the same word bearing two significations; so that these mysterious stones are only the children of such as escaped the general inundation.

CHAP.

---

(6) By the Arundelian marbles, Deucalion ruled at Lycerea, in the neighbourhood of Parnassus, about the beginning of the reign of Cecrops, king of Athens.

(7) The Phænician word Aben, or Eben, signifies both a stone and a child; and the Greek word Λαας, or Λαος, denotes either a stone or a people.

CHAP. IX.

OF SATURN.

Saturn was the youngest son of Cælus and Terra, and married his sister Vesta. Under the article of Cælus, we have taken notice how he treated his father. We find a new proof of his ambition in his endeavouring by the assistance of his mother, to exclude his elder brother Titan from the throne, in which he so far succeeded, that this prince was obliged to resign his birthright, on these terms, that Saturn should not bring up any male children, so that the succession might devolve to the right male line again.

Saturn, it is said, observed these conditions so faithfully, that he devoured all the sons he had by his wife, as soon as born. But his exactness in this point was at last frustrated by the artifice of Vesta. Having brought forth the twins, Jupiter and Juno, she presented the latter to her husband, and concealing the boy, sent him to be nursed on mount Ida in Crete, committing the care of him to the Curetes and Corybantes. Saturn, however, getting some intelligence of the affair, demanded the child, in whose stead his wife gave him a stone swaddled up, which he swallowed. This stone had the name of Ab-addir, (or the potent father) and received divine honours.

This fiction, of Saturn's devouring his sons, according to Mr. Le Clerc [8], was founded upon a custom which he had of banishing or confining his children for fear they should one day rebel against him. As to the stone which Saturn is said to swallow, this is another fiction, founded on the double meaning of the word Eben, which signifies both a stone and a child, and means no more than that Saturn was deceived by Rhea's substituting another child in the room of Jupiter.

Titan finding the mutual compact made between him and his brother thus violated, took arms to revenge the injury, and not only defeated Saturn, but made him and his wife Vesta prisoners, whom he confined

[8] Remarks upon Hesiod.

fined in Tartarus, a place so dark and dismal, that it afterwards became one of the appellations of the infernal regions. In the mean time Jupiter being grown up, raised an army in Crete for his father's deliverance. He also hired the Cecrops to aid him in his expedition; but on their refusal to join him after taking the money, he turned them into Apes. After this he marched against the Titans, and obtained a complete victory. The Eagle which appeared before the engagement, as an auspicious omen, was ever after chosen to carry his thunder. From the blood of the Titans, slain in the battle, proceeded serpents, scorpions, and all venomous reptiles. Having by this success freed his parents, the young prince caused all the gods assembled, to renew their oath of fidelity to Saturn, on an altar, which on that account has been raised to a constellation in the heavens. Jupiter, after this, married Metis, daughter of Oceanus, who, it is reported, gave Saturn a potion, which caused him to bring up Neptune and Pluto, with the rest of the children he had formerly devoured (9).

The merit of the son (as it often happens) only served to increase the father's jealousy, which received new strength from an ancient oracle or tradition, that he should be dethroned by one of his sons. Jupiter therefore secretly informed of the measures taken to destroy him, suffered his ambition to get the ascendant over his duty, and taking up arms, deposed his father, whom, by the advice of Prometheus, he bound in woollen fetters, and threw into Tartarus with Japetus his uncle. Here Saturn suffered the same barbarous punishment of castration he had inflicted on his father Cælus.

Macrobius searches into the reason why this god was bound with fetters of wool, and adds, from the testimony of Apolidorus, that he broke these cords once a year at the celebration of the Saturnalia (1). This he explains by saying, that this fable alluded to the corn, which being shut up in the earth, and detained by chains soft and easily broken, sprung forth and annually arrived at maturity. The Abbe Banier
says

(9) By this, Jupiter should be the youngest son of Saturn.
(1) Sat. lib. 1. c. 8.

says (2), that the Greeks looked upon the places situated to the east as higher than those that lay westward, and from hence concludes, that by Tartarus, or Hell, they only meant Spain. As to the castration of Saturn, Mr. Le Clerc conjectures (3), that it only means that Jupiter had corrupted his father's council, and prevailed upon the most considerable persons of his court to desert him.

The manner in which Saturn escaped from his prison is not related. He fled to Italy, where he was kindly received by Janus, then king of that country, who associated him in the government. From hence that part of the world obtained the name of Saturnia Tellus, as also that of *Latium*, from *latco*, to lie hid, because he found a refuge here in his distress. On this account money was coined with a ship on one side, to signify his arrival, and a Janus with a double head on the other, to denote his sharing the regal authority.

The reign of Saturn was so mild and happy, that the poets have given it the name of the GOLDEN AGE, and celebrated it with all the pomp and luxuriancy of imagination (4). According to Varro, this deity, from his instructing the people in agriculture and tillage, obtained his name (5) of Saturn. The sickle which he used in reaping being cast into Sicily, gave that island its ancient name of Drepanon, which in Greek signifies that instrument.

The historians give us a very different picture of Saturn. Diodorus represents him as a tyrannical, covetous, and cruel prince, who reigned over Italy and Sicily, and enlarged his dominions by conquest: he adds, that he oppressed his subjects by severe taxes, and kept them in awe by strong garrisons. This account agrees very well with those who make Saturn the first who instituted human sacrifices, which probably gave rise to the fable of his devouring his own children. Certain it is, that the Carthaginians

---

(2) Banier's Mythology, vol. 2. 185.
(3) Remarks upon Hesiod.
(4) The reader will see more on this head under the succeeding article.
(5) From Satus, that is, sowing or seed time.

nians (6) offered young children to this deity; and amongſt the Romans, his prieſts were clothed in red, and at his feſtivals gladiators were employed to kill each other.

The feaſts of this deity were celebrated with great ſolemnity amongſt the Romans about the middle of December. They were firſt inſtituted by Tullus Hoſtilius, though Livy dates them from the conſulſhip of Manilius and Sempronius. They laſted but one day till the time of Julius Cæſar, who ordered them to be protracted to three days; and in proceſs of time they were extended to five. During theſe, all public buſineſs was ſtopped, the ſenate never aſſembled, no war could be proclaimed, or offender executed. Mutual preſents of all kinds, (particularly wax lights) were ſent and received, ſervants wore the *pileus* or cap of liberty, and were waited on by their maſters at table. All which was deſigned to ſhew the equality and happineſs of mankind under the Golden Age.

The Romans kept in the temple of Saturn, the *libri elephantini*, or rolls, containing the names of the Roman citizens, as alſo the public treaſure. This cuſtom they borrowed from the Egyptians, who in the temple of Sudec, or Chrone, depoſited their genealogies of families and the public money.

Saturn, like the other heathen deities, had his amours. He fell in love with the nymph Phyllyra, the daughter of Oceanus, and was by his wife Rhea ſo near being ſurpriſed in her company, that he was forced to aſſume the form of a horſe. This ſudden transformation had ſuch an effect on his miſtreſs, that ſhe bore a creature whoſe upper part was like a man, and the reſt like a horſe. This ſon of Saturn became famous for his ſkill in muſic and ſurgery.

A modern author, M. La Pluche, has very juſtly accounted for this fabulous hiſtory of Saturn, which certainly derived its origin from Egypt. The annual meeting

(6) Mr. Selden, in his treatiſe of the Syrian gods, ſpeaking of Moloch, imagines, from the cruelty of his ſacrifices, he was the ſame as Saturn. In the reign of Tiberius, that prince crucified the prieſts of Saturn for offering young infants at his altars. This idea of Saturn's malignity is, perhaps, the reaſon why the planet, which bears this name, was thought ſo inauſpicious and unfriendly to mankind.

meeting of the Judges in that country was notified by an image with a long beard, and a scythe in his hand. The first denoted the age and gravity of the magistrates, and the latter pointed out the season of their assembling, just before the first hay-making or harvest. This figure they called by the names of Sudec (7), Chrone (8), Chiun (9), and Saterin (1); and in company with it, always exposed another statue representing Isis, with several breasts, and surrounded with the heads of animals, which they called Rhea (2), as these images continued exposed till the beginning of the new solar year, or the return of the Osiris (the Sun), so Saturn became regarded as the father of time. Upon other occasions the Egyptians depicted him with eyes before and behind, some of them open, others asleep; and with four wings, two shut and two expanded (3). The Greeks took these pictures in the literal sense, and turned into fabulous history what was only allegorical.

Bochart, and some other learned antiquaries, conceived Saturn to be the same with Noah, and drew a parallel, in many instances, which seem to favour their opinion.

Saturn was usually represented as an old man, bareheaded and bald, with all the marks of age and infirmity in his face. In his right hand they sometimes placed a sickle, or scythe, at others a key, and a serpent biting its own tail, and circumflexed in his left. He sometimes was pictured with six wings, and feet of wool, to shew how insensibly and swiftly time passes. The scythe denoted his cutting down and imparing all things, and the serpent the revolution of the year: *Quod in sese volvitur annus.*

CHAP.

(7) From Tsadic, or Sudec, justice, or the just.
(8) From Keron, splendor, the name given to Moses on his descent from the mount; hence the greek χρονος.
(9) From Cloen, a priest, is derived Keunah, or the sacerdotal office.
(1) From Seter, a judge, is the plural Seterim, or the judges.
(2) From Rahah, to feed, comes Rehea, or Rhea, a nurse.
(3) This figure seems borrowed from the Cherubim of the Hebrews.

CHAP. X.

OF THE GOLDEN AGE.

Difficult as it is, to reconcile the inconsistencies between the poets and historians in the preceding account of Saturn, yet the concurrent testimony of the former in placing the Golden Age in his time, seems to determine the point in his favour; and to prove that he was a benefactor and friend to mankind, since they enjoyed such felicity under his administration. We can never sufficiently admire the masterly description given by Virgil of these halcyon days, when peace and innocence adorned the world, and sweetened all the blessings of untroubled life. Ovid has yet heightened the description with those touches of imagination peculiar to him. Amongst the Greek poets, Hesiod has touched this subject with that agreeable simplicity which distinguishes all his writings.

By the Golden Age might be figured out the happiness of the primæval state before the first and universal deluge, when the earth, remaining in the same position in which it was first created, flourished with perpetual spring, and the air always temperate and serene, was neither discomposed by storms, nor darkened by clouds. The reason of affixing this time to the reign of Saturn, was probably this: the Egyptians held the first annual assembly of their judges in the month of February, and as the decisions of these sages were always attended with the highest equity, so the people regarded that season as a time of general joy and happiness, rather as all nature with them was then in bloom, and the whole country looked like one enamelled garden or carpet.

But after all it appears, that these halcyon times were but of a short duration, since the character Plato, Pythagoras, and others, give of this age, can only relate to that state of perfect innocence which ended with the fall.

CHAP. XI.

OF THE GIANTS.

THE giants were produced (as has been already obferved) of the blood which flowed from the wound of Saturn, when caftrated by his fon Jupiter. Proud of their own ftrength, and fired with a daring ambition, they entered into an affociation to dethrone Jupiter; for which purpofe they piled rocks on rocks, in order to fcale the fkies. This engagement is differently related by authors, both as to the place where it happened, and the circumftances which attended it; fome writers laying the fcene in Italy (4), others in Greece (5). It feems the father of the gods was apprized of the danger, as there was a prophetical rumour amongft the deities, that the giants fhould not be overcome, unlefs a mortal affifted in the war. For this reafon Jove, by the advice of Pallas, called up Hercules, and being affifted by the reft of the gods gained a complete victory over the rebels, moft of whom perifhed in the conflict. Hercules firft flew Alcyon with an arrow, but he ftill furvived and grew ftronger, till Minerva drew him out of the moon's orb, when he expired. This goddefs alfo cut off the heads of Enceladus and Pallantes, and afterwards encountering Alcyoneus at the Corinthian ifthmus, killed him in fpite of his monftrous bulk. Porphyris, about to ravifh Juno, fell by the hands of Jupiter and Hercules. Apollo and Hercules difpatched Ephialtes, and Hercules flew Eurytus, by darting an oak at him. Clytius was flain by Hecate, and Polybotes flying through the fea, came to the ifle of Coos, where Neptune tearing off part of the land, hurled it at him, and formed the ifle of Nifyros. Mercury flew Hyppolitus, Gratian was vanquifhed by Diana, and the Parcæ claimed their fhare in the victory, by the deftruction of Agryus and Thoan. Even Silenus's afs,

(4) In the Phlegræan plains, in Campania, near mount Vefuvius, which abounded with fubterraneous fires, and hot mineral fprings.

(5) Where they fet mount Offa on Pelion, in order to afcend the fkies.

afs, by his opportune braying, contributed to put the giants in confusion, and complete their ruin. During this war, of which Ovid has left us a short description, Pallas distinguished herself by her wisdom, Hercules by his strength, Pan by his trumpet, which struck a terror in the enemy, and Bacchus by his activity and courage. Indeed their assistance was no more than seasonable; for when the giants first made their audacious attempt, the gods were so astonished, that they fled into Egypt, where they concealed themselves in various shapes.

But the most dreadful of these monsters, and the most difficult to subdue, was Typhon or Typhæus; whom, when he had almost discomfited all the gods, Jupiter pursued to mount Caucasus, where he wounded him with his thunder; but Typhon turning upon him, took him prisoner; and after cutting with his own sickle the nerves of his hands and feet, threw him on his back, carried him into Cilicia, and imprisoned him in a cave, whence he was delivered by Mercury, who restored him to his former vigour. After this, Jove had a second engagement with Typhon, who flying into Sicily, was overwhelmed by mount Ætna.

The giants are represented by the poets as men of huge stature and horrible aspect, their lower parts being of a serpentine form. But above all, Typhon, or Typhæus, is described in the most shocking manner; Hesiod has giving him an hundred heads of dragons, uttering dreadful sounds, and having eyes that darted fire. He makes him, by Echidna, the father of the dog Orthus, or Cerberus, Hydra, Chimæra, Sphinx, the Nemæan lyon, the Hesperian dragon, and of storms and tempests.

Historians say, Typhæus was the brother of Osiris, king of Egypt, who, in the absence of this monarch, formed a conspiracy to dethrone him at his return; for which end he invited him to a feast, at the conclusion of which, a chest of exquisite workmanship was brought in, and offered to him who lying down in it should be found to fit it best. Osiris, not distrusting the contrivance, had no sooner got in but the lid was closed upon him, and the unhappy king thrown into the Nile. Isis, his queen, to revenge the death of her beloved husband, raised an army, the command

of

of which she gave to her son Orus, who, after vanquishing the usurper, put him to death. Hence the Egyptions, who detested his memory, painted him in their hieroglyphic characters in so frightful a manner. The length and multiplicity of his arms denoted his power; the serpents which formed his heads, signified his address and cunning; the crocodile scales which covered his body, expressed his cruelty and dissimulation; and the flight of the gods into Egypt, shewed the precautions taken by the great men to shelter themselves from his fury and resentment.

It is easy in this story of the giants to trace the Mosaic history which, informs us how the earth was afflicted with men of uncommon stature and great wickedness. The tradition of the tower of Babel, and the defeat of that impious design, might naturally give rise to the attempt of these monsters, to insult the skies and make war on the gods.

But there is another explication of this fable, which seems both more rational and curious. Amongst the names of the giants we find those of Briareus (6), Rœchus (7), Othus (8), Ephialtes (9), Prophyrion (1), Enceladus (2), and Mimas (3). Now the literal signication of these, leads us to the sense of the allegory, which was designed to point out the fatal consequences of the flood, and the considerable changes it introduced with regard to the face of nature. This is further confirmed by their tradition, that their Osiris vanquished the giants, and that Orus, his son, in particular, stopped the pursuit of Rœchus, by appearing before him in the form of a lion. By which they meant,

(6) From Beri, serenity; and Harcus, lost, to shew the temperature of the air destroyed.

(7) From Reuach, the winds.

(8) From Ouitta, or Othus, the times, to typify the vicissitude of the seasons.

(9) From Evi, or Ephi, clouds; and Altah, darkness, i. e. dark gloomy clouds.

(1) From Phau, to break, comes Pharpher, to separate minutely; to denote the general dissolution of the Primæval system.

(2) From Erceled, violent springs or torrents.

(3) From Maim, great and heavy rains. Now all these were phænomena new, and unknown before the flood. See La Pluche's history of the heavens, vol. 1. p. 60.

meant, that that induſtrious people had no way of ſecuring themſelves againſt the bad effects of the vernal winds, which brought on their annual inundation, but by exactly obſerving the ſun's entrance into Leo, and then retiring into the high grounds, to wait the going off of the waters.

It may not be improper to add, that from the blood of the giants defeated by Jupiter, were produced ſerpents and all kinds of venomous creatures.

CHAP. XII.
OF JANUS.

THE connection between Saturn and Janus, renders the account of the latter a proper ſupplement to the hiſtory of the former. Writers vary as to the birth of this deity, ſome making him the ſon of Cælus and Hecate, others the offspring of Apollo, by Creuſa, daughter of Erictheus, king of Athens. Heſiod is ſilent about him in his *Theogony*, and indeed Janus was a god little known to the Greeks. According to Cato, he was a Scythian prince, who, at the head of a victorious army, ſubdued and depopulated Italy. But the moſt probable opinion is, that he was an Etrurian king, and one of the earlieſt monarchs of that country, which he governed with great wiſdom, according to the teſtimony of Plutarch, who ſays, *Whatever he was, whether a king or a god, he was a great politician, who tempered the manners of his ſubjects, and taught them civility, on which account he was regarded as the god of peace, and never invoked during the time of war.* The Romans held him in peculiar veneration.

From Fabius Pictor, one of the oldeſt Roman hiſtorians, we learn, that the ancient Tuſcans were firſt taught by this good king to improve the vine, to ſow corn, and make bread, and that he firſt raiſed temples and altars to the gods, who were before worſhipped in groves. We have already mentioned Saturn as the introducer of theſe arts into Italy, where Janus aſſociated him into a ſhare of his power. Some ſay he was married to the youngeſt Veſta, the goddeſs of *fire*; others make his wife the goddeſs Carna, or Carma (4).

It

(4) Carna, or Carma, was a goddeſs who preſided over the vital parts, and occaſioned a healthy conſtitution of body.

It is certain that he early obtained divine honours at Rome, where Numa Pompilius inftituted an annual feftival to him in January, which was celebrated with manly exercifes. Romulus and Tatius had before erected him a temple, upon occafion of the union of the Romans with the Sabines. Numa ordained it fhould be opened in time of war, and fhut in time of peace (5), which happened but thrice for feveral centuries. 1. In the reign of Numa. 2. In the confulate of Attilus Balbus, and Manlius Torquatus; and, 3. By Auguftus Cæfar, affer the death of Antony, and reduction of Egypt.

Janus was the god who prefided over all new undertakings. Hence in all the facrifices the firft libations of wine and wheat were offered to him, as likewife all prayers were prefaced with a fhort addrefs to him. The peculiar offerings at his feftival were cakes of new meal and falt, with new wine and frankincenfe (6). Then all artificers and tradefmen began their works, and the Roman confuls for the new year folemnly entered on their office. All quarrels were laid afide, mutual prefents were made, and the day concluded with joy and mirth.

Janus was reprefented with two faces, and called Bifrons, Byceps, and Didymæus, as forming another image of himfelf on the difk of the moon, and looking to the paft and approaching year; with keys, as opening and fhutting up the day (7). He is faid to have regulated the months, the firft of which is diftinguifhed by his name, as the firft day of every month was alfo facred to him. He was therefore feated in the center of twelve altars; and had on his hands figures to the amount of days in the year. Sometimes his image had four faces, to exprefs the four feafons of the year over which he prefided.

Though Janus be properly a Roman deity, yet it is amongft the Egyptians we muft feek for the true explanation

(5) Hence Janus took the names of Patulcius and Clufius.
(6) Tooke contradicts Ovid, and fuppofes Pliny to prove, that the ancients did not ufe this gum in their facrifices; but the paffage of that author only fays, it was not ufed in the time of the Trojan war.
(7) *Quafi utriufque janua cæleftis potentum; qui exoriens aperiat diem, occidens claudat.* Macrob. l. 1. c. 9.

nation of his hiftory. That nation reprefented the opening of their folar year by an image, with a key in its hand, and two faces, one old, and the other young, to typify or mark the old or new year. King Picus with a hawk's head, who is ufually drawn near Janus, leaves no doubt but that the fymbol of this deity was borrowed from that people. The reader, after putting all this together, will reafonably conclude, that by this figure could only be intended the fun, the great ruler of the year.

CHAP. XIII.

Of the Elder VESTA, or CYBELE, the Wife of SATURN.

IT is highly neceffary, in claffing the Heathen divinities, to diftinguifh between this goddefs, who is alfo called Rhea, and Ops, from another Vefta, their daughter, becaufe the poets have been faulty in confounding them, and afcribing the attributes and actions of the one to the other.

The elder Vefta, commonly called Eftia by the Greeks, was the daughter of Cælus and Terra, and married to her brother Saturn, to whom fhe bore a numerous offspring. She had a multiplicity of names befides, of which the principal were Cybele, Magna Mater, or the great mother of the Gods; and Bona Dea, or the good goddefs, &c. under different facrifices.

Vefta is generally reprefented upon ancient coins fitting, though fometimes ftanding, with a lighted torch in one hand, and a fphere in the other.

Under the character of Cybele fhe makes a more magnificent appearance, being feated on a lofty chariot drawn by lions, crowned with towers, and having a key extended in her hand.

Some indeed make the Phrygian Cybele a different perfon from Vefta: they fay fhe was the daughter of Mœones, an ancient king of Phrygia and Dyndima, and that her mother, for fome reafons, expofed her on mount Cybelus, where fhe was nourifhed by lions. Her parents afterwards owned her, and fhe fell in love with Atys by whom conceiving, her father caufed her

C   lover

lover to be slain, and his body thrown to the wild beasts; Cybele upon this ran mad, and filled the woods with her lamentations. Soon after a plague and famine laying waste the country, the oracle was consulted, who advised them to bury Atys with great pomp, and to worship Cybele as a Goddess. Accordingly they erected a temple to her honour at Pessinus, and placed lions at her feet to denote her being educated by these animals.

Ovid relates the story a little more in the marvellous way: Atys was a boy so called by Cybele, whom she appointed to preside in her rites, enjoining him inviolate chastity; but the youth happening to forget his vow, in resentment the goddess deprived him of his senses; but at last pitying his misery she turned him into a *pine tree*, which as well as the *box*, was held sacred to her. The animal commonly sacrificed to Cybele was the sow, on account of its fecundity.

The priests of this deity were the Corybantes, Curetes, Idæi, Dactyli, and Telchines, who in their mystical rites made great use of Cymbals and other instruments of brass, attended with extravagant cries and howlings. They sacrificed sitting on the earth, and offered only the hearts of the victims.

The goddess Cybele was unknown to the Romans till the time of Hannibal, when, consulting the Sybilline oracles, they found that formidable enemy could not be expelled till they sent for the Idœan mother to Rome. Attalus, then king of Phrygia, at the request of their embassadors, sent her statue, which was of stone. But the vessel which carried it arriving in the Tyber, was miraculously stopped, till Claudia, one of the Vestal-Virgins, drew it ashore with her girdle.

This Vesta, to whom the living flame was sacred, is the same with the Ægyptian Isis, and represented the pure *æther*, inclosing, containing and pervading all things. Their expressings and attributes are alike. She was considered as the cause of generation and motion, the parent of all the luminaries, and is confounded with *nature* and the *world*. She obtained the name of Eftia, as being the life or essence of all things (8).

As to the priests of Cybele, the Corybantes, Curetes, &c. they are of the same original. Crete was a colony

(8) Plato in Cratylo.

colony of the Egyptians, confifting of three claffes of people. 1. The Corybantes or priefts (9). 2. The Curetes (1), or hufbandmen, and inhabitants of towns. 3. The Dactyli (2), or artificers and labouring poor. All which names are of Egyptian derivation.

Cybele was honoured at Rome by the title of Bona Dea, or good goddefs. But this devotion was only paid her by the matrons, and the rites were celebrated in fo fecret a manner, that it was no lefs than death for any man to be prefent at the affembly (3). Whence they were called Opertoria.

The Roman farmers and fhepherds worfhipped Cybele or Vefta, by the title of Magna Pales, or the goddefs of cattle and pafture. Her feftival was in April, at which time they purified their flocks and herds with the fumes of rofemary, laurel, and fulphur, offered facrifices of milk and millet cakes, and concluded the ceremony by dancing round ftraw fires. Thefe annual feafts were called Palilia, and were the fame with the Θησμο φορια of the Greeks, and probably of Phænician or Egyptian original.

The great feftival of Cybele, called Megalefia, was always celebrated in April, and lafted eight days at Rome.

CHAP. XIV.

OF VESTA THE YOUNGER.

COLLECTED fire is the offspring of æther. Hence we have another Vefta, faid to be the daughter of the other, by Saturn, or time, and the fifter of Ceres, Juno, Pluto, Neptune, and Jupiter. She was fo fond of a fingle life, that when her brother Jupiter afcended

the

---

(9) From Corban, a facrifice or oblation.

(1) From Keret, a city or town, comes the plural Keretim, to fignify the inhabitants.

(2) From *dac*, poor; and *tul* or *tyl*, a migration: hence our ultimma Thule. The Greeks for the fame reafon call the fingers Dactyli, becaufe they are the inftruments of labour.

(3) So we learn from Tibullus, Eclogue VI.

Sacra bonæ maribus non adeunda deæ.

the throne, and offered to grant whatever she asked, she desired only the preservation of her virginity, and that she might have the first oblation in all sacrifices (4) which she obtained. According to Lactantius, the chastity of Vesta is meant to express the nature of fire, which is incapable of mixture, producing nothing, but converting all things into itself.

Numa Pompilius, the great founder of religion among the Romans, is said first to have restored the ancient rites and worship of this goddess, to whom he erected a circular temple, which, in succeeding ages, was much embellished. He also appointed four priestesses to be chosen out of the noblest families in Rome, and of spotless character, whose office was to attend the sacred fire kept continually burning near her altar. These Vestal-Virgins continued in their charge for thirty years, and had very great privileges annexed to their dignity. This fire was annually renewed, with great ceremony, from the rays of the sun, on the kalends of March. It was preserved in earthen pots suspended in the air, and esteemed so sacred, that if by any misfortune it became extinguished (as happened once) a cessation ensued from all business, till they had expiated the prodigy. If this accident appeared to be owing to the neglect of the Vestals, they were severely punished; and if they violated their vow of chastity, they were interred alive.

As Vesta was the goddess of fire, the Romans had no images in her temple to represent her, the reason of which we learn in Ovid (5). Yet, as she was the guardian of couses or hearth, her image was usually placed in the porch or entry, and daily sacrifice offered her (6).

It is certain nothing could be a stronger or more lively symbol of the supreme Being, than fire. Accordingly we find this emblem in early use throughout all the east. The Persians held it in veneration long before

(4) It is a question if this privilege did not rather belong to the elder Vesta, in common with Janus.

(5) His words are these:
Effigiem nullam Vesta nec ignis habet. Fasti, lib. VI.
   No image Vesta's semblance can express,
   Fire is too subtile to admit of dress.

(6) Hence the word vestibulum, for a porch or entry; and the Romans called their round tables vestæ, as the Greeks used the common word Εςια, to signify chimnies in altars.

fore Zoroaster, who, in the reign of Darius Hystaspes, reduced the worship of it to a certain plan. The Prytanei of the Greeks were perpetual and holy fires. We find Æneas bringing with him to Italy his Penates (or houshold gods) the Palladium and the sacred fire. The Vesta of the Etrurians, Sabines, and Romans, was the same.

CHAP. XV.

OF JUPITER.

WE come now to the great king, or master of the gods. This deity was the son of Saturn, and Rhea, or Vesta, at least this is that Jupiter, to whom the actions of all the others were chiefly ascribed. For there were so many princes called by his name, that it seems to have been a common appellation in early times for a powerful or victorious prince (7). The most considerable of these was certainly the Cretan Jove above-mentioned, of whose education we have very various accounts, as well as the place of his birth. The Messenians pretended to shew in the neighbourhood of their city a fountain called Clepsydra, where Jupiter was educated by the nymphs Ithome and Neda, others say he was born at Thebes in Bœotia; but the most general and received opinion is, that he was brought up near mount Ida in Crete. Virgil tells us he was fed by the bees, out of gratitude for which he changed them from an iron to a golden colour. Some say his nurses were Amalthœa and Melissa, daughters of Melisseus king of Crete, who gave him goats milk and honey; others, that Amalthœa was the name of the goat that nursed him, whose horn he presented to those princesses with this privilege annexed, that whoever possessed it should immediately have whatever they desired; whence it came to be called the horn of Plenty. After this the goat dying, Jupiter placed her amongst the stars, and by the advice of Themis covered his shield with her skin to strike terror in the giants, whence it obtained the name

---

(7) Varro reckoned up 300 Jupiters, and each nation seems to have had one peculiar to itself.

name of Ægis. According to others, he and his sister Juno sucked the breasts of Fortune. Some alledge his mother Vesta suckled him; some, that he was fed by wild pigeons, who brought him ambrosia from Oceanus, and by an eagle, who carried nectar in his beak from a steep rock; in recompence of which services, he made the former the foretellers of winter and summer, and gave the latter the reward of immortality, and the office of bearing his thunder. In short, the nymphs and the bears claim a share in the honour of his education, nor is it yet decided which has the best title to it.

Let us now come to the actions of Jupiter. The first, and indeed the most memorable of his exploits, was his expedition against the Titans, for his father's deliverance and restoration, of which we have already spoken under the article of Saturn. After this he dethroned his father, and having possessed himself of his throne, was acknowledged by all the gods in quality of their supreme. Apollo, himself, crowned with laurel, and robed with purple, condescended to sing his praises to his lyre. Hercules, in order to perpetuate the memory of his triumphs, instituted the olympic games, where it is said that Pœbus carried off the first prize, by overcoming Mercury at the race. After this, Jupiter being fully settled, divided his dominions with his brothers Neptune and Pluto, as will be shewn in the sequel.

Jupiter, however, is thought to use his power in a little too tyrannical a manner, for which we find Juno, Neptune, and Pallas, conspired against, and actually seized his person. But the giants Cottus, Gyges, and Briareus, who were then his guards, and whom Thetis called to his assistance, set him at liberty. How these giants, with others of their race, afterwards revolted against him, and were overthrown, has been already mentioned in its place.

The story of Lycaon is not the least distinguishing of his actions. Hearing of the prevailing wickedness of mankind, Jove descended to the earth, and arriving at the palace of this monarch, king of Arcadia, declared who he was, on which the people prepared sacrifices, and the other honours due to him. But Lycaon, both impious and incredulous, killed one of his domestics, and served up the flesh dressed at the entertainment

entertainment he gave the god, who detefting fuch horrid inhumanity, immediately confumed the palace with lightening, and turned the barbarian into a wolf. Ovid has related this ftory with his ufual art.

But as ambition, when arrived at the height of its wifhes, feldom ftrictly adheres to the rules of moderation, fo the air of a court is always in a peculiar manner fatal to virtue. If any monarch deferved the character of encouraging gallantry by his example, it was certainly Jupiter, whofe amours are as numberlefs as the metamorphofes he affumed to accomplifh them, and have afforded an extenfive field of defcription to the poets and painters, both ancient and modern.

Jupiter had feveral wives: Metis, or Prudence, his firft, he is faid to have devoured, when big with child, by which himfelf becoming pregnant, Minerva iffued out of his head adult and completely armed. His fecond was Themis, or Juftice, by whom he had the Hours, meaning *regulation* of *time*; Eunomia, or *good order*; Diche, or *law*; Eirene, or *peace*, and the Deftinies. He alfo married Juno, his fifter, whom it is reported he deceived under the form of a cuckoo, who, to fhun the violence of a ftorm, fled for fhelter to her lap (8). She bore him Hebe, Mars, Lucina, and Vulcan. By Eurynome, he had the three Graces; by Ceres, Proferpine; Mnemofyne, the nine Mufes; by Latona, Apollo and Diana; by Maia, Mercury.

Of his intrigues we have a pretty curious detail. One of his firft miftreffes was Califto, the daughter of Lycaon, one of the nymphs of Diana. To deceive her, he affumed the form of the goddefs of chaftity, and fucceeded fo far as to make the virgin violate her vow. But her difgrace being revealed, as fhe was bathing with her patronefs, the incenfed deity not only difgraced her, but (9) turned her into a bear. Jove, in compaffion to her punifhment and fufferings, raifed her to a conftellation in the heavens (1). Califto, however, left a fon called Arcas, who having inftructed the Pelafgians in tillage and the focial

(8) At a mountain near Corinth, hence called Coceyx.
(9) Some fay it was Juno turned her into that animal.
(1) Called Urfa Major by the Latins, and Helice by the Greeks.

social arts, they from him took the name of Arcadians, and after his death he was, by his divine father, allotted also (2) a seat in the skies.

There is scarce any form which Jupiter did not at some time or other assume to gratify his desires. Under the figure of a satyr he violated Antiope, the wife of Lycus, king of Thebes, by whom he had two sons, Zethus and Amphion. In the resemblance of a swan he corrupted Leda, the spouse of Tyndaris, king of Laconia. Under the appearance of a white bull he carried off Europa, the daughter of Agenor, king of Phœnicia, into Crete, where he enjoyed her. In the shape of an eagle he surprised Asteria, the daughter of Cæus, and bore her away in his talons in spite of her modesty. Aided by the same disguise he seized the beauteous Ganymede, son of Tros, as he was hunting on mount Ida, and raised him to the joint functions of his cup-bearer and catamite.

It was indeed difficult to escape the pursuits of a god, who by his unlimited power made all nature subservient to his purposes. Of this we have a remarkable instance in Danae, whose father, Acrisius, jealous of her conduct, had secured her in a brazen tower; but Jupiter descending in a golden shower, found means to elude all the vigilance of her keepers. He inflamed Ægina, the daughter of Æsopus, king of Bœotia, in the similitude of a lambent fire, and then carried her from Epidaurus to a desert isle called Oenope, to which she gave her own name (3). Clytoris, a fair virgin of Thessaly, he debauched in the shape of an ant; but to corrupt Alcmena, the wife of Amphytrion, he was obliged to assume the form of her husband, under which the fair one, deceived, innocently yielded to his desires. By Thalia he had two sons called the Pallaci ; and two by Protogenia, viz. Æthlius, the father of Endymion, and Epaphus, the founder of Memphis in Egypt, and father of Lybia, who gave her name to the continent of Africk. Electra bore him Dardanus, Laodamia, Sarpedon, and Argus, Jodamus, Deucalion, with

many

(2) The Ursa Minor of the Latins, and Cynosura of the Greeks.

(3) The isle of Ægina, in the Archipelago.

many others too tedious to enumerate, though mentioned by the poets.

It is very evident that moft, if not all the ftories relating to the amours of the gods, were invented by their refpective priefts, to cover their corruption or debauchery. Of which this of Danae feems at leaft a palpable inftance, and may ferve to give fome idea of the reft: Acrifius was informed by an oracle, that his grandfon would one day deprive him of his crown and life; on which he fhut up his daughter Danae in a brazen tower, of the temple of Apollo at Delphos, the priefts of which oracle probably gave him this information, with no other view than to forward their fcheme, which tended to gratify the luft of Præteus, the king's brother, who being let through the the roof, pretending to be Jupiter, and throwing large quantities of gold amongft her domeftics, obtained his wifhes.

Two particular adventures of his are too remarkaable to be paffed in filence. He had deluded by his arts Semele, daughter of Cadmus, king of Thebes, who proved with child. Juno hearing of it, and intent on revenge, under the difguife of Beroe, nurfe to the princefs, was admitted to her prefence, and artfully infinuated to her that fhe might not be deceived in her lover, fhe advifed her, the next time he vifited her, to requeft, as a proof of his love, that fhe might fee him in the fame majefty with which he embraced Juno. Jupiter granted, not without reluctance, a favour he knew would be fo fatal to his miftrefs. The unhappy fair-one, unable to bear the dazzling effulgence, perifhed in the flames, and with her, her offspring muft have done fo too, if the god had not taken it out, and inclofed it in his thigh, where it lay the full time, when it came into the world, and was named Bacchus.

Jupiter next fell enamoured with Io, the daughter of Inachus, and, as fome fay, the prieftefs of Juno; having one day met this virgin returning from her father's grotto, he endeavoured to feduce her to an adjacent foreft; but the nymph flying his embraces, he involved her in fo thick a mift, that fhe loft her way, fo that he eafily overtook and enjoyed her. Juno, whofe jealoufy always kept her watchful, miffing her hufband, and perceiving a thick darknefs on the earth, descended, dispelled the cloud, and had certainly discovered the intrigue, had not Jupiter suddenly transformed Io into a white heifer. Juno, pleased with the beauty of the animal, begged her, and to allay her jealousy, he was obliged to yield her up. The goddess immediately gave her in charge to Argus, who had an hundred eyes, two of which only slept at a time. Her lover, pitying the misery of Io in so strict a confinement, sent Mercury down disguised like a shepherd, who with his flute charmed Argus to sleep, sealed his eyes with his *caduceus*, or rod, and then cut off his head. Juno, in regard to his memory, placed his eyes in the tail of the peacock, a bird sacred to her, and then turning her rage against Io, sent the furies to pursue her wherever she went (6); so that the wretched fugitive, weary of life, implored Jove to end her misery. Accordingly the god intreats his spouse to shew her compassion, swearing by Styx never to give her further cause of jealousy. Juno on this becomes appeased, and Io being restored to her former shape, is worshipped in Egypt by the name of Isis.

The fable of Io and Argus is certainly of Egyptian birth, and the true mythology is this: the art of weaving, first invented in Egypt, was by the colonies of that nation carried to Greece and Colchis, where it was practised with this difference, that the seasons for working were varied in each country according to to the nature of the climate. The months of February, March, April, and May, they employed in Egypt, in cultivating their lands; whereas these being winter months with the Grecians, they kept the looms busy. Now the Isis, which pointed out the *neomeniæ*, or monthly festivals in Egypt, was always attended with an *horus*, or figure expressive of the labour peculiar to the season. Thus the *horus* of the weaving months was a little figure stuck over with eyes, to denote the many lights necessary for working
by

(6) Dr. King relates this story a little differently. Io, pursued by Tisiphone (one of the furies) fell into the sea, and was carried first to Thracian Bosphorus, and thence into Egypt, where the monster still pursuing her, was repelled by the Nile. After this she was deified by Jupiter, and appointed to preside over winds and navigation. It is easy to see this agrees better with the Egyptian mythology.

by night. This image was called Argos (7), to signify his intention. Now the vernal Isis being depicted the head of a heifer, to exemplify the fertility and pleasantness of Egypt, on the sun's entrance into Taurus, at the approach of winter she quitted this form, and so was said to be taken into custody of Argos, from whom she was next season delivered by the *horus*, representing Anubis (or Mercury), that is, the rising of the dog-star. The taking these symbolical representations in a literal sense, gave rise to the fable.

It is no wonder if the number of Jupiter's gallantries made him the subject of detestation among the primitive Christians, as well as the ridicule of the wiser among the Heathens. Tertullian observes with judgment, *That it was no way strange to see all ranks so debauched, when they were encouraged in the most infamous crimes by the example of those they worshipped, and from whom they were to expect rewards and punishments.* Lucian, in his dialogues, introduces Momus pleasantly rallying Jove with regard to his amorous metamorphoses: *I have often trembled for you* (says he) *lest when you appeared like a bull, they should have carried you to the shambles, or clapped you in the plough; had a goldsmith catched you when you visited Danae, he would have melted down your godship in his crucible; or when you courted Leda like a swan, what if her father had put you on the spit?*

Jupiter had a multiplicity of names, either from the places where he was worshipped, or the attributes ascribed to him: He had the epithets of Xenius, or the hospitable; Elicious, on account of his goodness and clemency; and Dodonæus, on account of the oracular grove at Dodona, consecrated to him, and famous through all Greece.

Amongst the Romans he had the appellations of Optimus Maximus, on account of his beneficence and power; Almus, from his cherishing all things; Stabilitor, from his supporting the world; Opitulator, from his helping the distressed; Stator, from his suspending

(7) From *argoth*, or *argos*, weaver's work; whence the Greeks borrowed their Εγο·*opus*, or a work. Hence the isle of Amorgos, one of the Ægean isles, derives its name from Am, mother, and Orgin, weavers, or the mother or colony of weavers, being first planted from Egypt.

suspending the flight of the Romans at the prayer of Romulus; and Prædator, on account of part of the plunder being sacred to him in all victories. From the temple at the Capitol, on the Tarpeian rock, he was called Capitolinus and Tarpeius. When a Roman king or general slew an enemy of the same quality, the spoils were offered to him by the name of Feretrius.

The reign of Jupiter not having been so agreeable to his subjects as that of Saturn, gave occasion to the notion of the SILVER AGE; by which is meant an age inferior in happiness to that which preceded, though superior to those which followed.

This *Father of Gods and Men* is commonly figured as a majestic man with a beard, enthroned. In his left hand he holds a victory, and in his right hand grasps the thunder. At his feet an eagle with his wings displayed. The Greeks called him Ζηνα, and Δία, as the cause of life (8), the Romans, Jupiter, i.e. *juvans pater*, the assisting father.

The heathens had amongst their deities different representatives of the same thing. What Vesta, or the Idæan mother, was to the Phrygians, and Isis to the Egyptians; the same was Jupiter to the Greeks and Romans, the great symbol of Æther. So the author of the life of Homer, supposed to be the elder Dionysius of Halicarnassus, and the poet himself (9). So Ennius, as quoted by Cicero (1),

Lo the bright heav'n, which all invoke as Jove!
and Euripides (2),

—— *—See the sublime expanse,*
The boundless Æther, which enfolds this ball
That hold for Jove, the God supreme o'er all!

To conclude with the words of Orpheus; *Jove is omnipotent, he is the first and the last; the head and the*
middle;

(8) Plato in Cratylo.

(9) Ζεὺς δὲ ὁ αἰθὴρ, τουτέςιν ἢ τυ ωδης καὶ ἐνδεςμος ὑσιῶ; Ζεὺς δ' ἔλαχ' ὃ ξανὸν εὑρὶν ἐν αἰθέρι καὶ νεφέλεσιν.
Opusc. Mytholog. p. 326 & 327.

(1) *Aspice hoc sublime candens, quem invocant omnes* Jovem.
(2) *Vides sublime fusum, immoderatum æthera,*
Qui tenero terram circumjecta amplectitur,
Hunc summum habeto divum; hunc perhibeto Jovem,
Cicero de Nat. Deorum, l. 2.

middle; the giver of all things; the foundation of the earth and starry heavens; he is both male and female, and immortal. Jupiter is the source of enlivening fire, and the spirit of all things.

CHAP. XVI.

OF JUNO.

JUNO, the fifter and confort of Jupiter, was on that account ftiled the queen of heaven, and indeed we find her in the poets fupporting that dignity with an ambition and pride fuitable to the rank fhe bore.

Though the poetical hiftorians agree fhe came into the world at a birth with her hufband, yet they differ as to the place, fome placing her nativity at Argos, others at Samos near the river Imbrafus. Some fay fhe was nurfed by Eubæa, Porfymna, and Aræa, daughters of the river Afterion; others by the Nymphs of the ocean. Otes, an ancient poet, tells us fhe was educated by the Horæ or Hours: and Homer affigns this poft to Oceanus and Tethys themfelves.

It is faid that this goddefs, by bathing annually in the fountain of Canatho near Argos, renewed her virginity. The places where fhe was principally honoured were Sparta, Mycene, and Argos. At this place the facrifice offered to her confifted of 100 oxen.

Juno in a peculiar manner prefided over marriage and child-birth; on the firft occafion, in facrificing to her, the gall of the victim was always thrown behind the altar, to denote no fpleen fhould fubfift between married perfons. Women were peculiarly thought to be under her protection, of whom every one had her Juno, as every man had his guardian genius. Numa ordered, that if any unchafte woman fhould approach her temple, fhe fhould offer a female lamb to expiate her offence.

The Lacedemonians ftyled her Ægophaga, from the goat which Hercules facrificed to her. At Elis fhe was called Hoplofmia, her ftatue being completely armed.

armed. At Corinth she was termed Bunœa, from Buno, who erected a temple to her there. She had another at Eubœa, to which the emperor Adrian presented a magnificent offering, consisting of a crown of gold, and a purple mantle embroidered with the marriage of Hercules and Hebe in silver, and a large peacock whose body was gold, and his tail composed of precious stones resembling the natural colours.

Amongst the Romans, who held her in high veneration, she had a multiplicity of names. The chief were Lucina, from her first shewing the light to infants; Pronuba, because no marriage was lawful without previously invoking her; Socigena and Juga, from her introducing the conjugal yoke, and promoting matrimonial union; Domiduca, on account of her bringing home the bride; Unxia, from the anointing the door posts at the ceremony; Cinxia, from her unloosing the virgin zone, or girdle; Perfecta, because marriage completes the sexes; Opigena and Obstetrix, from the assisting women in labour; Populosa, because procreation peoples the world; and Sospita, from her preserving the female sex. She was also named Quiritus or Curitis, from a spear represented in her statues and medals; Kalendaris, because of the sacrifices offered her the first day of every month; and Moneta, from her being regarded as the goddess of riches and wealth.

It is said when the gods fled into Egypt, Juno disguised herself in the form of a white cow, which animal was, on that account, thought to be acceptable to her in her sacrifices.

Juno, as the queen of heaven, preserved a good deal of state. Her usual attendants were Terror and Boldness, Castor and Pollux, and fourteen nymphs; but her most faithful and inseparable companion was Iris, the daughter of Thaumas, who, for her surprising beauty, was represented with wings, borne upon her own rainbow, to denote her swiftness. She was the messenger of Juno, as Mercury was of Jove; and at death separated the souls of women from their corporeal chains.

This goddess was not the most complaisant of wives. We find in Homer, that Jupiter was sometimes obliged to make use of his authority to keep her in due subjection. When she entered into that

famous

famous conspiracy against him, the same author relates, that, by way of punishment, she had two anvils tied to her feet, golden manacles fastened to her hands, and so was suspended in the air or sky, where she hovered, on account of her levity, while all the deities looked on without a possibility of helping her. By this the mythologists say is meant the harmony and connection of the air with the earth, and the inability of the gods to relieve her, signifies that no force, human or divine, can dissolve the frame or texture of the universe. According to Pausanias, the temple of Juno at Athens had neither doors nor roof, to denote that Juno, being the air in which we breathe, can be inclosed in no certain bounds.

The implacable arrogant temper of Juno once made her abandon her throne in heaven, and fly into Eubæa. Jupiter in vain sought a reconciliation, 'till he consulted Citheron, king of the Platæans, then accounted the wisest of men. By his advice the god dressed up a magnificent image, seated it in a chariot, and gave out it was Platæa, the daughter of Æsopus, whom he designed to make his queen. Juno upon this resuming her ancient jealousy, attacked the mock bride, and by tearing off its ornaments found the deceit, quieted her ill humour, and was glad to make up the matter with her husband.

Though none ever felt her resentment more sensibly than Hercules, he was indebted to her for his immortality; for Pallas brought him to Jupiter while an infant, who, while Juno was asleep, put him to her breast. But the goddess waking hastily, some of her milk falling upon heaven formed the milky way. The rest dropped on the earth, where it made the lilies white, which before were of a saffron colour.

Juno is represented by Homer as drawn in a chariot adorned with precious stones, the wheels of ebony nailed with silver, and drawn by horses with reins of gold; but most commonly her car is drawn by peacocks, her favourite bird. At Corinth she was depicted in her temple as seated on her throne, crowned with a pomegranate in one hand, and in the other a sceptre with a cuckoo at top. This statue was of gold and ivory. That at Hierapolis was supported by lions, and so contrived as to participate of Minerva, Venus, Luna, Rhea, Diana, Nemesis, and the Destinies, according to the different points in view. She held in one hand a sceptre, in the other a distaff. Her head was crowned with rays and a tower; and she was girt with the cestus of Venus.

As Jupiter is the *æther*, Juno is the *atmosphere*. She is female on account of its softness; and is called the wife and sister of the other, to import the intimate conjunction between these two (3).

CHAP. XVII.

OF NEPTUNE.

THIS remarkable deity was the son of Saturn and Vesta, or Ops, and the brother of Jupiter. Some say he was devoured by his father. Others allege his mother gave him to some shepherds to be brought up amongst the lambs, and pretending to be delivered of a foal, gave it instead of him to Saturn. Some say his nurse's name was Arno; others, that he was brought up by his sister Juno.

His most remarkable exploit was his assisting his brother Jupiter in his expeditions, for which that god, when he arrived at the supreme power, assigned him the sea and the islands for his empire. Others imagine he was admiral of Saturn's fleet, or rather, according to Pamphus, generalissimo of his forces by sea and land.

The favourite wife of Neptune was Amphitrite, whom he courted a long time to no purpose, till he sent the dolphin to intercede for him, who succeeding, the god in acknowledgment placed him amidst the stars. By her he had Triton. Neptune had two other wives, the one called Salacia, from the salt-water, the other Venilia, from the ebbing and flowing of the tides.

Neptune

---

(3) *Aer autem, ut stoici disputant, inter mare & cælum, Junonis nomine consecratur, quæ est soror & conjux Jovis, quod & similitudo est ætheris & cum eo summa conjunctio. Effeminarunt autem eum, Junonique tribuerunt, quod nihil est eo mollius.* Cicero de Nat. Deor. l. 2.

Neptune is said to be the first inventor of horsemanship and chariot-racing. Hence Mithridates, king of Pontus, threw chariots drawn by four horses into the sea in honour of him, and the Romans instituted horse-races in the Circus during his festival, at which time all horses left working, and the mules were adorned with wreaths of flowers. Probably this idea of Neptune arose from the famous controversy between him and Minerva, when they disputed who should give name to Cecropia. The god, by striking the earth with his trident, produced a horse. Pallas raised an olive-tree, by which she gained the victory, and the new city was from her called Athens. But the true meaning of this fable is a ship, not a horse; for the question really was, whether the Athenians should apply themselves to navigation or agriculture, and as they naturally inclined to the first, it was necessary to shew them their mistake, by convincing them that husbandry was preferable to sailing. However, it is certain Neptune had some skill in the management of horses: for we find in Pamphus, the most ancient writer of divine hymns, this encomium of him, *That he was the benefactor of mankind in bestowing on them horses, and ships with decks resembling towers.*

When Neptune was expelled heaven for his conspiracy against Jupiter, he fled with Apollo to Laomedon, king of Troy, but he treated them differently, for having employed them in raising walls round this city, in which the lyre of Apollo was highly serviceable, he paid that deity divine honours, whereas he dismissed Neptune unrewarded; who, in revenge, sent a vast sea monster to lay waste the country, to appease which Laomedon was forced to expose his daughter Hesione.

On another occasion this deity had a contest with Vulcan and Minerva in regard to their skill. The goddess, as a proof of hers, made a house; Vulcan erected a man, and Neptune a bull; whence that animal was used in the sacrifices paid him. But it is probable, that as the victim was to be black, the design was to point out the raging quality and fury of the sea, over which he presided.

Neptune fell little short of his brother Jupiter in point of gallantry. Ovid in his epistles, has given a
catalogue

catalogue of his miftreffes. By Venus he had a fon called Eryx. Nor did he affume lefs different fhapes to fucceed in his amours. Ceres fled him in the form of a mare; he purfued in that of a horfe; but it is uncertain whether this union produced the Centaur, called Orion, or a daughter. Under the refemblance of the river Enipeus, he debauched Tyro, the daughter of Salmoneus, who bore him Peleus and Neleus. In the fame difguife he begot Othus and Ephialtes, by Ephimedia, wife of the giant Aloees. Melantho, daughter of Proteus, often diverting herfelf by riding on a dolphin, Neptune in that figure furprifed and enjoyed her. He changed Theophane, a beautiful virgin, into an ewe, and affuming the form of a ram, begot the golden fleeced ram, which carried Phryxus to Colchis. In the likenefs of a bird he had Pegafus by Medufa.

He was not only fond of his power of transforming himfelf, but he took a pleafure in beftowing it on his favourites: Proteus his fon poffeffed it in a high degree. He conferred it on Periclimenus, the brother of Neftor, who was at laft killed by Hercules, as he watched him in the form of a fly. He even obliged his miftreffes with it. We find an inftance of this in Metra, the daughter of Erificthon. Her father, for cutting down an oak-grove, confecrated to Ceres, was punifhed with fuch an infatiable hunger, that to fupply it he was forced to fell all he had. His daughter upon this intreated of her lover the power of changing her form at pleafure; fo that becoming fometimes a mare, a cow, or a fheep, her father fold her to relieve his wants, while the buyers were ftill cheated in their purchafe. Having ravifhed Cænis, to appeafe her he promifed her any fatisfaction, on which fhe defired to be turned into a man, that fhe might no more fuffer the like injury. Her requeft was granted, and by the name of Cæneus fhe became a famous warrior.

Neptune was a confiderable deity amongft the Greeks. He had a temple in Arcadia by the name of Proclyftius, or the *over-flower*; becaufe at Juno's requeft, he delivered the country from an inundation. He was called Hippius, Hippocourius, and Taraxippus, from his regulation of horfemanfhip. The places moft celebrated for his worfhip were Tænarus, Corinth,

Corinth, and Calabria, which laſt country was peculiarly dedicated to him. He had alſo a celebrated temple at Rome, enriched with many naval trophies; but he received a ſignal affront from Auguſtus Cæſar, who pulled down his ſtatue, in reſentment for a tempeſt, which had diſperſed his fleet and endangered his life. Some think Neptune the ſame with the ancient god Cenſus, worſhipped at Rome, and ſo called from his adviſing Romulus to the rape of the Sabines.

Let us now examine the mythological ſenſe of the fable. The Egyptians, to denote navigation, and the annual return of the Phænician fleet which viſited their coaſt, uſed the figure of an Oſiris carried on a winged horſe, or holding a three-forked ſpear or harpoon in his hand. To this image they gave the names of Poſeidon (4), or Neptune (5), which the Greeks and Romans afterwards adopted; but which ſufficiently prove this deity had his birth here. Thus the maritime Oſiris of the Egyptians became a new deity with thoſe who knew not the meaning of the ſymbol. But Herodotus, lib. ii. is poſitive that the Greeks received not their knowledge of Neptune from the Egyptians, but from the Lybians. The former received him not till afterwards, and even then, however they might apply the figure to civil purpoſes, paid him no divine honours. However, according to Plutarch, they called the maritime coaſt Nepthen. Bochart thinks he has found the origin of this god in the perſon of Japhet; and has given reaſons which render the opinion very probable.

Neptune, repreſented as god of the ſea, makes a conſiderable figure. He is deſcribed with black or dark hair, his garment of an azure or ſea-green colour, ſeated in a large ſhell drawn by whales or ſea horſes, with his trident in his hand (6), attended by the

(4) From *Paſh*, plenty, or proviſions, and *Jedaim*, the ſea-coaſt; or the proviſion of the maritime countries.

(5) From *Nouph*, to diſturb or agitate, and *Oni*, a fleet, which forms Neptoni, the arrival of the fleet.

(6) Some, by a far fetched alluſion, imagine the triple forks of the trident repreſent the three-fold power of Neptune in *diſturbing*, *moderating* or *calming* the ſeas. Others, his power over ſalt water, freſh water, and that of lakes or pools.

the sea gods Palæmon, Glaucus, and Phorcys; the sea goddesses Thetis, Melita, and Panopœa, and a long train of tritons and sea nymphs. In some ancient gems he appears on shore; but always holding in his hand the three forked trident, the emblem of his power, as it is called by Homer and Virgil, who have given us a fine contrast with regard to its use. The ancient poets all make this instrument of *brass*; the modern painters of *silver*.

CHAP. XVIII.

OF PLUTO.

WE now come to the third brother of Jupiter, and not the least formidable, if we consider his power and dominion. He was also the son of Saturn and Ops, and when his victorious brother had established himself in the throne, he was rewarded with a share in his father's dominions, which, as some authors say, was the eastern continent and lower part of Asia. Others make his division lie in the West, and that he fixed his residence in Spain, which being a fertile country, and abounding in mines, he was esteemed the god of wealth (7).

Some imagine that his being regarded as the *ruler* of the *dead*, and king of the infernal regions, proceeded from his first teaching men to bury the deceased, and inventing funeral rites to their honour. Others say he was a king of the Molossians in Epirus, called Aidoneus Orcus, that he stole Proserpine his wife, and kept a dog called Cerberus, who devoured Pirithous, and would have served Theseus in the same manner, if Hercules had not timely interposed to save him.

The poets relate the matter differently: they tell us that Pluto, chagrined to see himself childless and unmarried, while his two brothers had large families,

---

(7) The poets confounded Pluto, the god of hell, with Plutus, god of riches; whereas they are two very distinct deities, and were always so considered by the ancients.

lies, mounted his chariot to visit the world, and arriving in Sicily, chanced to view Proserpine, with her companions, gathering flowers (8). Urged by his passion he forced her into his chariot, and drove her to the river Chemarus, through which he opened himself a passage back to the realms of night. Ceres, disconsolate for the loss of her beloved daughter, lighted two torches at the flames of Mount Etna, and wandered through the world in search of her; till hearing at last where she was, she carried her complaint to Jupiter, who, on her repeated solicitations, promised that Proserpine should be restored to her, provided she had not yet tasted any thing in hell. Ceres joyfully bore this commission, and her daughter was preparing to return, when Ascalaphus, the son of Acheron and Gorgyra, gave information, that he saw Proserpine eat some grains of a pomegranate she had gathered in Pluto's orchard, so that her return was immediately countermanded. Ascalaphus was for this malicious intelligence transformed into a toad. But Jupiter, in order to mitigate the grief of Ceres, for her disappointment, granted that her daughter should half the year reside with her, and the other half continue in hell with her husband. It is easy to see, that this part of the fable alludes to the corn, which must remain all the winter hid in the ground, in order to sprout forth in the spring, and produce the harvest.

Pluto was extremely revered both amongst the Greeks and Romans. He had a magnificent temple at Pylos, near which was a mountain, that derived its name from the nymph Menthe, whom Proserpine, out of jealousy at Pluto's familiarity with her, changed into the herb called *mint*. Near the river Corellus, in Bœotia, this deity had also an altar in common with Pallas, for some mystical reason. The Greeks called him Agelestus, because all mirth and laughter were banished his dominions; as also Hades, on account of the gloominess of his dominions. Among the Romans he had the name of Februus, from the lustrations used at funerals, and Summanus, because he was the chief of ghosts, or rather the prince of the infernal deities. He was also called the terrestrial or infernal Jupiter.

His

(8) In the valley of Ætna, near mount Ætna.

His chief feftival was in February, and called Chariftia, becaufe then oblations were made for the dead, at which relations aſſiſted, and all quarrels were amicably adjuſted. Black bulls were the victims offered up, and the ceremonies were performed in the night, it not being lawful to facrifice to him in the daytime (9).

Pluto is generally repreſented in an ebony chair, drawn by four black horſes, whoſe names the poets have been careful to ſubmit (1) to us. Sometimes he holds a ſceptre to denote his power, at others a *wand*, with which he commands and drives the ghoſts. Homer ſpeaks of his helmet, as having the quality of rendering the wearer inviſſible; and tells us, that Minerva borrowed it when ſhe fought againſt the Trojans, to be concealed from Mars.

Let us now ſeek the mythology of the fable in that country where it firſt ſprung, and we ſhall find that the myſterious ſymbols of truth became, in the ſequel, thro' abuſe, the very ſources of idolatry and error. Pluto was indeed the funeral Oſiris of the Egyptians. Theſe people (2) every year, at an appointed ſeaſon, aſſembled to mourn over and offer ſacrifices for their dead. The image that was expoſed, to denote the approach of this ſolemnity, had the name of Peloutah (3) or the Deliverance, becauſe they regarded the death of the good, as a deliverance from evil. This figure was repreſented with a radiant crown, his body being entwined with a ſerpent, accompanied with the figns of the Zodiac, to ſignify the duration of one ſun, or ſolar year.

CHAP.

(9) On account of his averſion to the light.

(1) Orphæus, Æthon, Nycteus, and Alaſtor.

(2) The Jews retained this cuſtom, as we find by the annual lamentations of the virgins over Jeptha's daughter.

(3) From *Palat*, to free or deliver, comes *Peloutah*, deliverance, which is eaſily by corruption made Pluto.

C H A P. XIX.

OF PROSERPINE.

THIS goddess was the daughter of Jupiter and Ceres, and educated in Sicily; from whence she was stole by Pluto, as is related in the preceding chapter. Some say she was brought up with Minerva and Diana, and being extremely beautiful, was courted both by Mars and Apollo, who could neither of them obtain her mother's consent. Jupiter, it is said, was more successful, and ravished her in the form of a dragon. The Phænicians, on the other hand, affirm with more reason, that she was earlier known to them than to the Greeks or Romans; and that it was about 200 years after the time of Moses, that she was carried off by Aidoneus or Orcus, king of the Molossians.

Jupiter, on her marriage with Pluto, gave her the isle of Sicily as a dowry; but she had not been long in the infernal regions, when the fame of her charms induced Theseus and Pirithous to form an association to carry her off. They descended by way of Tænarus, but sitting to rest themselves on a rock in the infernal regions, they could not rise again, but continued fixed, till Hercules delivered Theseus, because his crime consisted only in assisting his friend, as bound by oath (4); but Pirithous was left in durance, because he had endangered himself through his own wilfulness and rashness.

Others made Proserpine the same with Luna, Hecate, and Diana, the same goddess being called Luna in heaven, Diana on earth, and Hecate in hell, when she had the name of Triformis or Tergemina. The Greeks called her Despoina, or the Lady, on account of her being queen of the dead. Dogs and barren cows were the sacrifices usually offered to her.

She is represented under the form of a beautiful woman enthroned, having something stern and melancholy in her aspect.

The

---

(4) They agreed to assist each other in gaining a mistress Pirithous had helped Theseus to get Helena, who in return attended him in this expedition.

The mythological sense of the fable is this: The name of Proserpine or Porsephone, amonst the Egyptians, was used to denote the change produced in the earth by the deluge (5), which destroyed its former fertility, and rendered tillage and agriculture necessary to mankind.

CHAP. XX.

OF THE INFERNAL REGIONS.

IT is evident that the Heathens had a notion of future punishments and rewards, from the description their poets have given of Tartarus and Elysium, though the whole is overloaded with fiction. According to Plato, Apollo and Ops brought certain brazen tablets from the Hyperboreans to Delos, describing the court of Pluto as little inferior to that of Jove; but that the approach to it was exceeding difficult on account of the rivers Acheron, Cocytus, Styx, and Phlegethon, which it was necessary to pass in order to reach these infernal regions.

Acheron was, according to some, the son of Titan and Terra, or, as others say, born of Ceres in a cave, without a father. The reason assigned for his being sent to hell is, that he furnished the Titans with water, during their war with the gods. This shews it was a river, not a person; but the place of it is not ascertained. Some fixing it amongst the Cimmerians near mount Circe (6), and in the neighbourhood of Cocytus; others making it that sulphureous and stinking lake near Cape Misenum in the bay of Naples (7), and not a few tracing its rise from the Acherusian fen in Epirus, near the city of Pandosia; from whence it flows till it falls into the gulph of Ambracia.

The

---

(5) From Peri, fruit, and Patat, to perish, comes Perephattah, or the fruit lost; from Peri, fruit, and Siphon, to hide, comes Persephoneh, or the corn destroyed or hid.
(6) On the coast of Naples.
(7) Near Cuma.

The next river of the Plutonian mansions is Styx, though whether the daughter of Oceanus or Terra, is uncertain. She was married to Pallas or Piras, by whom she had Hydra. To Acheron she bore Victory, who having assisted Jupiter against the giants, he rewarded her mother (8) with this privilege, that the most solemn oath amongst the gods should be by her deity, viz. the river Styx; so that when any of them were suspected of falshood, Iris was dispatched to bring the Stygian water in a golden cup, by which he swore; and if he afterwards proved perjured, he was deprived for a year of his nectar and ambrosia, and for nine years more separated from the celestial assembly. Some place Styx near the lake of Avernus in Italy; others make it a fountain near Nonacris in Arcadia, of so poisonous and cold a nature, that it would dissolve all metals (9), and could be be contained in no vessel.

Cocytus and Phlegethon are said to flow out of Styx by contrary ways, and re-unite to increase the vast channel of Acheron. The waters of Phlegethon were represented as streams of fire, probably on acaccount of their hot and sulphureous nature.

CHAP. XXI.

OF THE PARCÆ OR DESTINIES.

THESE infernal deities, who presided over human life, were in number three, and had each their peculiar province assigned: Clotho held the distaff, Lachesis drew or spun off the thread, and Atropos stood ready with her scissars to cut it asunder.

These were three sisters, the daughters of Jupiter and Themis, and sisters to the Horæ or Hours; according to others, the children of Erebus and Nox. They were secretaries to the gods, whose decrees they wrote.

(8) Some say it was on her own account, for discovering the combination of the giants against Jupiter.

(9) It is reported Alexander was poisoned with it at Babylon, and that it was carried for this purpose in an ass's hoof.

We are indebted to a late ingenious writer for the true mythology of these characters. They were nothing more originally than the mystical figure or symbols, which represented the months of January, February, and March, amongst the Egyptians. They depicted these in female dresses, with the instruments of spinning and weaving, which was the great business carried on in that season. These images they called (1) Parcæ, which signifies linen cloth, to denote the manufacture produced by this industry. The Greeks, who knew nothing of the true sense of these allegorical figures, gave them a turn suitable to their genius, fertile in fiction.

The Parcæ were described or represented in robes of white, bordered with purple, and seated on the thrones, with crowns on their heads, composed of the flowers of the Narcissus.

CHAP. XXII.

OF THE HARPIES.

THE next group of figures we meet in the shadowy realms are the Harpies, who were three in number, Celeno, Aello, and Ocypete, the daughters of Oceanus and Teria. They lived in Thrace, had the faces of virgins, the ears of bears, the bodies of vultures, with human arms and feet, and long claws. Pheneus, king of Arcadia, for revealing the mysteries of Jupiter, was so tormented by them, that he was ready to perish for hunger, they devouring whatever was set before him, till the sons of Boreas, who attended Jason in his expedition to Colchis, delivered the good old king, and drove these monsters to the islands called Echinades, compelling them to swear to return no more.

This fable is of the same original with the former one. During the months of April, May, and June, especially the two latter, Egypt was greatly subject to stormy winds, which laid waste their olive grounds, and brought numerous swarms of grashoppers and other

(1) From Parc, or Paroket, a cloth, curtain, or sail.

other troublesome insects from the shores of the Red Sea, which did infinite damage to the country. The Egyptians therefore gave figures which proclaimed these three months, a female face, with the bodies and claws of birds, and called them Harop (2), and a name which sufficiently denoted the true sense of the symbol. All this the Greeks realized, and embellished in their way.

CHAP. XXIII.

OF CHARON AND CERBERUS.

CHARON, according to Hesiod's theogany, was the son of Erebus and Nox, the parents of the greatest part of the infernal monsters. His post was to ferry the souls of the deceased over the waters of Acheron. His fare was never under one half-penny, nor exceeding three, which were put in the mouth of the persons interred; for as to such bodies who were denied funeral rites, their ghosts were forced to wander an hundred years on the banks of the river, Virgil's Æneid, VI. 330, before they could be admitted to a passage. The Hermonienses alone claimed a free passage, because their country lay so near Hell. Some mortal heroes also, by the favour of the gods, were allowed to visit the infernal realms, and return to light; such as Hercules, Orpheus, Ulysses, Theseus, and Æneas.

This venerable boatman of the lower world, is represented as a fat squalid old man, with a bushy grey beard and rheumatic eyes, his tattered rags scarce covering his nakedness. His disposition is mentioned as rough and morose, treating all his passengers with the same impartial rudeness, without regard to rank, age, or sex. We shall in the sequel see that Charon, was indeed a real person, and justly merited this character.

After crossing the Acheron, in a den adjoining to the entrance of Pluto's palace, was placed Cerberus, or the three-headed dog, born of Typhon and Echid-
ra,

(2) from Haroph, or Harop, a noxious fly; or from Arbeh, a locust.

na, and the dreadful maſtiff, who guarded theſe gloomy abodes. He fawned upon all who entered, but devoured all who attempted to get back; yet Hercules once maſtered him, and dragged him up to earth, where in ſtruggling, a foam dropped from his mouth, which produced the poiſonous herb, called aconite or wolf-bane.

Heſiod gives Cerberus fifty, and ſome a hundred heads; but he is more commonly repreſented with three. As to the reſt, he had a tail of a dragon, and inſtead of hair, his body was covered with ſerpents of all kinds. The dreadfulneſs of his bark or howl, Virgil's Æneid, VI. 416, and the intolerable ſtench of his breath, heightened the deformity of the picture, which of itſelf was ſufficiently diſagreeable.

CHAP. XXIV.

OF NOX, AND HER PROGENY, DEATH, SLEEP, &c.

NOX was the moſt ancient of the deities, and Orpheus aſcribes to her the generation of gods and men. She was even reckoned older than Chaos. She had a numerous offspring of imaginary children, as Lyſſa, or Madneſs, Erys, or Contention, Death, Sleep, and Dreams; all which ſhe bore without a father. From her marriage with Erebus, proceeded Old Age, Labour, Love, Fear, Deceit, Emulation, Miſery, Darkneſs, Complaint, Obſtinacy, Partiality, Want, Care, Diſappointment, Diſeaſe, War, and Hunger. In ſhort, all the evils which attend life, and which wait round the palace of Pluto, to receive his commands.

Death brings down all mortals to the infernal ferry. It is ſaid that her mother Nox beſtowed a peculiar care in her education, and that Death had a great affection for her brother Somnus, or Sleep, of whoſe palace Virgil has given us a fine deſcription, Æneid, VI. 894. Somnus had ſeveral children, of whom Morpheus was the moſt remarkable for his ſatyrical humour, and excellent talent in mimicking the actions of mankind.

Amongſt

Amongst the Eleans, the goddess Nox or Night, was represented by a woman holding in each hand a boy asleep: with their legs distorted; that in her right was white, to signify sleep, that in her left black, to figure or represent death. The sacrifice offered to her was a cock, because of its enmity to darkness, and rejoicing at the light. Somnus was usually represented with wings, to denote his universal sway.

CHAP. XXV.

OF THE INFERNAL JUDGES, MINOS, RHADAMANTHUS, AND EACUS.

AFTER entering the infernal regions, just at the separation of the two roads which lead to Tartarus and Elysium, is placed the tribunal of the three inexorable judges, who examine the dead, and pass a final sentence on departed souls. The chief of these was Minos, the son of Jupiter by Europa, and brother of Rhadamanthus and Sarpedon. After his father's death the Cretans would not admit him to succeed in the kingdom, till praying to Neptune to give him a sign, that god caused a horse to rise out of the sea, on which he obtained the kingdom. Some think this alludes to his reducing these islanders to subjection, by means of a powerful fleet. It is added, that Jove kept him nine years concealed in a cave, to teach him laws and the art of government.

Rhadamanthus, his brother, was also a great legislator. It is said that having killed his brother, he fled to Oechalia in Bœotia, where he married Alcmena, the widow of Amphytrion. His province was to judge such as died impenitent.

Æacus was the son of Jupiter by Ægina. When the isle of Ægina (so called from his mother) was depopulated by a plague, his father, in compassion to his grief, changed all the ants there into men and women. The meaning of which fable is, that when the pirates depopulated the country, and forced the people to fly to caves, Æacus encouraged them to come out, and by commerce and industry recover what they had lost. His character for justice was

such,

such, that in a time of universal drought he was nominated by the Delphic oracle to intercede for Greece, and his prayer was answered.

Rhadamanthus and Æacus were only inferior judges, the first of whom examined the Asiatics, the latter the Europeans, and bore only plain rods as a mark of their office. But all difficult cases were referred to Minos, who sat over them with a sceptre of gold. Their court was held in a large meadow, called the Field of Truth. Plato and Tully add Triptolemus to these as a fourth judge.

CHAP. XXVI.

OF TARTARUS, AND THE EUMENIDES, OR FURIES.

IN the recesses of the infernal regions lay the seat or abode of the wicked souls, called Tartarus, represented by the poets as a vast deep pit, surrounded with walls and gates of brass, and totally deprived of light. This dreadful prison is surrounded by the waters of Phlegethon, which emit continual flames. The custody of the unfortunate wretches doomed to this place of punishment, is given to the Eumenides, or Furies, who are at once their goalers and executioners.

The names of these avengeful sisters were Tisiphone, Alecto, and Megæra: but they went by the general appellation of the Furiæ, on account of the rage and distraction attending a guilty conscience; of Erynniæ, or Erynnis, because of the severity of their punishment; and Eumenides, because though cruel, they were capable of supplication, as Orestes found by following the advice of Pallas. Their birth is so differently related, that it is impossible to fix their genealogy or parentage. Indeed the theogany of the Greeks and Romans requires an uncommon clue to get out of the labyrinth which fiction has contrived.

Though the Furies were implacable, they were susceptible of love. We find an instance of this in Tisiphone, who growing enamoured of Cythæron an amiable youth, and fearing to affright him by her
form,

form, got a third person to disclose her flame. He was so unhappy as to reject her suit, on which she threw one of her snakes at him, which twining round his body strangled him. All the consolation he had in death was to be changed into a mountain, which still bears his name.

These goddesses were so terrible, that it was in some degree sacrilegious to invoke their name.. Yet however the objects of terror, they had their temples, as at Athens near the Areopagus, at Casina in Arcadia, and at Carnia in the Peleponnesus. But their highest solemnities were at Telphusia in Arcadia, where their priestesses went by the name of Hesyclidæ, and the sacrifices were performed at midnight, amidst a profound silence, a black ewe burnt whole being the victim. No wine was used in the libations, but only limpid water, or a liquor made of honey; and the wreaths used were of the flowers of the Narcissus and Crocus intermixed.

The mythologists have assigned each of these tormentresses their particular department. Tisiphone is said to punish the sins arising from hatred and anger; Megæra, those occasioned by envy; and Alecto, the crimes owing to ambition and lust. Some make but one fury, called Adrastia, the daughter of Jupiter and Necessity, and the avenger of all vice.

The furies are depicted with hair composed of snakes, and eyes inflamed with madness, carrying in one hand whips and iron chains, and in the other flaming torches, yielding a dismal light. Their robes are black, and their feet of brass, to shew their pursuit, though slow, is steady and certain.

Is it possible to conceive, that after this solemn and horrid representation, the Eumenides, or Furies, should be quite harmless beings? and the very deformities ascribed to them the symbols of national joy and repose? The Egyptians used these figures to denote the three months of autumn. The serpent was, with that people, the hieroglyphic of life, light, and happiness; the torch was the public indication of a sacrifice; and they placed two quails at the feet of the figure, to signify that the general security was owing to the plenty of the season. All this is elucidated by the names of these visionary beings, Tisiphone

phone (3), Alecto (4), and Megæra (5); which are all derived from circ instances relating to the vintage.

CHAP. XXVII.

OF THE FABULOUS PERSONS PUNISHED IN TARTARUS.

THE poets, in order to people this dismal region, have placed here the Giants or Titans, who rebelled against Jupiter, and who are bound in everlasting chains. They also mention several other notorious criminals condemned to suffer here, the chief of whom follow:

Titius was the son of Jupiter and Elara, daughter of the river Orchomenius in Thessaly. His father, apprehensive of Juno's jealousy, it is said, concealed him in the earth, where he grew to a monstrous bulk. He resided in Panopœa, where he became formidable for rapine and cruelty, till Apollo killed him for endeavouring to ravish Latona; though others say, he was slain by Diana, for an attempt on her chastity. He was next sent to Tartarus, and chained down on his back, his body taking up such a compass as to cover nine acres. In this posture a vulture continually preyed on his liver, which still grew again as fast as it was consumed.

Phlegyas was the son of Mars, and king of the Lapithœ, a people of Thessaly. Apollo having debauched his daughter Coronis, to revenge the injury he set fire to the temple of Delphos; for which sacrilege that god killed him with his arrows, and thrust him into Tartarus, where he is sentenced to sit under a huge rock, which hanging over his head, threatens him with perpetual destruction.

Ixion was the son of Mars and Pisidice, or, as others say, of Æthon and Pisione. Having married Dia, the daughter of Dioneus, he promised very considerable

(3) From Tsaphan, to inclose or hide, and Tseponeh, the time of putting wine into pitchers.
(4) From Leket, to gather.
(5) From Migherah, the sinking of the dregs, or the clarifying the wine.

siderable presents to her father for his consent; but to elude the performance, he invited him to a feast, and murdered him. Stung with remorse for the crime, he run mad, so that Jupiter in compassion not only forgave him, but took him up into heaven, where he had the impiety to endeavour to corrupt Juno. Jupiter, to be the better assured of his wickedness, formed a cloud in the shape of his wife, upon which Ixion begot the Centaurs. But boasting of his happiness, Jove hurled him down to Tartarus, where he lies fixed on a wheel encompassed with serpents, and which turns without ceasing.

Sisiphus was a descendant of Æolus, and married Merope, one of the Pleiades, who bore him Glaucus. His residence was at Epyra in Peleponnesus, and he was a crafty man. The reasons given for his punishment are various, though all the poets agree as to its nature, which was to roll a great stone to the top of a hill, from whence it constantly fell down again, so that his labour was incessantly renewed (6).

Tantalus, a Phrygian monarch, the son of Jupiter and the nymph Plota, had the impiety, in an entertainment he gave the gods, to kill his son Pelops, and serve him up as one of the dishes. All the deities perceived the fraud but Ceres, who eat one of his shoulders; but in compassion to his fate, she restored him to life, by boiling him in a cauldron, and gave him an ivory arm to supply the defect. The crime of the father did not pass unpunished. He was placed in Tartarus, where he was afflicted with eternal thirst and hunger, having water and the most delicious fruits still within his reach; but not being able to taste either, because they vanished before his touch. Ovid IV. 445.

Salmoneus, king of Elis, (Virgil, Æn. VI. 585) had the presumption to personate Jupiter, by driving a chariot over a bridge of brass, and casting flaming torches amongst the spectators, to imitate thunder and lightening. For this he was doomed to the tortures of this infernal dungeon.

The Belides complete this fabulous catalogue. They were the daughters of Danaus, the son of Belus,

(6) Some make Sisiphus a Trojan secretary who was punished for discovering secrets of state. Others say he was a notorious robber killed by Theseus.

lus, who was contemporary with Cecrops, king of Athens. This prince, who came from Egypt into Greece, expelled Sthenelus, king of the Argives, out of his kingdom, and by different wives had these fifty sisters. His brother Egyptus, with whom he had some difference, proposed a reconciliation, by marrying his fifty sons with their fair cousin germans. The wedding was agreed, but Danaus perfidiously directed each of his daughters to murder their husbands on the marriage night. Hypermnestra alone suffered Linceus to escape to Lyrcea, near Argos (7). The Belides, for this unnatural crime, were condemned to draw water out of a well with sieves, and pour it into a certain vessel; so that their labour was without end or success.

C H A P. XXVIII.

OF THE ELYSIAN FIELDS, AND LETHE.

BY way of contrast to Tartarus, or the prison of the wicked, let us place the Elysian Fields, or the happy abodes of the just and good; of which Virgil, of all the ancient poets, has given us the most agreeable picture. Virgil's Æneid, VI. 635. It were endless to give all the variety of descriptions, which a subject of this nature affords room for. An eternal spring of flowers and verdure, a sky always serene, and fanned by ambrosial breezes, an universal harmony and uninterrupted joy embalmed these delightful regions. But at the end of a certain period the souls placed here returned to the world to re-animate new bodies, before which they were obliged to drink at the river Lethe (8), whose waters had the virtue to create an oblivion of all that had passed in the former part of their lives.

To illustrate all this complexed chaos of fable, let us once more have recourse to the Egyptian mythology, where we shall find the whole secret of Tartarus, and the Elysian Fields unravelled. There was near each of the Egyptian towns a certain ground

appointed

(7) He afterwards dethroned Danaus.
(8) Απο της Ληθης, or oblivion.

appointed for a common burial-place. That at Memphis, as described by Diodorus, lay on the other side of the lake Acherusia (9), to the shore of which the deceased person was brought and set before a tribunal of judges appointed to examine into his conduct. If he had not paid his debts, his body was delivered to his creditors, till his relations released it, by collecting the sums due. If he had not faithfully observed the laws, his body was left unburied, or probably thrown into a kind of common shore called Tartarus (1). The same historian informs us, that near Memphis, there was a leaking vessel into which they incessantly poured Nile water, which circumstance gives ground to imagine, that the place where unburied bodies were cast out, was surrounded with emblems expressive of torture or remorse, such as a man tied on a wheel always in motion; another whose heart was the prey of a vulture, and a third rolling a stone up a hill with fruitless toil. Hence the fables of Ixion, Prometheus, and Sysiphus.

When no accuser appeared against the deceased, or the accuser was convicted of falshood, they ceased to lament him, and his panegyric was made; after which he was delivered to a certain severe ferryman, who by order of the judges, and never without it, received the body into his boat (2) and transported it across the lake, to a plain embellished with groves, brooks, and other rural ornaments. This place was called Elizout (3), or the habitation of joy. At the entrance of it, was placed the figure of a dog, with three pair of jaws, which they called Cerberus (4); and

(9) From Acharei, after, and ish, a man, comes Achariis, or the last state of man; or Acheron, that is the ultimate condition.

(1) From the Chaldaic Tarah, admonition, doubled comes Tartarah, or Tartarus, that is an extraordinary warning.

(2) Sometimes the judges denied even their kings funeral rites, on account of their mis-government.

(3) From Elizout, full satisfaction, or a place of repose and joy.

(4) They placed this image on account of that animals known fidelity to man. The three heads denoted the three funeral cries over the corpse, which is the meaning of the name. From Ceri or Cri, an exclamation, and Ber, the grave or vault, comes Cerber. or Cerberus, the cries of the grave.

and the ceremony of interment was ended by thrice (5) sprinkling sand over the aperture of the vault, and thrice bidding the deceased adieu. All these wise symbols addressed as so many instructions to the people, became the sources of endless fiction, when transplanted to Greece and Rome. The Egyptians regarded death as a deliverance (6). The boat of transportation they called Beris (7), or tranquillity; and the waterman who was impartial in the just execution of his office, they stiled Charon, which signifies inflexibility or wrath.

CHAP. XXIX.

OF APOLLO.

THIS deity makes one of the most conspicuous figures in the heathen theology, indeed not unjustly, from the glorious attributes ascribed to him of being the *god of light, medicine, verse,* and *prophecy.* Tully mentions four of this name, the most ancient of whom was the son of Vulcan, and tutelary god of the Athenians; the second a son of Corybas, and born in Crete; the third an Arcadian, called Nomion, from his being a great legislator; and the last, to whom the greatest honour is ascribed, the son of Jupiter and Latona (8), whose beauty having gained the affection of the king of the gods, Juno on discovering her pregnancy, drove her out of heaven, and commanded the serpent Python to destroy her, from whose pursuit Latona fled to the isle of Delos in the shape of a quail (9), where she was delivered of twins, called Diana and Apollo; the latter of whom, soon after his birth, destroyed the monster Python with

(5) *Injecto ter pulvere.* Horace, book I. ode 28.
(6) They called it Peloutah, alleviation or deliverance. Horace has the same thought.
Levare functum pauperum Laboribus. Carm. l. 2. Od. 18.
(7) Beri, quiet, serenity; whence Diodorus Siculus calls Charon's bark Baris.
(8) The daughter of Cæus the Titan, and Phœbe.
(9) Whence the isle was called Ortygia, though some say that Neptune raised it out of the sea to give her refuge

with his arrows (1), though some defer the time of
of this victory till he came to riper years. But Latona's troubles did not end here, for flying into Lycia with her children, she was denied the water of
the fountain Mela, by the shepherd Niocles and his
clowns, upon which she turned them into frogs.
After settling her son Apollo in Lycia, she returned
to Delos, and Diana went to reside in Crete.

The adventures of Apollo are pretty numerous.
The most remarkable are his quarrels with Jupiter,
on account of the death of his son Esculapius, killed
by that deity on the complaint of Pluto, that he decreased the number of the dead by the cures he
performed. Apollo, to revenge this injury, killed
the Cyclops, who forged Jove's thunderbolts, for
which he was banished heaven, and endured great suf-
ferings on earth, being forced to hire himself as a
shepherd to (2) Admetus, king of Thessaly, during
his excercising which office, he is said to have invented the lyre or lute, to sooth his trouble. In this re-
tirement an odd incident happened to him ; Mercury
was born in the morning, by noon he had learned
music, and composed the testudo ; and in the evening
coming to Apollo, he so amused him with this new
instrument, that he found an opportunity to steal his
cattle. Apollo discovering the theft, and insisting on
restitution, the sly deity stole his bow and arrows ;
so that he was forced to change his revenge into
laughter (3).

From Thessaly, Apollo removed to Sparta, and
settled near the river Eurotas, where he fell in love
with a fair boy called Hyacinthus, with whom being
at play, Zephyrus, through envy, blew Apollo's
quoit at his head, and killed him on the spot. To
preserve his memory, the god from his blood raised
the flower which bears his name (4). Though according

(1) Some assert that Diana assisted him in his fight.

(2) Some give this history another turn, and tell us that
Apollo being king of the Arcadians, and deposed for his ty-
ranny, fled to Admetus, who gave him the command of
the country lying near the river Amphrysas, inhabited by
shepherds.

(3) *Te boves olim, nisi redidisses*
    Per dolum amotas, puerum minaci
    Voce dum terret, Viduus Pharetra.
    Risit Apollo.   Horat. Lib. I. Ode X. l. 10.

(4) The Hyacinth or violet.

cording to others he only tinged with it the violet (which was white before) into a purple.

Cypariſſus, a beautiful boy, a favourite of Apollo, being exceſſively grieved for the death of a fawn or deer he loved, was changed by him into a cypreſs tree, which is ſince ſacred to funeral rites.

Apollo next viſited Laomedon, king of Troy, where finding Neptune in the ſame condition with himſelf, and exiled from heaven, they agreed with that king to furniſh bricks to build the wall of his capital; he alſo aſſiſted Alcathous in building a labyrinth, in which was a ſtone whereon he uſed to depoſit his lyre, and which emitted an harmonious ſound on the ſlighteſt ſtroke.

Though Apollo was diſtinguiſhed for his excellency in muſic, yet he was extremely jealous of rivalſhip on this head. The Muſes were under his immediate protection, and the graſhopper was conſecrated to him by the Athenians on account of its harmony (5). We find Midas, king of Phrygia, being conſtituted judge between him and Pan, who pretended to vie with him in harmony, and giving judgment for the latter, was rewarded with a pair of aſs's ears, to point out his bad taſte (6). Ovid has deſcribed this ſtory in an agreeable manner. Linus, who excelled all mortals in muſic, preſuming to ſing with Apollo, was puniſhed with death; nor did Marſyas the ſatyr eſcape much better, for having found a flute or pipe which Minerva threw away (7), he had the vanity to diſpute the prize with Apollo, who being decreed victor, hung up his antagoniſt on the next pine tree, and flayed him alive; but afterwards changed him into a river, which falls into the Meander.

This deity was ſo ſkilled in the bow, that his arrows were always fatal. Python and the Cyclops experienced their force. When the giant Tityus endeavoured to raviſh Diana, he transfixed and threw him into hell, where the vultures preyed on his liver.

Niobe,

(5) The Grecian poets celebrate the graſhopper as a very muſical inſect, that ſings amongſt the higheſt branches of the trees; ſo that it muſt have been a very different creature from the graſhopper known to us. See the notes in Cook's Heſiod.

(6) Ovid, Book XI. Fab. III. line 90.

(7) Becauſe as ſhe blew it, ſeeing herſelf in a fountain, ſhe found it deformed her face.

Niobe, the daughter of Tantalus, and wife of Amphion, being happy in seven sons and as many daughters, was so foolish as to prefer herself to Latona. This so enraged Apollo and Diana, that the former slew her sons with his darts, and the latter killed her daughters in the embraces of their mother, whom Jupiter, in compassion to her incessant grief, turned into a stone, which still emits moisture instead of tears (8).

The true meaning of the fable of Niobe is this, it signified the annual inundation of Egypt. The affront she offered to Latona was a symbol, to denote the necessity she laid that people under of retreating to the higher grounds. The fourteen children of Niobe are the fourteen cubits, that marked the increase of the Nile (9). Apollo and Diana killing them with their arrows, represents labour and industry, with the assistance of the sun's warm influence, overcoming these difficulties, after the retreat of the flood. Niobe's being turned to a stone, was owing to an equivocation. The continuance of Niobe was the preservation of Egypt. But the word Selau, which signified safety, by a small alteration (Selaw) expressed a stone. Thus Niobe became a real person metamorphosed to a rock.

Apollo resembled his father Jupiter, in his great propensity to love. He spent some time with Venus in the isle of Rhodes, and during their interview it is said the sky rained gold, and the earth was covered with lillies and roses. His most celebrated amour was with Daphne, (the daughter of the river Peneus) a virgin of Thessaly, who was herself prepossessed in favour of Lucippus, a youth of her own age. Apollo, to be revenged upon his rival, put it into his head to disguise himself amongst the virgins who went bathing, who discovering the deceit, stabbed him. After this the god pursued Daphne, who flying to preserve her chastity, was, on her intreaties to the gods, changed into a laurel (1), whose leaves Apollo immediately consecrated to bind his temples, and made that tree the reward of poetry.

The

(8) Ovid, Book VI. l. 310.
(9) The statue of Nile in the Thuilleries at Paris, has fourteen children placed by it, to denote these cubits.
(1) Ovid, Book I. l. 556.
——— *grasping at empty praise*
He snatch'd at Love, and filled his arms with bays. Waller.

The nymph Bolina, rather than yield to his suit, threw herself into the sea, for which he rendered her immortal: nor was he much more successful in his courtship of the nymph Castalia, who vanished from him in the form of a fountain, which was afterwards sacred to the muses (2). He debauched Leucothoe, daughter of Orchanus, king of Babylon, in the shape of her mother Eurynome. Clytia, her sister, jealous of her happiness, discovered the amour to their father, who ordered Leucothoe to be buried alive. Her lover, in pity to her fate, poured nectar on her grave, which turned the body into a tree which weeps the gum called frankincense. He then abandoned Clytia, who pined away, continually looking on the sun, till she became the Heliotrope or sunflower (3).

Of the children of Apollo we shall speak more at large in the following section.

Apollo had a great variety of names, either taken from his principal attributes, or the chief places where he was worshipped. He was called the Healer, from his enlivening warmth and cheering influence, and Pæan (4), from the pestilential heats; to signify the former, the ancients placed the graces in his right hand, and for the latter a bow and arrows in his left; Nomius, or the shepherd, from his fertilizing the earth, and thence sustaining the animal creation; Delius (5), from his rendering all things manifest; Pythias, from his victory over Python; Lycius, Phœbus, and Phaneta, from his purity and splendor.

The principal places where he was worshipped were Chrysus, Tenedos, Smyntha, Cylla, Cyrrha, Patrœa, Claros, Cynthius, Abæa, a city in Lycia, at Meletus, and amongst the Mæonians, from all which places he was denominated. He had an oracle and temple at Tegyra, near which were two remarkable fountains, called the Palm and the Olive, on account of the sweetness and transparency of the water. He had an oracle at Delos, for six months in the summer season, which for the rest of the year was removed to Patara in Lycia, and these removals were made
with

(2) Thence called Castalian sisters.
(3) Ovid, Book IV. l. 205.
(4) Ἀπὸ τῦ παίειν τάς ανίας.
(5) Ἀπὸ τῦ δῆλα πάντα ποιεῖν.

with great solemnity. But his most celebrated temple was at Delphos, the original of which was thus: Apollo being instructed in the art of divination by Pan, the son of Jupiter, and the nymph Thymbris, went to this oracle, where at that time Themis gave her answers; but the serpent Python hindering him from approaching the oracle he slew him, and so took possession of it. His temple here, in process of time, became so frequented, that it was called the oracle of the earth, and all the nations and princes in the world vied with each other in their munificence to it. Crœsus, king of Lydia, gave at one time a thousand talents of gold to make an altar there, besides presents of immense value at other times. Phalaris, the tyrant of Agrigentum, presented it a brazen bull, a master-piece of art. The responses here were delivered by a virgin priestess (6) called Pythia, or Phœbus, placed on a tripos (7) or stool with three feet, called also Cortina, from the skin of the Python with which it was covered. It is uncertain after what manner these oracles were delivered, though Cicero supposes the Pithoness was inspired, or rather intoxicated by certain vapours which ascended from the cave. In Italy, Apollo had a celebrated shrine at mount Soracte, where his priests were so remarkable for sanctity, that they could walk on burning coals unhurt. The Romans erected to him many temples. After the battle of Actium, which decided the fate of the world, and secured the empire to Augustus, this prince not only built him a chapel on that promontory, and renewed the solemn games to him, but soon after raised a most magnificent temple to him on mount Palatine, in Rome, the whole of Parian marble. The gates were of ivory exquisitely carved, and over the frontispiece were the solar chariot and horses of massy gold. The portico contained a noble library of the Greek and Latin authors. Within, the place was decorated with noble paintings, and a statue of the god by the famous Scopas, attended by a gigantic figure

(6) Some say the Pythoness being once debauched, the oracles were afterwards delivered by an old woman in the dress of a young maid.

(7) Authors vary as to the tripos, some making it a vessel in which the priests bathed.

figure in brass fifty feet high. In the area were four brazen cows, representing the daughters of Prætus, king of the Argives, who were changed into that form for presuming to rival Juno in beauty. These statues were wrought by Myron.

The usual sacrifices to Apollo were lambs, bulls, and oxen. The animals sacred to him were the wolf, from his acuteness of sight; the crow, from her augury, or foretelling the weather; the swan from its divining its own death; the hawk, from its boldness in flight; and the cock, from its foretelling his rise. The grashopper was also reckoned agreeable to him on account of its music. Of trees, the laurel, palm, olive, and juniper, were most in esteem with him. All young men, when their beards grew, consecrated their locks in his temple, as the virgins did theirs in the temple of Diana.

The four great attributes of Apollo were *divination, healing, music,* and *archery*; all which manifestly refer to the sun. Light dispelling darkness is a strong emblem of truth dissipating ignorance; what conduces more to life and health than the solar warmth, or can there be a juster symbol of the planetary harmony than Apollo's (7) lyre? As his darts are said to have destroyed the monster Python, so his rays dry up the noxious moisture, which is pernicious to vegetation and fruitfulness.

The Persians, who had a high veneration for this planet, adored it, and the light proceeding from it, by the names of Mithra and Orosmanes; the Egyptians by those of Osiris and Orus; and from their antiquities, let us now seek some illustration of the birth and adventures of Apollo.

The Isis which pointed out the *neomenia*, or monthly festival, before their annual inundation, was the symbolical figure of a creature with the upper part of a woman, and the hinder of a lizard, placed in a reclining posture. This they called Leto (8), and used it to signify to the people the necessity of laying in the provisions of olives, parched corn, and such other kinds of dry food, for their subsistence, during the flood. Now when the waters of the Nile decreased

(7) The seven strings of which are said to represent the seven planets.

(8) From Leto, or Letoah, a lizard.

decreased time enough to allow them a month, before the entrance of the sun into Sagittarius, the Egyptian farmer was sure of leisure enough to survey and sow his ground, and of remaining in absolute security till harvest. This conquest of the Nile was represented by an Orus, or image, armed with arrows, and subduing the monster Python. This they called Ores (9), or Apollo (1). The figure of Isis above-mentioned they also stiled Deione, or Diana (2), and they put in her hand the quail, a bird which with them was the emblem of security (3).

These emblems, carried by the Phænicians into Greece, gave rise to all the fable of Latona persecuted by the Python, and flying to Delos in the form of a quail, where she bore Orus and Dione, or Apollo and Diana. Thus (as on former occasions) the hieroglyphics, only designed to point out the regular festivals, and to instruct the people in what they were to do, became in the end the objects of a senseless and gross idolatry.

When Tyre was besieged by Alexander, the citizens bound the statue of Apollo with chains of gold; but when that conqueror took the place, he released the deity, who thence obtained the name of Philalexandrus, or the friend of Alexander. At Rhodes, where he was worshipped in a peculiar manner there was a colossal image of him at the mouth of the harbour seventy cubits high (4).

Phœbus (5) was very differently represented in different countries and times, according to the character he assumed. To depict the solar light, the Persians used a figure with the head of a lion covered with a Tiara, in the Persian garb, and holding a mad bull by the horns, a symbol plainly

of

(9) From Hores, a destroyer or waster.
(1) Apollo signifies the same
(2) From Dei, sufficiency, comes Deione, abundance.
(3) Selave in the Phænician signifies security, as also a quail; hence they used the quail to signify the thing. The Latin words Salus and Salvo are derived from hence.
(4) We shall speak of this hereafter.
(5) From Pheob, the source, and *ob*, the overflowing, or the *source of the inundation*, the Egyptians expressing the annual excess of the Nile by a sun, with a river proceeding from its mouth.

of Egyptian original. The latter people expressed him sometimes by a circle with rays; at other times by a sceptre with an eye over it; but their great emblem of the solar light, as distinguished from the orb itself, was the golden seraph, or fiery flying serpent (6). The Hicropolitans shewed him with a pointed beard, thereby expressing the strong emission of his rays downward; over his head was a basket of gold, representing the etherial light: he had a breast-plate on, and in his right hand held a spear, on the summit of which stood the image of victory (so that Mars is but one of his attributes); this bespoke him irresistible and ruling all things: in his left hand was a flower, intimating the vegetable creation nourished, matured, and continued by his beams: around his shoulders he wore a vest, depicted with gorgons and snakes; this takes in Minerva, and by it is expressed the virtue and vigour of the solar warmth, enlivening the apprehension and promoting wisdom; whence also he is with great propriety the president of the muses: close by were the expanded wings of the eagle, representing the æther, stretched out from him as from its proper center: at his feet were three female figures encircled by a seraph, that in the midst being the emblem of the earth rising in beauty from the midst of *nature* and *confusion* (the other two) by the emanation of his *light*, signified by the seraph or dragon.

Under the character of the sun, Apollo was depicted in a chariot drawn by four horses, whose names the poets have taken care to give us as well as those of Pluto. The poets feigned each night that he went to rest with Thetis in the ocean, and that the next morning the Hours got ready his horses for him to renew his course, (see Cambray's Telemaque for a picture) and unbarred the gates of day. It is no wonder they have been lavish on a subject, which affords such extensive room for the imagination to display itself, as the beauties of the sun-rising. When represented as Liber Pater (7), he bore a shield to
shew

(6) Vide Macrob. Saturn. l. 1, c. 17.
(7) Virgil gives him this name in his first Georgic.
―――*Vos, O clarissima mundi*
Lumina, labentum cælo qui ducitis annum,
Liber & alma Ceres.

shew his protection of mankind. At other times he was drawn as a beardless youth, his locks dishevelled, and crowned with laurel, holding a bow in his right hand with his arrows, and the lyre in his left. The palace of the sun has been admirably described by Ovid, as well as his car, in the second book of his Metamorphosis.

CHAP. XXX.

OF THE SONS OR OFFSPRING OF APOLLO, ÆSCULAPIUS, PHAETON, ORPHEUS, IDMON, ARISTÆUS, &c.

AS Apollo was a very gallant deity, so he had a very numerous issue, of which it is necessary to give some account, as they make a considerable figure in poetical history. The first and most noted of his sons was Æsculapius, whom he had by the nymph Coronis. Some say that Apollo shot his mother, when big with child of him, on account of her infidelity; but repenting the fact, saved the infant, and gave him to Chiron to be instructed (8) in physic. Others report, that as king Phlegyas, her father, was carrying her with him into Pelopennesus, her pains surprised her on the confines of Epidauria, where, to conceal her shame, she exposed the infant on a mountain. However this be, under the care of this new master he made such a progress in the medical art, as gained him a high reputation; so that he was even reported to have raised the dead. His first cures were wrought upon Ascles, king of Epidaurus, and Aunes, king of Daunia, which last was troubled with sore eyes. In short, his success was so great, that Pluto, who saw the number of his ghosts daily decrease, complained to Jupiter, who killed him with his thunderbolts.

Cicero reckons up three of his name. The first the son of Apollo, worshipped in Arcadia, who invented

(8) Ovid, who relates the story of Coronis in his fanciful way, tells us that Corvus, or the raven, who discovered her amour, had, by Apollo, his feathers changed from *black* to *white*.

vented the probe and bandages for wounds; the second, the brother of Mercury, killed by lightening; and the third, the son of Arsippus and Arsione, who frst taught the art of tooth-drawing and purging. Others make Æsculapius an Egyptian, king of Memphis, antecedent by a thousand years to the Æsculapius of the Greeks. The Romans numbered him amongst the Dii Adscititii, of such as were raised to heaven by their merit, as Hercules, Castor, and Pollux, &c.

The Greeks received their knowledge of Æsculapius from the Phænicians and Egyptians. His chief temples were at Pergamus, Smyrna, at Trica, a city of Ionia, and the isle of Coos; in all which, votive tablets were hung up (9), shewing the diseases cured by his assistance; but his most famous shrine was at Epidaurus, where every five years in the spring, solemn games were instituted to him nine days after the Isthmian games at Corinth.

The Romans grew acquainted with him by an accident; a plague happened in Italy, the oracle was consulted, and the reply was, that they should fetch the god Æsculapius from Epidaurus. An embassy was appointed of ten senators, at the head of whom was Q. Ogulnius. These deputies, on their arrival, visiting the temple of the god, a huge serpent came from under the altar, and crossing the city, went directly to their ship, and lay down in the cabin of Ogulnius; upon which they set sail immediately, and arriving in the Tiber, the serpent quitted the ship, and retired to a little island opposite the city, where a temple was erected to the god, and the pestilence ceased.

The animals sacrificed to Æsculapius were the goat; some say, on account of her nursing him; others, because this creature is unhealthy, as labouring under a perpetual fever. The dog and the cock were sacred to him, on account of their fidelity and vigilance. The raven was also devoted to him for its forecast, and being skilled in divination. Authors are not agreed as to his being the inventor of physic, some affirming that he only perfected that part which relates to the regimen of the sick.

Let

(9) From these tablets or votive inscriptions, Hippocrates is said to have collected his aphorisms.

Let us now seek for the origin of this fable. The public sign or symbol exposed by the Egyptians in their assemblies, to warn the people to mark the depth of the inundation, in order to regulate their ploughing accordingly, was the figure of a man with a dog's head carrying a pole with serpents twisted round it, to which they gave the names of Anubis (1), Thaaut (2), and Æsculapius (3). In process of time they made use of this representation for a real king, who, by the study of physic, sought the preservation of his subjects. Thus the dog and the serpents became the characteristics of Æsculapius amongst the Romans and Greeks, who were entirely strangers to the original meaning of these hieroglyphics.

Æsculapius had, by his wife Epione, two sons, Machaon and Podalirius, both skilled in surgery, and who are mentioned by Homer as present at the siege of Troy, and were very serviceable to the Greeks. He had also two daughters, called Hygiœa and Jaso.

This deity is represented in different attitudes. At Epidaurus his statue was of gold and ivory (4), seated on a throne of the same materials, his head crowned with rays, and a long beard, having a knotty stick in one hand, the other entwined with a serpent, and a dog lying at his feet. The Phliasians depicted him as beardless; and the Romans crowned him with laurel, to denote his descent from Apollo. The knots in his staff signify the difficulties that occur in the study of medicine.

Phaeton was the son of Apollo and the nymph Clymene. Having a dispute with Epaphus, the son of Jupiter and Io, the latter upbraided him, that he was not really the son of his father, and that his mother only made use of that pretence to cover her infamy. The youth, fired at this reproach, by his mother's advice carried his complaint to his father Phœbus, who received him with great tenderness, and, to allay his disquietude, swore by Styx to grant him

(1) From Hannobeach, which in Phœnician signifies the barker, or warner, Anubis.

(2) The word Tayant, signifies the dog.

(3) From Aish, man, and Caleph, dog, comes Æscaleph, the mandog, or Æsculapias.

(4) This image was the work of Thrasymedes, the son of Arignotus, a native of Paros.

him whatever he requested, as a mark of his acknowledging him for his son. Phaeton boldly asked the direction of the solar chariot for one day. The father, at once grieved and surprised at the demand, used all arguments in vain to dissuade him from the attempt; but being by his oath reduced to submit to his obstinacy, he gave him the reins, with the best directions he could how to use them. The ambition of our young adventurer was too fatal to himself. He lost his judgment and way together; and Jupiter, to prevent his setting the world on fire, was obliged with his thunderbolts to hurl him from his seat into the river Eridanus or the Po. His sisters Phaethusa, Lampetia, and Phœbe, lamented his loss so incessantly upon the banks, that the gods changed them into black poplar trees, whose juice produces the electrum or amber. Cycnus, king of Liguria, no less grieved for his loss, was changed into a swan, a bird which became after sacred to Apollo. This story makes a very considerable figure in Ovid (5), who has out-done himself on this subject.

A late author offers an ingenious conjecture, with regard to this fable (6). Linen-cloth was the great manufacture of Egypt, and the bleaching of it consequently of great importance. The image exposed for directing this, was a youth with rays round his head, and a whip in his hand, seated on an orb, to which they gave the name of Phaeton (7), and Ben-Climmah (8). Probably the months of May, June, and July, were the three sisters of Phaeton, because during these months they washed their linen white; of which Cygnus, or the swan, the friend of Phaeton, is a further symbol. Now as the word Albanoth, applied to these months (9), signifies also poplar trees, it gave rise to this metamorphoses.

Orpheus

(5) Ovid Metamorph. lib. II. in principio.
(6) La Pluche hist. de Cieux.
(7) From Pha the month, and Eton linen, is made Phaeton; that is, the indiction of the linen works.
(8) Ben-Climmah, the son of hot weather. Hence the story of Phaeton's burning the world.
(9) Albanoth, or Lebanoth, signifies the whitening fields or yards for bleaching.

Orpheus was the son of Phœbus, by the muse Calliope (1). He was born in Thrace, and resided near mount Rhodope, where he married Eurydice, a princess of that country. Aristeus, a neighbouring prince, who fell in love with her, attempted to surprise her, and in her flight, to escape his violence, she was killed by the bite of a serpent. Her disconsolate husband was so affected at his loss, that he descended by the way of Tænarus to hell, in order to recover her. As music and poetry were to him hereditary talents, he exerted them in so powerful a manner, that Pluto and Proserpine were so far touched, as to restore him his beloved consort on *one* condition, that he should not look back on her, till they came to the light of the world. His impatient fondness made him break this article, and he lost her for ever. Grieved at her loss, he retired to the woods and forests, which it is said were sensible of his harmony (2). But the Mænades or Bacchæ, either incensed at his vowing a widowed life, or, as others say, instigated by Bacchus, whose worship he neglected (3), tore him in pieces, and scattered his limbs about the fields, which were collected and buried by the Muses. His head and harp, which were cast into the Hebrus, were carried to Lesbos, and the former interred there. His harp was transported to the skies, where it forms one of the constellations. He himself was changed into a swan, and left a son called Methon, who founded in Thrace a city of his own name. Ovid has given us this whole story (4); but contrary to his usual method, has broke the thread of it, by intersperfing it in different parts of his work.

It is certain that Orpheus may be placed as the earliest poet of Greece, where he first introduced *astronomy*, *divinity*, *music*, and *poetry*, all which he had learned in Egypt. He wrote many volumes in natural philosophy and antiquities (5), of which only a few
imperfect

(1) Some make him the son of Oeagrus and Calliope.
(2) Ovid Metam. lib. XI. in principio.
(3) Others say by Venus, on account of his despising her rites, and that the nymphs, excited by her, tore him in pieces in struggling who should have him.
(4) In his Xth and XIth books.
(5) He wrote a book of hymns, and treatises on the generation of the elements; on the giants war: on the rape of Proserpine; on the labours of Hercules; of stones; on the rites and mysteries of the Egyptians.

imperfect fragments have escaped the rage of time. In his book of stones, he says of himself, *He could understand the flight and language of birds, stop the course of rivers, overcome the poison of serpents, and even penetrate the thoughts of the heart* (6).

Let us seek the origin of this fable once more in Egypt, the mother-country of fiction. In July, when the sun entered Leo, the Nile overflowed all the plains. To denote the public joy at seeing the inundation rise to its due height, they exhibited a youth playing on the lyre or sistrum, and sitting by a tame lion. When the waters did not increase as they should, this Horus was represented stretched on the back of a lion as dead. This symbol they called Oreph or Orpheus (7), to signify that agriculture was then quite unseasonable and dormant. The songs they amused themselves with at this dull season, for want of exercise, were called the hymns of Orpheus; and as husbandry revived immediately after, it gave rise to the fable of Orpheus returning from hell. The Isis placed near this Horus, they called Eurydice (8), and as the Greeks took all these figures in the literal, and not in the emblematical sense, they made Eurydice the wife of Orpheus.

Idmon was the son of Apollo by Asteria, and attended the Argonauts in their expedition to Colchis, being famed for his skill in augury; but wandering from his companions, as they occasionally landed, he was killed by a wild boar.

Another of the children of Apollo was Linus, whom he had by the nymph Terpsichore. He was born at Thebes, and eminent for learning, if it be true that Thamyris, Orpheus, and Hercules, were all his scholars. Some say he was slain by the latter for ridiculing him; but if Orpheus (as others affirm) lived a hundred years before Hercules, it is rather probable that Linus was the disciple of Orpheus. However this be, Linus wrote on the origin of the world, the course of the sun and moon, and the production of animals.

After

(6) This probably gave rise to the fable of his making rocks and forests move to his lyre.

(7) From Oreph, occiput, or the back part of the head.

(8) From Eri, a lion, and Daca, tamed, is formed Eridaca, Eurydice, or the lion tamed, i. e. the violence or rage of the inundation overcome.

After all, Linus was only a symbol of the Egyptians, which the Greeks, according to custom, personated. At the end of autumn or harvest, the Egyptians fell to their night-work, of making linen-cloth (9), and the figure then exposed was called Linus (1), and denoted the sitting up or watching during the night.

Aristæus was the son of Apollo, by Cyrene, a virgin nymph, who used to accompany him in hunting, and whom he first fell in love with on seeing her encounter a lion. He was born in Lybia. He received his education from the nymphs, who taught him to extract oil from olives, and to make honey, cheese, and butter; all which arts he communicated to mankind. On this account he was regarded as a rural deity. From Africa he passed into Sardinia and Sicily, from whence he travelled into Thrace, where Bacchus initiated him in his mysteries. We have already mentioned how his passion occasioned the death of Eurydice, to revenge which the wood-nymphs destroyed his bee-hives. Concerned at this loss, he advised with his mother, and was told by the oracle to sacrifice bulls to appease her shade; which counsel following, the bees which issued from the carcases fully supplied the damages he had sustained (2). He died near mount Hæmus, and was deified on account of the services he had done to mankind by his useful inventions. He was also honoured in the isle of Coos, for his calling the Etesian winds to relieve them in an excessive time of heat. Herodotus says, that he appeared at Cyzicum after his death, and three hundred and forty years after, was seen in Italy, at Metapontum, where he enjoined the inhabitants to erect a statue to him near that of Apollo; which, on consulting the oracle, they performed.

Circe was the daughter of Phœbus, by Persis, the child of Oceanus, and a celebrated sorceress. Her first husband was a king of the Sarmatæ, whom she poisoned,

---

(9) This was their chief manufacture.

(1) Linus, from Lyn, to watch, whence our word linen, that is, the work, for the time of doing it.

(2) Virgil has introduced this story with great elegance and propriety, in his IVth Georgic, l. 314.

foned, for which she was expelled the kingdom, and fled to a promontory on the coast of Tuscany, which afterwards took her name. Here she fell in love with Glaucus, one of the sea deities, who preferring Scylla to her, she changed her into a sea monster. Picus, king of the Latins, her next favourite, for rejecting her addresses, was metamorphosed into a woodpecker.

The most remarkable of Circe's adventures, was with Ulysses. This prince returning from Troy, was cast away on her coast, and his men, by a drink she gave them, were transformed to swine, and other beasts. Ulysses was preserved by Mercury, who gave him the herb moly, to secure him from her enchantments, and instructed him, when she attempted to touch him with her wand, to draw his sword, and make her swear by Styx, she would use him as a friend, otherwise he would kill her. By this means, he procured the liberty of his companions, and continued a year with Circe, who bore him two children, viz. Agrius and Latinus. Circe had a sepulchre in one of the isles, called Pharmacusæ, near Salamis.

Circe was no other than the Egyptian Isis, whose Horus, or attending image, every month assuming some different form, as a human body, with the head of a lion, dog, serpent, or tortoise, gave rise to the fable of her changing men by her inchantments into these animals. Hence the Egyptians gave her the name of Circe, which signifies the Ænigma.

Apollo had many other children. Æthusa, the daughter of Neptune, bore him Elutherus. By Evadne he had Janus; by Atria, Miletus, Oaxus, and Arabus, who gave his name to Arabia; by Melia, he had Ismenious and Tænarus; by Aglaia, Thestor; by Manto, Mopsus; by Anathrippe, Chius; by Achalide, he had Delphus, and many others too tedious to enumerate.

CHAP.

CHAP. XXXI.

OF THE MUSES, AND PEGASUS, THE GRACES, AND THE SYRENS.

THESE celebrated goddesses, the Muses, were the daughters of Jupiter and Mnemosyne, though some think them born of Cœlus. Their number at first was only three or four (3), but Homer and Hesiod have fixed it at nine (4), which it has never since exceeded. They were born on mount Pierus, and educated by the nymph Eupheme.

They had many appellations common to them all, as Pierides, from the place of their birth; Heliconides, from mount Helicon, in Bœotia; Pernassides, from the hill of Parnassus, in Phocis; Citherides, from mount Citheron, a place they much frequented; Aonides, from Aonia; Hippocranides, Agannipides, and Castalides, from different fountains consecrated to them, or to which they were supposed to resort.

In general they were the tutelar goddesses of all sacred festivals and banquets, and the patronesses of all polite and useful arts. They supported virtue in distress, and preserved worthy actions from oblivion. Homer calls them mistresses and correctresses of manners (5). With regard to the sciences, these sisters had each their particular province or department, though poetry seemed more immediately under their united protection.

Calliope (so called from the sweetness of her voice) presided over rhetoric, and was reckoned the first of the nine sisters.

Clio,

---

(3) *Mneme, Aede, Melete*, that is, Memory, Singing, and Meditation, to which some add Thelexiope.

(4) Some assign as a reason for this, that when the citizens of Sicyon directed three skilful statuaries, to make each three statues of the three muses, they were all so well executed, that they did not know which to choose, but erected all the nine, and that Hesiod only gave them names.

(5) Hence the old bards and poets were in such high esteem, that when Agamemnon went to the siege of Troy, he left one with Clytemnestra, to keep her faithful, and Egisthus could not corrupt her, till he had destroyed this counsellor.

Clio, the second (6), was the Muſe of hiſtory, and takes her name from her immortaliſing the actions ſhe records.

Erato (7), was the patroneſs of elegiac, or amorous poetry, and the inventreſs of dancing. To Thalia (8), belonged comedy, and whatever was gay, amiable, and pleaſant. Euterpe (named from her love of harmony) had the care of tragedy.

Melpomene (ſo ſtiled from the dignity and excellency of her ſong) was the guardian Muſe of lyric and epic poetry (9).

Terpſichore was the protectreſs of muſic, particularly the flute (1). The chorus of the ancient drama was her province, to which ſome add logic.

To Polyhymnia (2) (belonged that harmony of voice and geſture, which gives a perfection to oratory and poetry, and which flows from juſt ſentiments and a good memory.

Urania was the Muſe whoſe care extended to all divine or celeſtial ſubjects, ſuch as the hymns in praiſe of the gods, the motions of the heavenly bodies, and whatever regarded philoſophy or aſtronomy (3).

The Muſes, though ſaid to be virgins, were no enemies to love (4). We have already taken notice of Calliope and Terpſichore yielding to the addreſſes of Apollo. If their complaiſance was ſolely owing to the reſentment of Venus, who inſpired the flames of love, to revenge the death of her favourite Adonis; it muſt be owned that the Muſes have ſince been ſufficiently devoted to her ſervice.

The Muſes were themſelves not wholly free from revenge, as appears in the ſtory of Thamyris. This perſon was the ſon of Philammon, and the nymph Agriopa, and born at Oderſæ, once a famous city of Thrace. He became ſo excellent a proficient in muſic,

(6) From κλίω, Glory. (7) From ἔρας, Love.
(8) From θάλλειν, to flouriſh or revive.
(9) From μελος ποιειν, to make a concert or ſymphony.
(1) Τερπειν τοις χοροις, to delight in choruſes.
(2) From πολυς and μνεια, a great memory.
(3) From ὐρανῶ, Heaven.
(4) The virginity or chaſtity of the Muſes, is a point diſputed by the ancient writers, though the majority inclines in their favour.

music, that he had the courage or vanity to contend (5) with the Muses; but being overcome, they not only punished him with the loss of sight and memory, but caused Jupiter to cast him into hell, to expiate his impiety.

The Muses were represented crowned with flowers, or wreaths of palm, each holding some instrument or token of the science or art over which she presided. They were depicted as young, and the bird sacred to them was the swan (6).

To trace the origin of these fabulous deities, it is necessary to observe, that the nine emblematical figures, which were exhibited amongst the Egyptians to denote the nine months, during which that country was freed from the inundation, had each some instrument, or symbol, peculiar to the business of the months, as a pair of compasses, a flute, a mask, a trumpet, &c. All these images were purely hieroglyphical, to point out to the people what they were to do, and to ascertain their use, they were called the nine Muses (7). The Greeks, who adopted this group of emblems as so many real divinities, took care to give each a particular name, suited to the instruments they bore, and which threw a new disguise upon the truth.

The Graces are also attendants of the Muses, though placed in the train of Venus (8). Some make them the daughters of Jupiter and Eurynome, others of Bacchus and Venus. They were three, Aglaia, Thalia, and Euphrosyne, names relative to their nature (9). The Lacedemonians and Athenians knew

(5) Thamyris wrote a poem on the wars of the gods with the Titans, which exceeded every thing that appeared of the kind before.

(6) Perhaps because it was consecrated to their master Apollo

(7) From the word Mose, that is, saved or disengaged from the waters; whence the name of Moses given to the Hebrew lawgiver: so near did the Phœnician and Egyptian languages agree, which with some small difference of pronunciation only, made two distinct tongues.

(8) I choose to place them here on account of the explanation of the fable under one view.

(9) Aglaia, or honesty, to shew that benefits should be bestowed freely; Thalia, or flourishing, to denote that the

sense

knew but two, to whom they gave different appellations (1). Eteocles, king of the Orchomenians, was the firſt who erected a temple to them.

Pegaſus was a winged horſe produced by the blood which fell from Meduſa's head, when ſhe was killed by Perſeus. He flew to mount Helicon, the ſeat of the Muſes, where, with a ſtroke of his hoof, he opened a fountain called Hippocrene, or the horſe's ſpring (2).

The unravelling theſe figures will convince us how juſtly they belong to this article, as they complete its illuſtration. Near the nine female figures which betokened the dry ſeaſon, were placed three others, repreſenting the three months of inundation, and were drawn ſometimes ſwathed, as incapable of uſing their hands and feet. Theſe were called Charitout (3), or the divorce. The reſemblance of this word to the Greek Charities, which ſignifies thankſgivings or favours, gave riſe to the fable of the Graces, or three goddeſſes preſiding over benefits and outward charms.

Yet, as during the inundation, all parts could not be ſo fully ſupplied, but that ſome commerce was neceſſary, they had recourſe to ſmall barks, to ſail from one city to the other. Now the emblematical figure of a ſhip or veſſel, in Egypt and Phœnicia, was a winged horſe (4), by which name the inhabitants of Cadiz, a Phœnician colony, called their veſſels. Now, if the Muſes and Graces are the goddeſſes which preſide over arts and gratitude, this emblem becomes unintelligible; but if we take the nine Muſes from the months of action and induſtry, and the three Graces for the three months of inundation and reſt, the winged horſe, or boat with ſails, is a true picture of the end of navigation, and the return of rural toils. To this figure the Egyptians gave the

ſenſe of kindneſs ought never to die; Euphroſyne, or chearfulneſs, to ſignify that favours ſhould be conferred and received with mutual pleaſure.

(1) The Spartan Graces were Clito and Phaena; thoſe of Athens, Auro and Hegemo.

(2) Fons Caballinus. See Perſius, ſatyr I.

(3) From Charat, to divide, comes Charitout, the ſeparation of commerce.

(4) Strabo Geograph. Lib. II. p. 99. edit. Reg. Paris.

the name of Pegasus (5), expressive of its true meaning. All these images transplanted to Greece, became the source of endless confusion and fable.

By the Latin and Greek poets, the Graces are represented as beautiful young virgins, naked, or but very slightly cloathed (6), and having wings on their feet. They are also joined hand in hand, to denote their unity.

The Syrens were the daughters of Achelous. Their lower parts were like fishes, and their upper like women; but they were so skilled in music, that they insnared all who heard them to destruction. Presuming to contend with the Muses, they were vanquished, and stripped at once of their feathers and voices, as a punishment for their folly.

The Egyptians sometimes represented the three months of inundation by figures half female and half fish, to denote to the inhabitants their living in the midst of the waters. One of these images bore in her hand the sistrum, or Egyptian lyre, to shew the general joy at the flood's arriving to its due height, which was the assurance of a succeeding year of plenty. To these symbols they gave the name of Syrens (7), expressive of their real meaning. The Phœnicians, who carried them into Greece, represented them as real persons, and the Greeks and Romans had too strong a taste for the fabulous, not to embellish the story (1).

CHAP. XXXII.

OF DIANA, LUNA, OR HECATE.

HAVING treated of the god of wit and harmony, with his offspring and train, let us now come to his twin-sister Diana, the goddess of chastity, and the

daughter

(5) From Pag, to cease, and Sus, a ship, Pegasus, or the cessation of navigation.
(6) *Solutis Gratiæ, Zonis.* Ode XXX. 5.
Junctæque nymphis Gratiæ decentes
Alterno terram quatiunt pede. Horace, Lib. I. Ode IV. 5.
(7) From Shur, a hymn, and Ranan, to sing.
(1) Hence our imaginary form of the Mermaid.

daughter of Jupiter and Latona. Her father, at her requeſt, granted her perpetual virginity, beſtowed on her a bow and arrows, appointed her queen of the woods and foreſts (2), and aſſigned her a guard of nymphs to attend her (3). She became the patroneſs of hunting thus: Britomartis, a huntreſs-nymph, being one day entangled in her own nets, while the wild boar was approaching her, vowed a temple to Diana, and ſo was preſerved. Hence Diana had the name of Dictynna. Others relate the ſtory differently, and ſay that Britomartis, whom Diana favoured on account of her paſſion for the chace, flying from Minos her lover, fell into the ſea, and was by her made a goddeſs.

The adventures of Diana made a pretty conſiderable figure in poetical hiſtory, and ſerve to ſhew that the virtue of this goddeſs, if inviolable, was alſo very ſevere. Actæon experienced this truth to his coſt. He was a young prince, the ſon of Ariſtæus and Autonoe, the daughter of Cadmus, king of Thebes. As he was paſſionately fond of the ſport, he had the misfortune one day to diſcover Diana bathing with her nymphs. The goddeſs, incenſed at the intruſion, changed him into a ſtag; ſo that his own dogs miſtaking him for their game, purſued and tore him in pieces. Ovid has wrought up this ſcene with great art and imagination (4).

The truth of this fable is ſaid to be as follows: Actæon was a man of Arcadia, a great lover of dogs and hunting, and by keeping many dogs, and ſpending his time in hunting on the mountains, he entirely neglected his domeſtic affairs, and being brought to ruin, was generally called the wretched Actæon, who was devoured by his own dogs.

Meleager was another unhappy victim of her reſentment, and the more ſo as his puniſhment was owing to no crime of his own. Oeneus, his father, king of Ætolia, in offering ſacrifices to the rural deities, had forgot Diana. The goddeſs was not of a character to put up with ſuch a neglect. She ſent a huge wild boar into the fields of Calcedon, who laid every thing

---

(2) *Montium cuſtes nemorumque virgo.* Horat. Lib. III.
(3) Sixty nymphs, called Oceaninæ, and twenty of the Aſiæ.
(4) Ovid, Lib. III. 131.

thing waste before him. Meleager, with Theseus, and the virgin Atalanta, undertook to encounter it. The virgin gave the monster the first wound, and Meleager, who killed it, presented her the skin, which his uncles took from her, for which he slew them. Althæa, his mother, hearing her two brothers had perished in this quarrel, took an uncommon revenge. She remembered at the birth of her son the Fates had thrown a billet into the chamber, with an assurrance the boy would live, as that remained unconsumed. The mother had till now carefully saved a pledge on which so much depended; but inspired by her present fury, she threw it into the flames, and Meleager instantly seized with a consuming disease, expired as soon as it was burnt. His sisters, who excessively mourned his death, were turned into henturkies. Ovid has not forgot to embellish his collection with this story (5). Others relate the story of Meleager thus: Diana had, to avenge herself of Oeneus, raised a war between the Curetes and Ætolians. Meleager, who fought at the head of his father's troops, had always the advantage, till killing two of his mother's brothers, his mother Althea loaded him with such imprecations, that he retired from the field. The Curetes upon this advanced, and attacked the capital of Ætolia. In vain Oeneus presses his son to arm and repel the foe; in vain his mother forgives and intreats him. He is inflexible, till Cleopatra, his wife, falls at his feet, and represents their mutual danger. Touched at this, he calls for his armour, issues to the fight, and repels the enemy.

Nor was Diana less rigorous to her own sex. Chione, the daughter of Dædalion, being caressed both by Apollo and Mercury, bore twins, Philamon, the son of Apollo, a famous musician, and Autolycus, the son of Mercury, a skilful juggler or cheat. The mother was so imprudent to boast of her shame, and prefer the honour of being mistress to two deities, to the modesty of Diana, which she ascribed to her want of beauty; for this the goddess pierced her tongue with an arrow, and deprived her of the power of future boasting or calumny.

The river Alpheus fell violently enamoured of Diana, and having no hopes of success, had recourse to

(5) Ovid, Lib. VIII. 261.

to force. The goddefs fled to the Letrini, where fhe amufed herfelf with dancing, and with fome art fo difguifed herfelf and her nymphs, that Alpheus no longer knew them. For this, thefe people erected a temple to her.

During the chafe one day, Diana accidentally fhot Chenchrius, fon of the nymph Pryene, who bewailed him fo much, that fhe was turned into a fountain.

Diana had a great variety of names; fhe was called Cynthia and Delia, from the place of her birth; Artemis, on account of her honour and modefty. By the Arcadians fhe was named Orthofia; and by the Spartans, Orthia. Her temples were many, both in Greece and Italy; but the moft confiderable was at Ephefus, where fhe was held in the higheft veneration. The plan of this magnificent edifice was laid by Ctefiphon, and the ftructure of it employed for 220 years the ableft architects and ftatuaries in the world. It was fet on fire by Eroftratus, on the day that Alexander the Great came into the world; but was foon rebuilt with equal fplendor under Dinocrates, who alfo built the city of Alexandria.

The facrifices offered to Diana, were the firft fruits of the earth, oxen, rams, and white hinds; human victims were fometimes devoted to her in Greece, as we find in the cafe of Iphigenia. Her feftival was on the ides of Auguft, after which time all hunting was prohibited.

Diana was reprefented of an uncommon high ftature, her hair difhevelled, a bow in her hand, and a quiver at her back, a deer-fkin faftened to her breaft, and her purple robe tucked up at her knees, with gold buckles or clafps, and attended by nymphs in a hunting-drefs, with nets and hounds.

Diana was alfo called Dea Triformis or Tergemina, on account of her triple character, of Luna in heaven, Diana on earth, and Hecate in the infernal regions; though the actions of the firft and laft are afcribed to her under the fecond name (6).

Luna was thought to be the daughter of Hyperion and Theia. The Egyptians worfhipped this deity both as male and female, the men facrificing to it as Luna, the women as Lunus, and each fex on thefe occafions

---

(6) Hefiod makes Luna, Diana, and Hecate, three diftinct goddeffes.

occasions assuming the dress of the other. Indeed this goddess was no other than the Venus Urania, or Cælestis of the Assyrians, whose worship and rites the Phœnicians introduced into Greece. Under this character Diana was also called Lucina, (a name she held in common with Juno) and had the protection of women in labour (7), though some make Lucina a distinct goddess from either (8). By this name she was adorned by the Æginenses and Eleans.

If Diana was so rigid in point of chastity on earth, her virtue grew a little more relaxed when she got to the skies. She bore Jupiter a daughter there, called Ersa, or the Dew; and Pan, who was not the most pleasing of the gods, deceived her in the shape of a white ram. But her most celebrated amour was with Endymion (1), the son of Æthlius, and grandson of Jupiter, who took him up in to heaven, where he had the insolence to solicit Juno, for which he was cast into a profound sleep. Luna had the kindness to conceal him in a cave of mount Latmos in Caria, where she had fifty daughters by him, and a son called Ætolus, after which he was again exalted to the skies.

The fable of Endymion had its origin in Egypt. These people in the neomenia, or feast, in which they celebrated the ancient state of mankind, chose a grove or some retired shady grotto, where they placed an Isis, with her crescent or moon, and by her side an Horus asleep, to denote the security and repose which mankind then enjoyed. This figure they called Endymion (2), and these symbolical figures, like the rest, degenerated into idolatry, and became the materials for fabulous history.

As the moon, Diana was represented with a crescent on her head, in a silver chariot drawn by white hinds,

(7) It is said she assisted Latona, her mother, at the birth of Apollo, but was so terrified at the pains, that she vowed perpetual virginity.

(8) Some make Lucina the daughter of Jupiter and Juno, and born in Crete.

(1) Others affirm, that Endymion was a king of Elis, much given to astronomy and lunar observations, for which he was said to be in love with the moon, and caressed by her.

(2) From En, a grotto or fountain, and Dimion, resemblance, is made Endymion, or the *grotto of the representation*.

hinds, with gold harnefs, which fome change to mules, becaufe that animal is barren (3). Some make her conductors a white and black horfe (4), others oxen, on account of the lunar horns.

Hecate was the daughter of Jupiter and Ceres. As to the origin of the name there is fome variation (5). She was the goddefs of the infernal regions, and on that account is often confounded with Proferpine. She prefided over ftreets and highways; for which caufe fhe was called Trivia, as alfo Propyla, becaufe the doors of houfes were under her protection (6). The appellation of Brimo was given her on account of her dreadful fhrieks, when Mars, Apollo, and Mercury meeting her in the woods, attempted to ravifh her. She was alfo famous for botany, efpecially in difcovering baneful and poifonous herbs and roots; as alfo for her fkill in enchantments and magical arts, in the practice of which her name was conftantly invoked (7). Hefiod has given a very pompous defcription of the extent of her power (8). She was filed in Egypt, Bubaftis.

As Hecate, Diana was reprefented of an exceffive height, her head covered with frightful fnakes, and her feet of a ferpentine form, and furrounded with dogs, an animal facred to her, and under whofe form fhe was fometimes reprefented. She was alfo efteemed the goddefs of inevitable fate.

If we have recourfe to the Egyptian key, we fhall find this threefold goddefs the fame fymbol with the Juno and Cybele we have already treated of. The Greek fculptors had too good a tafte to endure the head of the bull or goat on their deities, which they borrowed from that country. They therefore altered

(3) To exprefs that the moon had no light of her own, but what fhe borrowed from the fun.

(4) To exprefs the wane and full of the moon.

(5) Either from ἑκαθεν, at a diftance, becaufe the moon darts her rays afar off; or from ἑκατον, a hundred, becaufe a hecatomb was the ufual victim.

(6) At every new moon the Athenians made a fupper for her in the open ftreet, which in the night was eaten up by the poor people.

(7) So Dido, in Virgil, calls on
Tergeminam Hecaten, tria virginis ora Dianæ. Æneid IV.

(8) Theogony, l. 411.

ed thefe hieroglyphical figures to their own mode; but took care to preferve the attributes by difpofing them in a more elegant manner. The lunar fymbol amongft the Egyptians was called Hecate, or (9) Achete, and by the Syrians, Achot. The latter alfo ftiled her Deio, or Deione (1), and Demeter. The crefcent and full moon over her head at the *neomenia*, made her miftaken for that planet; and the time of the interlunia, during which fhe remained invifible, fhe was fuppofed to take a turn to the invifible world, and fo got the name of Hecate. Thus the tripartite goddefs arofe. The meaning of the ancient fymbols was confounded and forgot, and a fenfelefs jargon of fable and fuperftition introduced in its place, a point which can never be too exactly attended to on this occafion.

CHAP. XXXIII.

OF MERCURY.

PASS we now to a deity neither famous for his truth or honefty, though he makes no inconfiderable figure in the celeftial catalogue. Mercury was the fon of Jupiter and Maia, daughter of Atlas, and born on mount Cyllene in Arcadia. He was fuckled by Juno, fome of whofe milk falling befides his mouth on the heavens, produced the Galaxy. He began to difplay early his talents for theft, as we have obferved under the article of Apollo. Being careffed when an infant in Vulcan's arms, he ftole away his tools. The fame day he defeated Cupid at wreftling, and while Venus praifed him after his victory, he found means to convey away her ceftus. He pilfered Jupiter's fceptre, and had done the fame thing by his thunderbolts, but they were too hot for his fingers. He ferved Battus a very flippery trick. This man faw him ftealing king Admetus's cows from Apollo his herdfman.

(9) Achate, the only or excellent, or Achot, (in the Syriac) the fifter.

(1) Deio, or Deione, from Dei, fufficiency; or Demeter, from Dei, and Mater, rain, i. e. plenty of rain.

herdsman. To bribe him to silence, he gave him a fine cow, and the clown promised to keep it secret. Mercury, to try him, assumed another shape, and offering a higher reward, the fellow told all he knew, on which (2) the god turned him into a touch-stone.

Mercury had several appellations. He was called Hermes (3) and Cyllenius, from his temple upon mount Cyllene. Nor were his employments less various. He was the cupbearer of Jupiter till Ganymede took his place. He was the messenger of the gods, and the tutelar god of roads and cross-ways (4), the inventor of weights and measures, and the guardian of all merchandize and commerce, though this office seems but ill to agree with the actions ascribed to him. He was in a peculiar manner the protector of learning, being the first discoverer of letters, and the god of rhetoric and oratory. He was also famous for his skill in music, and so eloquent, that he was not only the arbitrator in all quarrels amongst the gods, but in all leagues and negociations particular regard was paid (5) to him.

Together with Tellus and Pluto, Mercury was invoked amongst the terrestrial gods. In conjunction with Hercules he presided over wrestling and the gymnastic exercises, to shew that address on these occasions should always be joined to force. He was also believed to preside over dreams, though Morpheus claims a share with him in this department.

Annually, in the middle of May, a festival was celebrated to his honour at Rome, by the merchants and traders, who sacrificed a sow to him, intreating he would prosper their business, and forgive their frauds. In all sacrifices offered to him, the tongues of the victims were burnt, which custom was borrowed

(2) Ovid has given a fine description of this incident. Metam. lib. II. 680.

(3) Ἑρμῆς, the interpreter, because he interpreted the minds of the gods and men.

(4) Where the Greeks and Romans placed certain figures, called Hermæ, from him, being of marble or brass, with the head of a Mercury, but downwards of a square figure.

(5) As the Feciales, or priests of Mars, proclaimed war; so the Caduceatores, or priests of Mercury, were employed in all embassies and treaties of peace.

rowed from the Megarenses. Persons who escaped imminent danger sacrificed to him a calf with milk and honey. The animals sacred to him were the dog, the goat, and the cock.

By his sister Venus he had a son called Hermaphroditus, a great hunter; a wood nymph, called Salamacis, fell in love with him, but had the mortification to be repulsed. Upon this, inflamed by her passion, she watched near a fountain where he used to bathe, and when she saw him naked in the water, rushed to embrace him; but the youth still avoiding her, she prayed the gods their bodies might become one, which was immediately granted; and what was yet more wonderful, the fountain retained the virtue of making all those Hermaphrodites who used its waters (6).

A late author gives this story another turn. He says, the fountain Salmacis (7) being inclosed with high walls, very indecent scenes passed there; but that a certain Greek of that colony building an inn there for the entertainment of strangers, the barbarians, who resorted to it, by their intercourse with the Greeks, became softened and civilized, which gave rise to the fable of their changing their sex.

Mercury had other children, particularly Pan, Dolops, Echion, Caicus, Erix, Bunus, Phares, and the Lares, with several others. Such was the Mercury of the Greeks and Romans.

But the origin of this deity must be looked for amongst the Phœnicians, whose image is the symbolical figure of their great ancestor and founder, and the proper arms of that people. By the bag of money which he held, was intimated, the gains of merchandize. By the wings with which his head and feet were furnished, was shadowed the shipping of that people, their extensive commerce and navigation. The caduceus, with which (8) he was said to conduct the spirits of the deceased to Hades, pointed out the great principles of the soul's immortality, a state of (9) rewards and punishments

after

(6) See Ovid's description of this adventure. Metam. book IV.

(7) In Caria, near the city of Halicarnassus.

(8) *Virgaque levem coerces*
——— *Aurea turbam.*

(9) *Tu pias lætis animas reponis*
——— *Sedibus.* HORACE.

(1) after death, and a (2) refuscitation of the body. It is described as producing three leaves together; hence called by Homer the *golden three-leaved wand*. The doctrine alluded to by this, was more distinctly taught by the emblems adorning the hermetic wand: for to the extremity of it was annexed the ball or CIRCLE. Two SERAPHS entwined the rod; over which were the EXPANDED WINGS, forming the complete hieroglyphic of THE MIGHTY ONES. The name of Mercury is a compound of the Celtic Merc, merchandize (3), and Ur, a man; and corresponds very exactly with the Hebrew Etymology, rendering the meaning of the word Cnaan, or Canaan, a merchant or trader.

This symbolical figure (like many others, which at first were very innocent) became in time the object of idolatrous worship to most nations. We are not to wonder that the Egyptians particularly, whose country was the land of Ham, the father of Canaan, should do honour to this figure, and apply it to their purposes: for it is more than probable, that, being so near at hand, he might be greatly assisting to his brother Mizraim in the settlement of that country; besides the consideration of their after-obligations to his descendant the Phœnician, who is also called the Ægyptian Hercules.

CHAP. XXXIV.

OF VENUS.

THE next deity that offers, is that powerful goddess whose influence is acknowledged by Gods and men. Cicero mentions four of this name (4); but the Venus generally known is she who is fabled to have sprung from the froth or fermentation raised by the genitals of Saturn, when cut off by his son Jupiter, and thrown into the sea. Hence she gained the

(1) *Hæc alias sub tristia Tartara mittit.*
(2) *Dat somnos adimitque.*   VIRGIL.
(3) From Racal, to trade, comes Marcolet, merchandize.
(4) The first the daughter of Cælum; the second Venus Aphrodita; the third born of Jupiter and Dione, and the wife of Vulcan; and the fourth Astarte, or the Syrian Venus, the mistress of Adonis.

the name of Aphrodite (5). As soon as born she was laid in a beautiful couch or shell, embellished with pearl, and by gentle zephyrs wafted to the isle of Cythera, in the Ægean sea, from whence she sailed to Cyprus, which she reached in April. Here, as soon as she landed, flowers rose beneath her feet, the Hours received her, and braided her hair with golden fillets, after which she was by them wafted to Heaven. Her charms appeared so attractive in the assembly of the gods, that scarce one of them but what desired her in marriage. Vulcan, by the advice of Jupiter, put poppy in her nectar, and, by intoxicating her, gained possession.

Few of the deities have been so extensively worshipped, or under a greater variety of names. She was called Cytherea, Paphia, Cypria, Erycina, Idalia, Acidalia, from the places where she was in a particular manner adored. Other appellations were given her from her principal attributes. She was stiled Victrix (6), to denote her resistless sway over the mind; Amica, from her being propitious to lovers; Apaturia, from the deceit and inconstancy of her votaries; Ridens, from her love of mirth and laughter (7); Hortensis, from her influencing the vegetation of plants and flowers; Marina, from her being born of the sea; Melanis, from her delighting in nocturnal (8) amours; Meretrix, from the prostitution of her votaries; and Genetrix, from her presiding over the propagation of mankind. The epithet of Migonitis, was given her from her power in the management of love (9); and that of Murica and Myrtea, on account of the myrtle consecrated to her. She was named Verticordia, from her power of changing

the

(5) From 'Αφρός, froth, though some derive it from αφραίνω, run mad, because all love is infatuation or frenzy.

(6) Under this character she is represented leaning on a shield, and carrying victory in her right hand, and a sceptre in her left. At other times with a helmet, and the apple of Paris in her hand.

(7) Horace, lib. I. ode 2, *Sive tu mavis Erycina ridens*; so Homer calls her φιλομειδης, or the *laughter-loving queen*.

(8) From μελας, black, because lovers choose the night.

(9) From μιγνυμι, to mix or mingle; so Virgil,
——— *Mixta Deo Mulier.*

the heart; for which reafon the Greeks ſtiled her
Επιστροφια. The Spartans called her Venus Armata,
becauſe when befieged by the Meſſenians, their wives,
unknown to their huſbands, raifed the fiege. The
Romans alſo termed her Barbata, becauſe when a
difeafe had feized the women, in which they loſt all
their hair, on their prayers to Venus it grew again.
A temple was dedicated to her by the appellation of
Calva; becauſe when the Gauls inveſted the capitol,
the women offered their hair to make ropes for the
engines. She had alſo the epithet of Cluacina (1),
from her image being erected in the place where the
peace was concluded between the Romans and
Sabines.

Let us now enquire a little into the actions afcribed
to this goddefs. Her conjugal behaviour we ſhall fee
under the article of Vulcan, and find it was none of
the moſt edifying. Her amours were numerous.
Not to mention Apollo, Neptune, Mars, and Mercury, who all boafted of her favours (2). She had
Æneas (3) by Anchifes; but her principal favourite
was Adonis, the fon of Cynaras, king of Cyprus and
Myrrha, and a youth of incomparable beauty, un-
fortunately in hunting killed by a wild boar. Venus,
who flew to his affiftance, received a prick in her foot
with a thorn, and the blood which dropped from it
produced the damafk rofe (4); but coming too late
to fave him, ſhe changed him into the flower Anemone, which ſtill retains a crimfon colour (5). After
this ſhe obtained of Proferpine, that Adonis ſhould
continue fix months with her on earth, and fix months
remain in the lower regions.

The

(1) From Cluo, to hear, liften, or agree.

(2 By Apollo ſhe had Elefiryon, and five fons; by Neptune, Eryx, and Meligunis, a daughter; by Mars, Timor
and Pallor; and by Mercury, Hermaphroditus.

(3 She immortalized Æneas, by purifying and anointing
his body with ambrofial effence, and the Romans deified him
by the name of Indiges. We have feveral ancient infcrip-
tions. *Deo Indigeti.*

(4 Ovid, lib. X. 505.

5 Some mythologize this ſtory, to fignify by Adonis the
Sun, who, during the fummer figns, refides with Venus on
the earth, and during the winter with Proferpine. The
wild boar which killed him is the Cold.

The moſt remarkable adventure of Venus, was her famous conteſt with Juno and Minerva for beauty. At the marriage of Peleus and Thetis, the goddeſs Diſcord reſenting her not being invited, threw a golden apple amongſt the company with this inſcription, *Let it be given to the faireſt* (6). The competitors for this prize were the three deities abovementioned. Jupiter referred them to Paris, youngeſt ſon of Priamus, king of Troy, who then kept his father's flocks on mount Ida. Before him the goddeſſes appeared, as moſt ſay, naked. Juno offered him empire or power; Minerva, wiſdom; and Venus endeavoured to bribe him with the promiſe of the *faireſt woman in the world*. Fatally for himſelf and family, the ſhepherd was more ſuſceptible of love than of ambition or virtue, and decided the point in favour of Venus. The goddeſs rewarded him with Helen (7), whom he carried off from her huſband Menelaus, king of Sparta, and the rape gave riſe to that formidable aſſociation of the Greek princes, which ended in the deſtruction of his family, and the ruin of Troy.

Venus, however propitious ſhe was to lovers, was very ſevere to ſuch as offended her. She changed the women of Amathus, in Cyprus, into oxen for their cruelty. The Propætides, who denied her dignity, grew ſo ſhameleſsly impudent, that they were ſaid to be hardened into ſtones (8). Hippomenes and Atalanta were another inſtance of her reſentment; for after ſhe had aſſiſted him to gain the virgin, on their neglect to pay her the due offerings, ſhe infatuated them ſo, that they lay together in the temple of Cybele, who, for that profanation, turned them into lions (9).

Nor was ſhe leſs favourable to her votaries. Pygmalion, a famous ſtatuary, from a notion of the inconveniences of marriage, reſolved to live ſingle. He had, however, formed a beautiful image of a virgin in ivory, with which he fell ſo deeply enamoured, that he treated it as a real miſtreſs, and continually
ſolicited

(6) *Detur Pulchriori.*
(7 *Such Helen was, and who can blame the boy,*
  Who in ſo bright a flame conſum'd his Troy? WALLER.
(8) See Ovid, lib. X. l. 238.
(9) See the article Cybele, and Ovid, lib. X. 560.

solicited Venus, by prayers and sacrifices, to animate his beloved statue. His wishes were granted, and by this enlivened beauty he had a son called Paphos, who gave his name to the city of Paphos in Cyprus (1).

A goddess so universally known and adored could not fail of temples. That of Paphos in Cyprus was the principal. In that of Rome, dedicated to her by the title of Venus Libitina, were sold all things necessary for funerals. She had also a magnificent shrine, built for her by her son Æneas, on mount Eryx in Sicily. The sacrifices usually offered to her were white goats and swine, with libations of wine, milk, and honey. The victims were crowned with flowers or wreaths of myrtle. The birds sacred to her were the swan, the dove, and the sparrow.

So far for the Venus Pandemos, or Popularis, the goddess of wanton and effeminate love; but the ancients had another Venus, whom they stiled Urania and Celestis, (who was indeed no other than the Syrian Astarte) and to whom they ascribed no attributes but such as were strictly chaste and virtuous. Of this deity they admitted no corporeal resemblance; but she was represented by the form of a globe ending conically (2), and only pure fire was burnt on her altars. Her sacrifices were called Nephalia, on account of her sobriety, only honey and wine being offered; but no animal victims except the heifer, nor was the wood of figs, vines, or mulberries, suffered to be used in them.

This distinction of two Venuses, the *chaste* and the *impure* one, leads us to the true explication of the fable. In the different attributes of the Egyptian Isis, we see these contradictory characters explained. The Isis crowned with the crescent star of some of zodiacal signs, is the celestial Venus. The Isis with the terrestrial symbols, such as the heads of animals, a multitude of breasts, or a child in her lap, became the goddess of fruitfulness and generation, and consequently the Venus Pandemos. As the latter was regarded as a divinity propitious to luxury and pleasure,

(1) Ovid, lib. ". 245.
(2) This manner of representation was borrowed from the Arabians and Syrians, who thought the deity was not to be expressed by any corporeal form.

fure, it is no wonder if she soon gained the ascendant over her rival. In Phœnicia and Egypt, the young girls (3) consecrated to the service of the terrestrial Isis, usually resided in a tent or grove near the temple, and were common prostitutes; whereas those devoted to the celestial Isis, or Venus Urania, were strictly chaste. These tabernacles were called the *pavillion of the girls* (4), and gave rise to the name of Venus, ascribed to the goddess of love. The Syrians also called the terrestrial Isis Mylitta, or Illithe (5), and the Greeks and Romans adopted the same name. Thus the symbolical Isis of Egypt, after producing the different deities of Cybele, Rhea, Vesta, Juno, Diana, Luna, Hecate, and Proserpine, formed also the different characters of the common and celestial Venus; so easily does superstition and invention multiply the objects of idolatry.

As Venus was the goddess of love and pleasure, it is no wonder if the poets have been lavish in the description of her beauties. Homer and Virgil have (6) given us fine pictures of this kind. Nor were the ancient sculptors and painters negligent on so interesting a subject. Phidias formed her statue of ivory and gold, with one foot on a tortoise (7). Scopias represented her riding on a he-goat, and Praxiteles wrought

(3) They were called the Κιστοφοροι, or basket-bearers, because they carried the offerings.

(4) Succoth Venoth, the tabernacle of the girls. The Greeks and Romans, who could not pronounce the word Venoth, called it Venos, or Venus, and hearing the tent of Venus so often mentioned, took it for the name of the goddess herself.

(5) From Jeled, to beget, comes Illitta, generation, which the Latins well expressed by Diva Genetrix, or Genitalis. See Horace, carmen seculare, l. 14.

(6, *She said, and turning round her neck she show'd,*
That with celestial charms divinely glow'd;
Her waving locks immortal fragrance shed,
And breath'd ambrosial sweets around her head;
In flowing pomp her radiant robe was seen,
And all the goddess sparkled in her mien.
PITT's Virgil, Æneid I. 402.

(7) This statue was at Elis, and the tortoise was designed to shew, that women should not go much abroad, but attend their domestic affairs.

wrought her ftatue at Cnidos of white marble, half opening her lips and fmiling. Apelles drew her as juft emerged from the fea, and preffing the water out of her hair, a piece that was reckoned ineftimable. It were endlefs to mention the variety of attitudes in which fhe is reprefented in antique gems and medals (8); fometimes fhe is cloathed in purple, glittering with gems, her head crowned with rofes, and drawn in her ivory car, by fwans, doves, or fparrows. At others fhe is reprefented ftanding, with the Graces attending her; but in all pofitions, Cupid, her fon, is her infeparable companion. I fhall only add, that the ftatue called the Medicean Venus, is the beft figure of her which time has preferved.

CHAP. XXXV.

OF THE ATTENDANTS OF VENUS, VIZ. CUPID, HYMEN, AND THE HORÆ, OR HOURS.

BEFORE we clofe the article of Venus, it is neceffary to give fome account of the deities who were ufually reprefented in her train, and formed a part of that ftate in which fhe ufually appeared.

The firft of thefe is Cupid. Some make him one of the moft ancient of the deities, and fay he had no parents, but fucceeded immediately after Chaos. Others report, that Nox, or Night, produced an egg, which having hatched under her fable wings, brought forth Cupid, or Love, who, with golden pinions, immediately flew through the whole world (9). But the common opinion is, that Cupid was the fon of Mars and Venus, and the favourite child of his mother, who, without his aid, as fhe confeffes in

in

---

(8) See a great number of thefe in Mr. Ogle's antiquities, illuftrated by ancient gems, a work which, it is a great lofs to the public, that ingenious and worthy gentleman did not live to finifh.

(9) Others make him the fon of Porus, the god of counfel, who being drunk begot him on Penia, the goddefs of poverty. Others the fon of Cælus and Terra; and fome of Zephyrus and Flora.

in Virgil, could do little execution. Indeed the poets, when they invoke the mother, feldom fail to make their joint addreſſes to the fon (1). Perhaps this confcioufnefs of his own importance, rendered this little divinity fo arrogant, that, on many occafions, he forgets his filial duty. This Cupid belonged to the Venus Pandemos, or Popularis, and was called Anteros, or Luſt.

But the ancients mention another Cupid, fon of Jupiter and Venus, of a nobler character, whofe delight it was to raife refined fentiments of love and virtue, whereas the other infpired bafe and impure defires. His name was Eros, or true Love. Eros bore a golden dart, which caufed real joy and affection; Anteros a leaden arrow, which raifed a fleeting paſſion, ending in faticty and difguſt.

Cupid was reprefented ufually naked, to ſhew that love has nothing of its own. He is armed with a bow and quiver full of darts, to ſhew his power of the mind; and crowned with rofes, to ſhew the delightful but tranfitory pleafures he beſtows. Sometimes he is depicted *blind*, to denote that love fees no faults in the object beloved; at others he appears with a rofe in one hand, and a dolphin in the other; fometimes he is feen ſtanding between Hercules and Mercury, to fignify the prevalence of eloquence and valour in love; at others he is placed near Fortune, to exprefs how much the fuccefs of lovers depends on that inconſtant goddefs. He is always drawn with wings, to typify, that nothing is more fleeting than the paſſion he excites.

The Egyptian Horus, which attended the terreftrial Ifis, or the Venus Popularis, or Pandemos, was, according to the cuſtom of the neomenia, reprefented with different attributes; fometimes with the wings of the Etefian wind, at others with the club of Hercules (2), the arrows of Apollo, fitting on a lion, driving a bull, tying a ram, or having a large fiſh in his nets. Thefe figns of the different feafons of the year, gave rife to as many fables. The empire of

Eros,

(1) See Horace, lib. 1. ode xxx. & paſſim.
(2) There is a gem in Mr. Ogle's poſſeſſion, anfwering this defcription.

Eros, or Love, was made to extend to heaven and earth, and even to the depths of the ocean; and this little but powerful child difarmed gods and men.

Hymen, the fecond attendant of Venus, was the god of marriage, and the fon of Bacchus and that goddefs (3). He is faid to be born in Attica, where he made it his bufinefs to refcue virgins carried off by robbers, and to reftore them to their parents. On this account all maids newly married offered facrifices to him; as alfo to the goddefs of concord. He was invoked in the nuptial ceremony (4) in a particular manner.

This god was reprefented of a fair complexion, crowned with amaricus, or the herb fweet marjoram, and robed in a veil of faffron colour (reprefentative of the bridal blufhes) with a torch lighted in his hand, becaufe the bride was carried always home by torchlight.

Every one knows it was a conftant cuftom of the oriental nations, on the wedding-day, to attend the bride-groom and bride with torches and lamps. The chorus on thefe occafions was, *Hu! Humeneh! Here he comes! This is the feftival!* (5) The figure exhibited on this occafion in Egypt, was a young man bearing a lamp or torch, placed near the female figure, which denoted the day of the month fixed for the ceremony.

The Graces, who always attended Venus, have been already defcribed with the Mufes under the article of Apollo.

The Horæ, or Hours, were the daughters of Jupiter and Themis, and the harbingers of Apollo. They were alfo the nurfes of Venus, as well as her dreffers, and made a neceffary part of her train.

CHAP.

(3) Hymen is thought to be the fon of the goddefs Venus Urania, or the celeftial Venus.

(4) They repeated often words, O Hymen! O Hymenæ!

(5) From Hu! Io! or here he is, and Meneh, the feaft or facrifice, comes Hymenæus.

CHAP. XXXVI.

OF VULCAN.

THOUGH the husband should usually precede the wife, yet Vulcan was too unhappy in wedlock to obtain this distinction. There were several of the name (6); the principal, who arrived at the honour of being deified, was the son of Jupiter and Juno, or, as others say, of Juno alone; however this be, he was so remarkably deformed, that his father threw him down from heaven to the isle of Lemnos, and in the fall he broke his leg (7). Others report, that Juno herself, disgusted at his sight, hurled him into the sea, where he was nursed by Thetis (8).

The first residence of Vulcan on earth was the isle of Lemnos (9), where he set up his forge, and taught men how to soften and polish brass and iron. From thence he removed to the Liparean isles, near Sicily, where, with the assistance of the Cyclops, he made Jupiter fresh thunderbolts, as the old grew decayed. He also wrought an helmet for Pluto, which rendered him invisible; a trident for Neptune, that shook both land and sea; and a dog of brass for Jupiter, which he animated, so as to perform (1) all the natural functions of the animal. Nor is this a wonder, when we consider, that, at the desire of the same god, he formed Pandora, who was sent with the fatal box to Prometheus, as has been related in its place. In short, Vulcan was the general armourer of the gods. He made Bacchus a golden crown, to present Ariadne;

(6) The first, said to be the son of Cælus; the second, the son of Nilus, called Opas; the third, the Vulcan, son of Jupiter and Juno, mentioned above; and the fourth, the son of Mænalius, who resided in the Vulcanian or Liparean isles.

(7) He was caught by the Lemnians, or he had broke his neck. It is added, he was a whole day in falling.

(8) Others report that he fell on the land, and was nursed by apes; and that Jupiter expelled him the skies for attempting to rescue Juno, when she conspired against him.

(9) Because Lemnos abounds in minerals and hot springs.

(1) Jupiter gave this dog to Europa, she to Procris, and by her it was given to Cephalus her husband, and by Jupiter after turned to a stone.

Ariadne; a chariot for the Sun, and another for Mars. At the requeſt of Thetis, he fabricated the divine armour of Achilles, whoſe ſhield is ſo beautifully deſcribed by Homer (2); as alſo the invincible armour of Æneas, at the entreaty of Venus. To conclude, with an inſtance of his ſkill this way, in revenge for his mother Juno's unkindneſs, he preſented her a golden chair, managed by ſuch unſeen ſprings, that when ſhe ſat down in it ſhe was not able to move, till ſhe was forced to beg her deliverance from him.

Vulcan, like the reſt of the gods, had ſeveral names or appellations: he was called Lemnius, from the iſle of Lemnos, conſecrated to him; Mulciber, or Mulcifer, from his art of ſoftening ſteel and iron. By the Greeks, Hephaiſtos, from his delighting in flames, or fire; and Ætneus and Lipareus, from the places ſuppoſed to be his forges (3). As to his worſhip, he had an altar in common with Prometheus (4), and was one of the gods who preſided over marriage, becauſe he firſt introduced the uſe of torches at the nuptial rites. It was cuſtomary with many nations after victory, to gather the enemy's arms in an heap, and offer them to Vulcan. His principal temple was in a conſecrated grove at the foot of Mount Ætna, guarded by dogs, who had the diſcernment to diſtinguiſh his votaries, to tear the vicious, and fawn upon the virtuous.

The proper ſacrifice to this deity was a lion, to denote the reſiſtleſs fury of fire. His feſtivals were different: at thoſe called Protervia (amongſt the Romans) they ran about with lighted torches. The Vulcania were celebrated by throwing living animals into the fire. The Lampadophoria were races performed to his honour, where the contention was to carry lighted torches to the goal; but whoever overtook the perſon before him, had the privilege of delivering him his torch to carry, and to retire with honour.

Vulcan, however diſagreeable his perſon, was ſenſible of love: his firſt paſſion was for Minerva, and he

(2) See Iliad, lib. 18.
(3) On account of the volcanoes and fiery eruptions there.
(4) Prometheus firſt invented fire, Vulcan the uſe of it, in making arms and utenſils.

he had Jupiter's confent to make his addreffes to her; but his courtfhip was too ill placed to be fuccefsful. He was more fortunate in his fuit to Venus, though he had no great reafon to boaft his lot. The goddefs was too great a beauty to be conftant, and Vulcan too difagreeable to be happy. She chofe Mars for her gallant, and the intrigue for fome time went on fwimmingly. As Apollo, or the Sun, had a friendfhip for the hufband, Mars was particularly fearful of his difcovering the affair, and therefore fet a boy called Alectryon, or Gallus, to warn him and his fair miftrefs of the Sun's approach. The fentinel unluckily fell afleep, and fo the Sun faw them together, and let Vulcan prefently into the fecret. The blackfmith god, to revenge the injury, againft their next meeting, contrived fo fine and imperceptible a net-work, that they were taken in their guilt, and expofed to the ridicule of the gods, till releafed at the interceffion of Neptune. Mars, to punifh Alectryon for his neglect, changed him into a cock, who, to atone for his fault, by his crowing, gives conftant notice of the fun-rife (5).

This deity, as the god of fire, was reprefented varioufly in different nations. The Egyptians depicted him proceeding out of an egg, placed in the mouth of Jupiter, to denote the radical or natural heat diffufed through all created beings. Some hiftorians make him one of the firft Egyptian kings, who for his goodnefs was deified; and add, that king Menes erected a noble temple to him at Thebes with a coloffal ftatue feventy-five feet high. The Phœnicians adored him by the name of Chryfor, and thought him the author and caufe of lightning and all fiery exhalations. Some writers confound him with the Tubal Cain of fcripture. In ancient gems and medals of the Greeks and Romans, he is figured as a lame, deformed, and fqualid man, working at the anvil, and ufually attended by his men the Cyclops, or by fome god or goddefs who come to afk his affiftance.

To examine into the ground of this fable, we muft have once more recourfe to the Egyptian antiquities. The Horus of the Egyptians was the moft mutable figure on earth; for he affumed fhapes fuitable to all

feafons

(5) See Ovid, Lib. IV. 167.

seasons of time and ranks of people: to direct the husbandman he wore a rural dress. By a change of attributes, he became the instructor of the smiths and other artificers, whose instruments he appeared adorned with. This Horus of the smiths had a short or lame leg, to signify that agriculture or husbandry halt without the assistance of the handicraft or mechanic arts. In this apparatus he was called Mulciber (6), Hephaistos (7), and Vulcan (8), all which names the Greeks and Romans adopted with the figure, which as usual they converted from a symbol to a god. Now as this Horus was removed from the side of the beautiful Isis (or the Venus Pandemos) to make room for the martial Horus, exposed in time of war, it occasioned the jest of the assistants, and gave rise to the fable of Vulcan's being supplanted in his wife's affections by the god of war.

CHAP. XXXVII.

OF THE OFFSPRING OF VULCAN.

THOUGH Vulcan had no issue with Venus, yet he had a pretty numerous offspring. We have already mentioned his passion for Minerva: this goddess coming one day to bespeak some armour of him, he attempted to ravish her, and in the struggle his seed fell on the ground, and produced the monster Erichthonius (9). Minerva nourished him in her thigh, and afterwards gave him to be nursed by Aglauros, Pandrosus, and Herse, but with a strict caution not to look in the cradle or coffer which held him. The first and last neglecting this advice ran mad. Erichthonius

---

(6) From Malac, to direct and manage, and Ber or Beer, a cave, or mine, comes Mulciber, the king of the mines or forges.

(7) From Aph, father, and Esto, fire, is formed Ephaisto, or Hepheftion, the father of fire.

(8) From Wall, to work, and Canan, to hasten, comes Wolcan, or work finished.

(9) Derived from Ερίδος and χθων, or Earth and Contention.

thonius being born with deformed, or as some say, serpentine legs, was the first inventor of chariots to ride in. He was the fourth king of Athens, and a prince of great justice and equity.

Cacus, another son of Vulcan, was of a different character. He was a notorious robber, and received his name from his consummate villainy (1). He fixed himself on mount Aventine, and from thence infested all Italy with his depredations; but having stolen some oxen from Hercules, he dragged them backwards to his cave (2), that the robbery might not be discovered by the track. Hercules, however, passing that way, heard the lowing of his cattle, broke open the doors, and seizing the wretch, put him to death.

A third son of Vulcan, Cæculus (3), so called from his little eyes, resembled his brother Cacus, and lived by prey. It is said his mother sitting by the fire, a spark flew into her lap, upon which she conceived. Others say some shepherds found him in the fire as soon as born. He founded the city Prænefte.

By his wife Aglaia, one of the Graces, Vulcan had several sons, as Ardalus, the inventor of the pipe, called Tibia; Brotheus, who being deformed like his father, destroyed himself in the fire, to avoid the reproaches he met with; Æthiops, who gave his name to the Æthiopians, before called Æthereans; Olenus, the founder of a city of his own name in Bœotia; Ægyptus, from whom Egypt was called; Albion; Periphenus; Morgion; Acus, and several others.

CHAP. XXXVIII.

OF THE CYCLOPS AND POLYPHEMUS.

THE Cyclops were the sons of Neptune and Amphitrite. The principal weee Brontes, Steropes, and

(1) From κακ☉, bad or wicked.
(2) Virgil has given a fine description of this cave, but he makes him but half a man. See Æneid VIII. 194.
(3) It is thought the noble Roman family of Cæcilii derive their name from him. See Virgil, Æneid X. 544, and Æneid VII. 680.

and Pyracmon, though their whole number was above a hundred. They were the journeymen of Vulcan. It is said, as soon as they were born, Jupiter threw them into Tartarus, but that they were delivered at the interceffion of Tellus, and so became the affistants of our god. They had each but one eye (4) placed in the middle of their foreheads, and lived on such fruits and herbs as the earth brought forth without cultivation. They are reported to have built the walls of Mycenæ and Tyrinthe with such maffy stones, that the smallest required two yoke of oxen to draw it. The dealers in mythology say, that the Cyclops signify the vapours raised in the air, which occasion thunder and lightning.

With these we may clafs Polyphemus, though he was the son of Neptune, having like the Cyclops but one eye; but of so gigantic a stature, that his very aspect was terrible. His abode was in Sicily, where he surprised Ulyffes, and his companions, of whom he devoured six; but Ulyffes making him drunk, blinded him with a firebrand, and so escaped with the rest. Virgil has given us a fine description of this scene (5).

CHAP. XXXIX.

OF MINERVA OR PALLAS.

WE come next to Minerva or Pallas, one of the most diftinguished of the Dii Majores, as being the goddess of sciences and wisdom. Cicero mentions five (6) of this name; but the most confiderable was the daughter of Jupiter, not by an infamous amour, nor

(4) From Κυκλο-, Circules, and ωψ, Oculus, that is, the one-eyed men.

(5) See Virgil's Æneid, Lib. III. 620, but the whole description, though admirable, is too long to be copied.

(6) The firft, the mother of Apollo, or Latona; the second produced from the Nile, and worshipped at Sais, in Egypt; the third, the child of Jupiter's brain; the fourth, the daughter of Jupiter and Croypha, who invented chariots with four wheels; and the fifth, the child of Pallas, whom she killed, because he attempted her chastity.

nor even by the conjugal bed, but the child of his brain. It is said her father, seeing Juno barren, through grief, struck his forehead, and three months after came forth Minerva (7). On the day of her nativity it rained gold at Rhodes (8). Her first appearance on the earth was in Libya, were beholding her own beauty in the lake Triton, she from thence gained the name of Tritonis (9).

She had beside several other appellations amongst the Greeks and Romans. She was called Pallas from the brandishing her spear in war. Athena, because she was born full grown, and never suckled; whence also she obtained the name of Ametrosis, or Motherless. The epithet of Parthenis, or the virgin, was given her on account of her perpetual chastity; that of Ergatis, or the workwoman, for her excellency in spinning and weaving; Musica, from her inventing the pipe; Pylotis, because her image was set up in the gates; and Glaucopis, or green-eyed, because her eyes were of that cast (1), like those of the owl.

Minerva was the goddess of war, wisdom and arts, such as weaving, the making oil, music, especially the pipe (2); of building castles, over which she presided; and, in short, was the patroness of all
those

(7) It is said Vulcan was the midwife, by cleaving his skull with a hatchet; but that seeing an armed virago come out, instead of a child, he ran away. Others report, that when Jupiter swallowed Metis, one of his wives, she was with child of Pallas.

(8) Hence the Rhodians were the first who worshipped her, as Claudian remarks:

Auratos Rhodiis imbres, nascente Minerva
Induxisse Jovem ferunt.

Some say it was because she taught them the art of making colossal statues.

(9) An annual ceremony was performed at this lake by the virgins, who in distinct bodies attacked each other with various weapons. The first that fell was esteemed not a maid, and thrown into the lake; but she who received most wounds was carried off in triumph.

(1) Yet Homer, and all the poets, call her the blue-eyed maid. See Pope.

(2) It is said, seeing her cheeks reflected in the water as she played, she threw away the pipe, with this expression, *That music was too dear if purchas'd at the expence of beauty.*

those sciences which render men useful to society and themselves, and entitle them to the esteem of posterity.

We have already had occasion to observe how this goddess vowed a perpetual virginity, and in what manner she rejected the addresses of Vulcan. She was indeed very delicate on this point, for she deprived Tiresias of his sight, because he accidentally saw her bathing in the fountain of Helicon; but at the intercession of his mother Chariclc, she relented so far, that, to compensate his loss, she endued him with the gift of prophecy (3). Nor was she less severe to Medusa, who being ravished by Neptune in her temple, she revenged the sacrilege, by turning her locks into snakes, and causing all who beheld her after to be changed into stones.

She was equally jealous of her superiority in the arts she invented. Arachne, a Libyan princess, the daughter of Idmon, had the presumption to challenge her at spinning. The folly cost her dear; for Minerva struck her with the spindle on the forehead, for which attempting to hang herself, through despair, the goddess turned her into a spider, in which shape she still exercises the profession she so much boasted of (4). The reader may consult Ovid, if he would see this story set in a beautiful light.

As conduct is opposite, in military affairs, to brutal valour, so Minerva is always by the poets placed in contrast to Mars. Thus we see Homer makes her side with the Greeks in the Trojan war, while the other deity takes the part of the enemy. The success is answerable to this disposition (5), and we see prudence and discipline victorious over valour without counsel, and force under no direction.

One of the most remarkable of Minerva's adventures, was her contest with Neptune, of which notice has been taken under the article of that deity. When Cecrops founded Athens, it was agreed, that whoever of these two deities should produce the most beneficial gift to mankind, should give name to the new city. Neptune with a stroke of his trident formed

(3) Ovid relates the story of Tiresias very differently: for which see Metamorph. Lib. III. 316.
(4) See Ovid, Lib. VI. 1.
(5) See the preface to Mr. Pope's Homer.

formed a horse; Pallas caused an olive to spring from the ground, and carried the prize. The meaning of this fable was to point out, that agriculture was to a rising colony of more importance than navigation.

Minerva was highly honoured, and had several temples both in Greece and Italy. The Athenians, who always had a particular devotion to her, as the patroness of their city, in the flourishing state of their republic, erected a magnificent temple to her by the name of Parthenis, or the virgin goddess, in which they placed her statue of gold and ivory thirty-nine feet high, wrought by the hand of Phidias. She had a stately temple at Rome, on mount Aventine, where her festival, called Minervalia, or Quinquatria, was celebrated for five days successively in the month of March. She had sometimes her altars in common with Vulcan, sometimes with Mercury. The usual victim offered her was a white heifer never yoked. The animals sacred to her were the cock, the owl, and the basilisk.

We must not here omit the Palladium (6) or that sacred statue of her which fell down from heaven, and was preserved in Troy, as a treasure on whose safety that of the city depended. Diomedes and Ulysses found means to steal it, and the city was soon after taken and destroyed (7). However, it is certain that Æneas brought either this or another of the same kind with him into Italy, and deposited it at Lavinium, from whence it was removed to Rome, and placed in the temple of Vesta. When this edifice was consumed by fire, Metellus, a noble Roman, rushed in, and brought it off, though with the loss of his eyes; in recompence for which heroic action, he had the privilege of coming to the senate in a chariot, that the honour might in some degree allay the sense of his misfortune. The Romans, indeed, vain of their Trojan descent, regarded the Palladium in

---

(6) Authors differ as to this Palladium, some making it of wood, and adding, it could move its eyes and shake its spear. Others say, it was composed of the bones of Pelops, and sold by the Scythians to the Trojans.

(7) Some assert it was a counterfeit Palladium the Greek generals stole away, and that Æneas saved the true one. Others make two Palladiums.

in the fame light with their anceftors, and thought the fecurity and duration of their empire were annexed to the poffeffion of this guardian image.

Come we next to enquire into the mythological birth and origin of this fabled goddefs, who is no other than the Egyptian Ifis under a new drefs or form, and the fame with the Pales, or rural goddefs of the Sabines (8). The Athenians, who were an Egyptian colony from Sais, followed the cuftoms of their anceftors, by particularly applying themfelves to raifing flax for linen cloth, and the cultivation of the olive (9). Now the figure worfhipped at Sais, prefiding over thefe arts, was a female in complete armour. This, as Diodorus tells us, was becaufe the inhabitants of this dynafty, were both the beft hufbandmen and foldiers in Egypt. In the hand of this image they placed a fhield with a full moon depicted on it, furrounded by ferpents, the emblems of life and happinefs. And at the feet of this fymbol they placed an owl, to fhew it was a nocturnal facrifice. To this they gave the name of Medufa (1), expreffive of what fhe was defigned to reprefent. The Greeks who were ignorant of the true meaning of all this, did not think fit to put fuch a favourable fenfe on the head of Medufa, which feemed to them an object of horror, and opened a fine field for poetical imagination. The prefling of the olives did indeed turn fruit into ftones in a literal fenfe; hence they made the ægis or fhield of Minerva petrify all who beheld it.

To remind the people of the importance of their linen manufactory, the Egyptians expofed in their feftivals another image, bearing in her right hand the beam or inftrument round which the weavers rolled the warp of their cloth. This image they called Minerva (2). Now there are ancient figures of Pallas extant,

---

(8) To whofe honour the feafts called Palilia were celebrated. Now this word is manifeftly of Egyptian derivation, being taken from Pillel, to govern the city; whence comes Pelilah, the public order.

(9) The city of Sais derives its name from this tree, Zaith or Sais fignifying the olive.

(1) From Dufh, to prefs, comes Medufha, or Medufa, the prefling. See Ifaiah xxv. 10.

(2) From Manevra, a weaver's loom.

extant, which correspond with this idea (3). What still heightens the probability of this is, that the name of Athene, given to this goddess, is the very word in Egypt for the flaxen thread (4) used in their looms. Near this figure, which was to warn the inhabitants of the approach of the weaving, or winter season, they placed another of an insect, whose industry seems to have given rise to this art, and to which they gave the name of Arachne (5), to denote its application. All these emblems, transplanted to Greece by the genius of that people, fond of the marvellous, were converted into real objects, and indeed afforded room enough for the imagination of their poets to invent the fable of the transformation of Arachne into a spider.

Minerva, by the poets and sculptors, is usually represented in a standing attitude completely armed, with a composed but smiling countenance, bearing a golden breast-plate, a spear in her right hand, and her terrible ægis in her left, having on it the head of Medusa entwined with snakes. Her helmet was usually entwined with olives, to denote peace is the end of war, or rather because that tree was sacred to her. See her picture in Cambray's Telemaque. At her feet is generally placed the owl or the cock; the former being the emblem of wisdom, the latter of war.

CHAP. XL.

OF MARS AND BELLONA.

MARS was the son of Juno alone, who being chagrined that Jupiter should bear Minerva without her help, to be even with him consulted Flora, who shewed her a flower in the Olenian fields, on touching of which she conceived, and became the mother of this dreadful deity (6). Thero, or Fierceness, was his

(3) In the collection of prints made by M. de Crozat.
(4) Atona, linen thread. See Proverbs vii. 16.
(5) From Arach, to make linen cloth.
6) Others make him the son of Jupiter and Juno, or of Jupiter and Erys.

his nurse, and he received his education amongst the Scythians, the most barbarous nation in the world, amongst whom he was adored in a particular manner, though they acknowledged no other god.

This deity had different appellations. The Greeks called him Ares (7), from the destruction he causes. He had the name of Gradivus, from his majestic port; of Quirinus, when on the defensive, or at rest. By the ancient Latins he was stiled Salisubsulus, or the dancer, from the uncertainty that attends all martial enterprises.

Mars was the god of war, and in high veneration with the Romans, both on account of his being the father of Romulus, their founder, and because of their own genius, always inclined to conquest. Numa, though otherwise a pacific prince, having implored the gods, during a great pestilence, received a small brass buckler, called ancile, from heaven, which the nymph Egeria advised him to keep with the utmost care, the fate of the Roman people and empire depending on its conservation. To secure so valuable a pledge, Numa caused eleven more shields of the same form to be made, and intrusted the care of these to an order of priests he instituted, called Salii, or the priests of Mars, in whose temple the twelve ancilia were deposited. The number of these priests were also twelve, chosen out of the noblest families, who, on the first of March annually, the festival of Mars, carried the ancilia with great ceremony round the city, clashing their bucklers, and singing hymns to the gods, in which they were joined by a chorus of virgins chosen to assist on this occasion, and dressed like themselves. This festival was concluded with a grand supper (8).

Augustus erected a magnificent temple to Mars at Rome, by the title of Ultor, which he vowed to him, when he implored his assistance against the murderers of Julius Cæsar. The victims sacrificed to him were the wolf for his fierceness, the horse on account of its usefulness in war, the woodpecker and vulture for their ravenousness, the cock for his vigilance. He was crowned with grass, because it grows in cities depopulated by war, and thickest in places moistened with human blood.

The

(7) From αρειν, to kill.
(8) Called Cœna Saliaris.

The history of Mars furnishes few adventures. We have already related his amour with Venus, by whom he had Hermione, contracted to Orestes, and afterwards married to Pyrrhus, king of Epirus.

By the nymph Bistonis, Mars had Tereus, who reigned in Thrace, and married Progne, the daughter of Pandion, king of Athens. This princess had a sister called Philomela, a great beauty; and being desirous to see her, she requested her husband to go to Athens, and bring her sister, with her father's permission to her. Tereus, by the way, fell in love with his charge, and on her rejecting his solicitations, ravished her, cut out her tongue, and enclosed her in a strong tower, pretending to his wife she died in the journey. In this condition the unhappy princess found means to embroider her story, and sent it to her sister, who, transported with rage, contrived how to revenge the injury. First she brought her sister home privately; next she killed her son Itys, and served up his flesh to his father, for supper: after he had eat it, she exposed the head, and told him what she had done; Tereus, mad with fury, pursued the sisters, who in their flight became transformed, Progne to a swallow, and Philomela to a nightingale. Itys was by the gods changed into a pheasant, and Tereus himself into a lapwing. Ovid has (9) given us this story with his usual embellishments.

Mars married a wife called Nerio, or Nerione (1), which in the Sabine tongue signifies valour or strength. He had several children, the principal of whom were Bythis, who gave his name to Bythinia; Thrax, from whom Thrace was so called; Ænomaus, Ascalaphus, Biston, Chalybs, Strymon, Parthenopæus, Tmolus, Pylus, Euenus, Calydon, &c.

This deity having killed Halirothus, the son of Neptune, was indicted before the assembly of the gods for the murder, as well as for the crime of debauching Alcippe, sister to the deceased. Twelve gods were present, of whom six were for acquitting him; so that by the custom of the court, when the voices were equal, the favourable side carrying it,

he

---

(9) See Ovid, Lib. VI. 413.

(1) Hence the Claudian family at Rome are said to derive the surname of Nero.

he came off. Some say this trial was in the famous Areopagus, or hill of Mars, at Athens, a court which, in succeeding time, gained the highest reputation, for the justice and impartiality of its proceedings (2).

Mars was neither invulnerable nor invincible, for we find him in Homer both wounded and pursued by Diomedes; but then it must be considered, that Homer was so good a patriot, that he always affects to disgrace the gods who took the Trojan's part.

Mars, whatever his appearance be, was of Egyptian original. This nation was divided into three classes, the priests, the husbandmen, and the artificers; of these, the first were by their profession exempt from war, and the latter reckoned too mean to be employed in defence of the state; so that their militia was wholly taken from the second body. We have already observed, that in the sacrifices which preceded their military expeditions, their Isis appeared in a warlike dress, and gave rise to the Greek Pallas, or Minerva. The Horus which accompanied this figure, was also equipped with this helmet and buckler, and called by the name of Harits (3), or the formidable. The Syrians softened this word to Hazis (4); the Greeks changed it to Ares; the Gauls pronounced it Hesus; and the Romans and Sabines, Warets or Mars. Thus the military Horus of the Egyptians became personified, and made the god of combats or war.

Mars is usually described in a chariot drawn by furious horses, completely armed, and extending his spear with one hand, while with the other hand he grasps a sword embrued in blood. His aspect is fierce and savage. Sometimes Discord is represented as preceding his car, while Clamour, Fear, and Terror, appear in his train. Virgil has given a description of this god pretty much agreeable to this idea (5).

Bellona

(2) These judges were chosen out of persons of the most blameless characters. They suffered no verbal pleadings before them, lest a false eloquence might varnish a bad cause; and all their sentences were given in writing, and delivered in the dark.

(3) From Harits, violence and enraged. See Job. xv. 20.

(4) Hazis, (Syr) the terrible in war, Psalm xxiv. 8. The Syrians also called him Ab Gueroth, or the father of combats; whence the Romans borrowed their Gradivus Pater.

(5) Virgil, Æneid VIII. 700.

Bellona is usually reckoned the sister of Mars, though some call her both his sister and wife. As her inclinations were equally cruel and savage, she took a pleasure in sharing his dangers, and is commonly depicted as driving his chariot with a bloody whip in her hand. Appius Claudius built her a temple at Rome, where, in her sacrifices called Bellonaria, her priests used to slash themselves with knives. Just opposite stood the Columna Bellica, a pillar from whence the herald threw a spear, when war was proclaimed against any nation. She is said to be the inventress of the needle (6), from whence she took her name.

This goddess is represented sometimes holding a lighted torch or brand, at others with a trumpet; her hair composed of snakes clotted with gore, and her garments stained with blood, in a furious and distracted attitude.

CHAP. XLI.
OF CERES.

IT may not be improper now to pass to softer pictures, whose agreeableness may serve as a contrast to the stronger images just displayed. As plenty and abundance repair the waste and havock of war, we shall next to Mars, introduce Ceres, a divinity friendly and beneficent to mankind.

This goddess was the daughter of Saturn and Rhea. Sicily, Attica, Crete, and Egypt, claim the honour of her birth, each country producing its reasons, though the first has the general suffrage. In her youth she was so beautiful, that her brother Jupiter fell in love with her, by whom she had Proserpine. Neptune next enjoyed her; but the fruit of this amour is controverted, some making it a daughter called Hira, others a horse called Arion. Indeed as this last deity caressed her in that form, the latter opinion seems best founded. However this be, she was so ashamed of this last affair, that she put on mourning garments,

(6) From Βελόνη, a needle.

garments, and retired to a cave, where she continued so long, that the world was in danger of perishing for want (7). At last Pan discovered her retreat, and informed Jupiter, who, by the intercession of the Parcæ, or Fates, appeased her, and prevailed on her to return to the world.

For some time she took up her abode in Corcyra, from whence she removed to Sicily, where the misfortune befell her of the rape of Proserpine her daughter by Pluto. The disconsolate mother immediately carried her complaints to Jupiter, upbraiding him with his permitting such an injustice to be committed especially on the person of his own daughter. But obtaining little satisfaction, she lighted her torches at mount Ætna, and mounting her car drawn by winged dragons, set out in search of her beloved daughter. As her adventures in this journey were pretty remarkable, we shall mention them in their order.

Her first stop was at Athens, where being hospitably received by Celeus, she in return taught him to sow corn, and nourished his son Triptolemus with celestial milk by day, at night covering him with fire, to render him immortal. Celeus, out of curiosity, discovering this last particular, was so affrighted, that he cried out and revealed it himself, on which the goddess killed him. As to his son, Ceres lent him her chariot, and sent him through the world to instruct mankind in the art of agriculture.

She was next entertained by Hypothoon and Meganira (8) his wife, who set wine before her, which she refused, as unsuitable to her mournful condition; but she prepared herself a drink from an infusion of meal or corn, which she afterwards used. Iambe (9), an attendant of Meganira, used to divert the goddess with stories and jests, which she repeated in a certain kind of verse. It happened, during a sacrifice made her here, that Abbas, son to Meganira, derided the ceremony, and used the goddess with opprobrious language; whereupon sprinkling him with a certain mixture she held in her cup, he became a newt or water lizard. Erisichton also, for cutting down a grove consecrated to her, was punished

(7) Because during her absence the earth produced no corn or fruits.

(8) Hypothoon was the son of Neptune and Asope.

(9) The daughter of Pan and Echo, and the inventress of Iambic verse.

ed with such an insatiable hunger, that nothing could satisfy him, but he was forced to gnaw his own flesh.

From thence Ceres passed into Lycia, where being thirsty, and desiring to drink at a spring, the clowns not only hindered her, but sullied and disturbed the water, reviling her for her misfortunes; upon which she turned them into frogs. These frogs, though already punished for affronting his sister, had the folly to ask Jupiter to grant them a king. He sent them a frog, whom they rejected, and desired another; upon which the god sent them a water serpent, who devoured them, and effectually convinced them of their weakness.

It is disputed, who first informed Ceres where her daughter was; some ascribe the intelligence to Triptolemus, and his brother Eubuleus; but the most part agree in giving the honour of it to the nymph Arethusa (a fountain in Sicily) (1) who flying the pursuit of the river Alpheus, saw this goddess in the infernal regions.

We have but one amour of Ceres recorded. Finding Jason, the son of Jupiter and Electra, asleep in a field newly ploughed up, she acquainted him with her passion, and bore him Plutus the god of riches; but Jove, incensed to see his son become his rival, killed him with a thunderbolt.

Ceres had several names; she was called Magna Dea, or the great goddess, from her bounty in supporting mankind; Melaina, from her back cloathing; Euchlæa, from her verdure; Alma, Altrix, and Mammosa, from her nourishing and impregnating all seeds and vegetables, and being as it were the common mother of the world. The Arcadians, by way of excellence, stiled her Despoina, or the Lady. She was also honoured with the peculiar epithet of Thesmophoris, or the Legislatress, because husbandry first taught the use of landmarks, and the value of ground, the source of all property and law.

It must be owned this goddess was not undeserving the highest titles given her, considered as the deity who first taught men to plough and sow, to reap and house their corn, to yoke oxen, to make bread, to cultivate all sorts of pulse and garden-stuff (except beans), though some make Bacchus the first inventor of

(1) The daughter of Nereus and Doris, and a companion of Diana.

of agriculture. She also instructed mankind to fix limits or boundaries, to ascertain their possessions.

There was none of the celestial assembly to whom more solemn sacrifices were instituted than to Ceres. The place where she was principally worshipped was at Eleusis, where her rites were performed in the most solemn and mysterious manner. They were celebrated only once in five years; all the matrons initiated, were to vow a perpetual chastity. At the commencement of the festival, a feast was kept for several days, during which wine was banished the altars. After this the procession began, which consisted in the carriage of the sacred baskets or canisters, in one of which was inclosed a child with a golden seraph, a van, grains, cakes, &c.

The representation of the mysteries, during which a profound silence (2) was to be observed, concluded thus: after a horrid darkness, thunder, lightning, and whatever is most awful in nature, succeeded a calm and bright illumination, which discovered four persons splendidly habited. The first was called the Hierophant, or the *expounder of sacred things*, and represented the Demiurgus, or supreme being; the second bore a torch, and signified Osiris; the third stood near the altar, and signified Isis; the fourth, whom they call the Holy Messenger, personated Mercury (3). To these rites none were admitted but persons of the first character, for probity or eminence. Only the priests were suffered to see the statue of the goddess. All the Assembly used lighted torches, and the solemnity concluded with games, in which the victors were crowned with ears of barley.

According to Herodotus, these rites were brought from Egypt to Greece, by the daughters of Danaus. Others say, that Eumolpus, the son of Triptolemus and Driope, transferred them from Eleusis to Athens.

The Thesmophoria, or lesser festivals of Ceres, were celebrated annually at Argos, and in many points resembled the Eleusinian mysteries, though they fell short of them very much in the dignity and grandeur of the celebration.

Q. Memmius

(2) It was death to speak, or to reveal what passed in these religious rites.

(3) The whole purport of this representation, was designed to allegorize the desolate state of mankind after the flood, and shew the benefits of agriculture and industry.

Q. Memmius the ædile firſt introduced theſe rites into Rome by the title of Cerealia (4). None were admitted to the ſacrifices guilty of any crime; ſo that when Nero attempted it, the Roman matrons expreſſed their reſentment, by going into mourning. This feſtival was cloſed by a banquet and public horſe-races.

The Ambarvalia were feaſts celebrated by the Roman huſbandmen in ſpring, to render Ceres propitious, by luſtrating their fields. Each maſter of a family furniſhed a victim with an oaken wreath round its neck, which he led thrice round his ground, followed by his family ſinging hymns, and dancing in honour of the goddeſs. The offerings uſed in the luſtration were milk and new wine. At the cloſe of the harveſt there was a ſecond feſtival, in which the goddeſs was preſented with the firſt fruits of the ſeaſon, and an entertainment provided for the relations and neighbours.

The beginning of April the gardeners ſacrificed to Ceres, to obtain a plentiful produce of their grounds, which were under her protection. Cicero mentions an ancient temple of hers at Catanea, in Sicily, in which the offices were performed by matrons and virgins only, no man being admitted. The uſual ſacrifices to this goddeſs were a ſow with pig, or a ram. The garlands uſed by her in her ſacrifices were of myrtle or rape-weed: but flowers were prohibited, becauſe Proſerpine was loſt as ſhe gathered them. The poppy alone was ſacred to her, not only becauſe it grows amongſt corn, but becauſe in her diſtreſs Jupiter gave it her to eat, that ſhe might ſleep and forget her troubles.

Let us now endeavour to find ſome explanation of this hiſtory of Ceres. If we have recourſe to our former key, we ſhall find the Ceres of Sicily and Eleuſis, or of Rome and Greece, is no other than the Egyptian Iſis, brought by the Phœnicians into thoſe countries. The very name of myſtery (5) given to the Eleuſinian rites, ſhews they are of Egyptian origin. The Iſis, which

---

(4) This appears from a medal of this magiſtrate, on which is the effigy of Ceres holding in one hand three ears of corn, in the other a torch, and with her left foot treading on a ſerpent.

(5) From Miſtor, a veil or covering.

which appeared at the feast appointed for the commemoration of the state of mankind after the flood, bore the name of Ceres (6), suitable to her intention. She was figured in mourning, and with a torch, to denote the grief she felt for the loss of Persephone (7) her favourite daughter, and the pains she was at to recover her. The poppies with which this Isis was crowned, signified the joy men received at their first abundant crop (8). Triptolemus was only the attendant Horus (9), bearing in his hand the handle of a plough, and Celeus his father was no more than (1) the name of the tools used in the forming this useful instrument of agriculture. Eumolpus expressed (2) the regulation or formation of the people to industry and tillage; and Proserpina or Persephone being found again, was a lively symbol of the recovery of corn almost lost in the deluge, and its cultivation with success. Thus the emblems, almost quite simple, of the most important event which ever happened in the world, became, when transplanted to Greece and Rome, the sources of the most ridiculous fable and grossest idolatry.

.Ceres was usually represented of a tall majestic stature, fair complexion, languishing eyes, and yellow or flaxen hair; her head crowned with poppies, or ears of corn, her breasts full and swelling, holding in her right hand a bunch of the same materials with her garland, and in her left a lighted torch. When in a car or chariot, she is drawn by winged dragons, or lions.

CHAP.

(6) From Cerets, dissolution or overthrow, Jeremiah xlvi. 20.
(7) From Peri, fruit or corn, and Saphan, lost, comes Persephone, or the corn lost.
(8) Bobo signifies a double crop, and is also the name for the poppy.
(9) From Tarap, to break, and Telem, a furrow, comes Triptolem, or the act of ploughing.
(1) Celeus, from Celi, a tool or vessel.
Virgea præterea Celei *vilisque supellex.* VIRGIL GEO.
(2) From Wam, people, and Alep, to learn, is derived Eumolep or Eumolpus, i. e. the people regulated or instructed.

CHAP. XLII.

OF BACCHUS.

As corn and wine are the nobleft gifts of nature, fo it is no wonder, in the progrefs of idolatry, if they became deified, and had their altars. It is therefore no unnatural tranfition, if from Ceres we pafs to Bacchus.

This deity was the fon of Jupiter and Semele, (as has been obferved in the article of Jupiter) and was born at Thebes. Cicero mentions five (3) of the name. It is faid the nymphs took care of his education, though fome afcribe this office to the Horæ or Hours; others to the Naides. Mercury after this carried him into Eubæ to Macris, the daughter of Arifteus (4), who anointed his lips with honey; but Juno, incenfed at his finding a protection in a place facred to her, banifhed him thence; fo that Macris fled with him into the country of the Phœnicians, and nourifhed him in a cave. Others fay, that Cadmus, father to Semele, difcovering her crime, put her and the child into a wooden ark, which by the tides was carried to Oreatæ, a town of Laconia, where Semele being found dead, was buried with great pomp, and the infant nurfed by Ino in a cave. During this perfecution, being tired in his flight, he fell afleep, and an Amphifbena, or two-headed ferpent, of the moft poifonous kind, bit his leg; but awaking, he ftruck it with a vine twig, and that killed it.

In his infancy fome Tyrrhenian merchants found him afleep on the fhore, and attempted to carry him away; but fuddenly he transformed himfelf into monftrous fhapes; at the fame time their mafts were encompaffed with vines, and their oars with ivy, and, ftruck with madnefs, they jumped into the fea, where the god changed them into dolphins. Homer has made this the fubject of one of his hymns.

Bacchus,

(3) The 1ft fon of Jupiter and Proferpine; the 2d the Egyptian Bacchus, the fon of Nile, who killed Nyfa; the 3d the fon of Caprius, who reigned in Afia; the 4th the fon of Jupiter and Luna; and the 5th born of Nifus and Thione.

(4) Others fay Mercury carried him to Nyfa, a city of Arabia, near Egypt.

Bacchus, during the giants war, distinguished himself greatly by his valour in the form of a lion, while Jupiter, to encourage his son, used the word Euhoe, which became afterwards frequently used in his sacrifices. Others say, that in this rebellion the Titans cut our deity to pieces; but that Pallas took his heart, while yet panting, and carried it to her father, who collected the limbs, and re-animated the body, after it had slept three nights with Proserpine (5).

The most memorable exploit of Bacchus was his expedition to India, which employed him three years. He set out from Egypt, where he left Mercurius Trismegistus to assist his wife in quality of co-regent, and appointed Hercules his viceroy. Busiris he constituted president of Phœnicia, and Antæus of Libya; after which he marched with a prodigious army, carrying with him Triptolemus and Maro, to teach mankind the arts of tillage and planting the vine. His first progress was westward (6), and during his course he was joined by Pan and Lusus, who gave their names to different parts of Iberia. Altering his views he returned through Ethiopia, where the Satyrs and Muses increased his army, and from thence crossing the red sea, he penetrated through Asia to the remotest parts of India, in the mountains of which country, near the source of the Ganges, he erected two pillars, to shew that he had visited the utmost limits of the habitable world (7). After this returning home with glory, he made a triumphant entry into Thebes, offered part of his spoils to Jupiter, and sacrificed to him the richest spices of the east. He then applied himself solely to affairs of government, to reform abuses, enact good laws, and consult the happiness of his people, for which he not only obtained

(5) The Mythologists say, this is to denote that the cuttings of vine will grow, but that they will be three years before they come to bear.

(6) Pan gave his name to Spain, or Hispania, Lusus to Lusitania, or Portugal.

(7) In his return he built Nysa, and other cities, and passing the Hellespont he came into Thrace, where he left Maro, who founded the city Maronæa. To Macedo he gave the country from him called Macedonia, and left Triptolemus in Attica to instruct the people.

ed the title of the law-giver, by way of excellence, but was deified after death.

Juno having struck him with madnefs, he had before this wandered through part of the world. Proteus, king of Egypt, was the firſt who received him kindly. He next went to Cybella in Phrygia, where being expiated by Rhea, he was initiated in the myſteries of Cybele. Lycurgus, king of the Edoni, near the river Strymon, affronted him in this journey, for which Bacchus deprived him of his reaſon; ſo that when he thought to prune his vines, he cut off the legs of his ſon Dryas and his own. By command of the oracle, his ſubjects impriſoned him, and he was torn in pieces by wild horſes. It is eaſy to ſee how inconſiſtent theſe accounts of the ſame perſon are, and that the actions of different Bacchuſes are aſcribed to one.

We have two other inſtances recorded of the reſentment of this deity. Alcithoe, a Theban lady, derided his prieſteſſes, and was transformed into a bat; Pentheus, the ſon of Echion and Agave, for ridiculing his ſolemnities, called Orgia, was torn in pieces by his own mother and ſiſters (8), who in their madneſs took him for a wild boar.

The favourite wife of Bacchus was Ariadne, whom he found in the iſle of Naxos, abandoned by Theſeus; he loved her ſo paſſionately, that he placed the crown ſhe wore as a conſtellation in the ſkies. By her he had Staphilus, Thyoneus, Hymenæus, &c.

Ciſſus, a youth whom he greatly eſteemed, ſporting with the Satyrs, was accidentally killed. Bacchus changed him into the plant ivy, which became in a peculiar manner conſecrated to his worſhip. Silenus, another of his favourites, wandering from his maſter, came to Midas, king of Phrygia, at whoſe court he was well received. To requite this favour, Bacchus promiſed to grant whatever he requeſted. The monarch, whoſe ruling paſſion was avarice, deſired all he touched might be turned to gold; but he ſoon felt the inconveniency of having his wiſh granted, when he found his meat and drink converted into metal. He therefore prayed the god to recall his bounty, and releaſe him from his miſery. He

G was

(8) Ovid, Lib. II. 630.

was commanded to wash in the river Pactolus, which, from that time, had golden sands (9).

(1) Bacchus had a great variety of names; he was called Dionysius (2), from his father's lameness while he carried him in his thigh: the appellation of Biformis was given him, because he sometimes was represented as old, sometimes as young; that of Brisæus, from his inventing the wine press (3); that of Bromius, from the crackling of fire heard when Semele perished by the lightning of Jupiter; that of Bimater, from his having two mothers, or being twice born. The Greeks stiled him Bugenes, or born of an ox, because he was drawn with horns; and for the same reason the Latins called him Tauriformis. He was named Dæmon Bonus, because in all feasts the last glass was drank to his honour. Evius, Evous, and Evan, were names used by the Bacchanals in their wild processions, as were those of Eleus and Eleleus. He was stiled Iacchus, from the noise (4) made by his votaries in their drunken frolics; Lenæus, because wine assuages the sorrows and troubles of life (5); Liber, and Liber Pater, because he sets men free from constraint, and puts them on an equality; and on the same account he was surnamed Lyæus, and Lycæus (6); Nyctilius was an appellation given him, because his sacrifices were often celebrated in the night; from his education on mount Nysa, he gained the epithet of Nisæus, as also that of Thyoneus, from Thyo his nurse; and that of Triumphus, from his being the first who instituted triumphs.

The principal festivals of Bacchus were the Oscophoria, instituted by the Phœnicians. The Trieterica cele-

(9) Ovid, Lib. XI. 86.

(1) From Βακχειν, to run mad, because wine inflames, and deprives men of their reason.

(2) From Διος, God, and νυσος, lame or crippled.

(3) Some derive it from Brisa his nurse; others from the promontory Brisa, in the isle of Lesbos, where he was chiefly worshipped.

(4) From ιακχυν, to exclaim or roar. See Claudian's rape of Proserpine.

(5) From lenio, to soften; but Servius gives the epithet a Greek etymology, from ληνος a wine-press. The first conjecture is best-supported by the poets.

Cura fugit, multo a viturque mero. OVID.

(6) From λυω, to unloose or set free.

(7), celebrated in remembrance of his three years expedition to India. The Epilœnea were games appointed at the time of vintage, in which they contended who should tread out most must or wine, and sung hymns to the deity. The Athenians observed a certain feast called Apaturia; as also others called Ascolia and Ambrosia. The latter were celebrated in January, the month sacred to Bacchus; the Romans called them Brumalia, and kept them in February and August (8); but the most considerable of the Romans, with regard to this god, were the Bacchanali, Dionysia or Orgia, solemnized at mid-day in February, by women only at first, but afterwards by both sexes. These rites were attended with such abominable excesses and wickedness, that the senate abolished them by a public decree (9).

The victims agreeable to Bacchus, were the goat and swine, because these animals are destructive to the vines; the dragon and the pye on account of its chattering. The trees and plants used in his garlands were the ivy, the fir, the oak, and the herb rapeweed; as also the flower Daffodil or Narcissus.

Bacchus was the god of mirth, wine, and good cheer, and as such the poets have not been sparing in his praises. On all occasions of pleasure and social joy they never failed to invoke his presence, and to thank him for the blessings he bestowed. To him they ascribed the forgetfulness of their cares, and the soft transports of mutual friendship and chearful conversation. It would be endless to repeat the compliments paid him by the Greek and Latin poets, who, for the most part, were hearty devotees to his worship.

Bacchus, by the poets and painters, is represented as a corpulent youth (1) naked, with a ruddy face, wanton look, and effeminate air. He is crowned with ivy and vine leaves, and bears in his hand a

thyrsus

---

(7) Virgil, Æneid IV. 303.
(8) See Cœl. Rhodog. Lib. XVII. cap. 5.
(9) See Horace, Book II. Ode XIX. wholly consecrated to his praise.
(1) Bacchus was sometimes depicted as an old man with a beard, as at Elis in Greece, and it was only then he had horns given him; sometimes he was cloathed with a tyger's skin.

thyrfus (2), encircled with the fame. His car is drawn fometimes by lions, at others by tigers, leopards, or panthers, and furrounded by a band of Satyrs and Mænades, or wood-nymphs, in frantic poftures; and, to clofe the mad proceffion, appears old Silenus riding on an afs, which was fcarcely able to carry fo fat and jovial a companion.

But on the great farcophagus of his Grace the Duke of Beaufort, at Badminton, he is expreffed as a young man mounted on a tyger, and habited in a long robe. He holds a thyrfus in one hand, and with the other pours wine into a horn. His foot refts upon a bafket. His attendants are the feafons properly reprefented, and intermingled with Fauns, Genii, &c.

To arrive at the true original of this fabled deity, we muft once more revifit Egypt, the mother-country of the gods, where he was indeed no other than the Ofiris of that people. Whence fprung another Bacchus, diftinguifhed from him, will prefently appear. We have already had fufficient occafion to remark how their Horus changed his name and attributes, according to the feafons, and the circumftances or operations he was intended to direct. To commemorate the ancient ftate of mankind, he appeared under the fymbol of a child, with a feraph by his fide, and affumed the name of Ben-Semele (3). This was an image of the weaknefs and imperfection of hufbandry after the deluge. The Greeks, who knew nothing of the true meaning of the figure, called it the fon of Semele, and to heighten its honour made Jupiter his father, or, according to the eaftern ftile (4), produced him out of his thigh. They even embellifhed the ftory with all the marvellous circumftances of his mother's death, and fo effectually compleated the fable.

Let us add to this, that in all the ancient forms of invocation to the fupreme being, they ufed the expreffions afterwards appropriated to Bacchus, fuch
as

---

(2) The thyrfus was a wooden javelin with an iron head.
(3) Ben-Semele, or the child of the reprefentation.
(4) See Genefis xlvi. 26, fpeaking of Jacob's children, or who came out of his thigh.

as Io Terombe (5)! Io Bacche (6)! or Io Baccoth! Jehova! Hevan, Hevoe, and Eloah 7)! and Hu Eſh! Atta Eſh (8). Theſe exclamations were repeated in after-ages by the people, who had no longer any ſenſe of their true ſignification, but applied them to the objects of their idolatry. In their huntings they uſed the outcries of Io Saboi (9)! Io Niſſi! which, with a little alteration, became the titles of the deity we are ſpeaking of. The Romans or Latins, of all theſe, preferred the name of Baccoth, out of which they compoſed Bacchus. The more delicate ear of the Greeks choſe the word Io Niſſi, out of which they formed Dionyſius. Hence it is plain, that no Bacchus ever exiſted, but that he was only a maſque or figure of ſome concealed truth. In ſhort, whoever attentively reads Horace's inimitable ode to Bacchus (1), will ſee that Bacchus meant no more than the improvement of the world, by the cultivation of agriculture, and the planting of the vine.

CHAP. XLIII.

OF THE ATTENDANTS OF BACCHUS; SILENUS, SYLVANUS, AND THE MÆNADES OR BACCHÆ, THE SATYRS, FAUNI, AND SELENI.

As Bacchus was the god of good-humour and fellowſhip, ſo none of the deities appeared with a more numerous or ſplendid retinue.

Silenus, the principal perſon in his train, had been his preceptor, and a very ſuitable one for ſuch a deity; for the old man had a very hearty affection for his

---

(5) Io Terombe! let us cry to the Lord; hence Dithyrambus.

(6) Io Baccoth! God ſee our tears! whence Bacchus.

(7) Jehova! Hevan or Hevoe, the author of exiſtence; Eloah, the mighty God! hence Evoe, Evous, &c.

(8) Hu Eſh! thou art the fire! Atta Eſh! thou art the life! hence Attes and Ves.

(9) Io Saboi! Lord thou art an Hoſt to me! Io Niſſi! Lord be my guide! hence Sebaſius and Dionyſius, the names of Bacchus.

(1) Horace, Lib. II. Ode XIX.

his bottle; yet Silenus diftinguifhed himfelf in the giant's war, by appearing on his afs, whofe braying put thofe daring rebels into confufion (2). Some fay he was born at Malea, a city of Sparta; others, at Nyfa in Arabia; but the moft probable conjecture is, that he was a prince of Caria, noted for his equity and wifdom (3). However this be, he was a conftant attendant and companion of his pupil in all his expeditions. Silenus was a notable good moralift in his cups, as we find in Virgil, who has given us a beautiful oration of his on the nobleft fubjects (4), in the fine eclogue which bears his name.

Silenus is depicted as a fhort corpulent old man, bald-headed, with a flat nofe, prominent forehead, and big ears. He is ufually defcribed as over-loaded with wine, and feated on a faddle-backed afs, upon which he fupports himfelf with a long ftaff; and in the other hand carries a cantharus or jug, with the handle worn out almoft by frequent ufe.

Silvanus was a rural deity, who often appears in the train of Bacchus; some fuppofe him the fon of Saturn, others of Faunus. He was unknown to the Greeks; but the Latins received the worfhip of him from the Pelsigi, who, upon their migration into Italy, confecrated groves to his honour, and appointed folemn feftivals, in which milk was offered to him. Indeed the worfhip of this imaginary deity feems wholly to have rifen out of the ancient facred ufe of woods and groves.

The Mænades were the prieftesses and nymphs who attended Bacchus, and were alfo called Thyades, from their fury; Bacchæ, from their intemperance; and Mimallones, from their difpofition to ape and mimic others, which is one of the qualities of drunken people. Thefe bore thyrfufes bound with ivy, and in their proceffion fhocked the ear and eye with their extravagant cries and ridiculous and indecent contortions.

The

(2) For which it was raifed to the fkies, and made a conftellation.

(3) On this account arofe the fable of Midas lending him his ears. It is faid, that being once taken prifoner, he purchafed his liberty with this remarkable fentence, *That it was beft not to be born; and next to that, moft eligible to die quickly.*

(4) Virgil, Eclogue VI. 14.

The life-guards or trained bands of Bacchus were the Satyrs. It is uncertain whence these half creatures sprung; but their usual residence was in the woods and forests, and they were of a very wanton and lustful disposition; so that it was very dangerous for a stray nymph to fall into their hands. Indeed it was natural for them to use compulsion, for their form was none of the most inviting, having deformed heads, armed with short horns, crooked hands, rough and hairy bodies, goats feet and legs, and tails as long as horses.

We are now to seek some explanation of this groupe of figures, and to do this we must have recourse to the Egyptian key. As idolatry improved, the feasts or representations of those people grew more pompous and solemn, show degenerated into masquerade, and religion into farce or frenzy. The Ben-Semele, or child or representation, mentioned in the explanation of Bacchus, became a jolly rosy youth, who, to adorn the pomp, was placed in a chariot, drawn by actors in tigers or leopards skins, while others, dressed in those of bucks or goats, surrounded him; and, to shew the dangers they had gone through in hunting, they smeared their faces with dregs of wine, or juice of mulberries, to imitate the blood of the beasts they killed. These assistants were called Satyrs (5), Fauns (6), and Thyades (7), and Mænades (8), and Bassaridas (9). To close the procession, appeared an old man on an ass, offering wine to the tired youth, who had returned from a prosperous chace, and inviting them to take some rest. This person they called Sylen (1), or Sylvan, and his dress was designed to shew, that old men were exempt from those toils of youth, which, by extirpating beasts of prey, secured the approaching harvest.

All these symbols were by the Greeks and Romans adopted in their way, and the actors of masks of Egypt, became the real divinities of nations, whose inclination to the marvellous made them greedily embrace whatever flattered that prepossession.

CHAP.

(5) From Satur, hidden or disguised.
(6) From Phanim, a masque or false face.
(7) From Thouah, to wander or run about wildly.
(8) From Manoua, to intoxicate or drive mad.
(9) From Batsar, to gather the grapes.
(1) From Selau, safety or repose.

CHAP. XLIV.

OF HERCULES AND HIS LABOURS.

HAVING gone through the Dii Majores, or celestial deities of the firſt rank; we ſhall proceed to the demi gods, who were either thoſe heroes whoſe eminent actions and ſuperior virtues raiſed them to the ſkies, or thoſe terreſtrial divinities, who for their bounty and goodneſs to mankind, were claſſed with the gods.

To begin with the former, Hercules undoubtedly claims the foremoſt place. There were ſeveral of this name (2); but he to whom, amongſt the Greeks, the greateſt glory is attributed, was the ſon of Jupiter and Alcmena, wife of Amphitryon king of Thebes. This monarch being gone on an expedition againſt the Ætolians, Jove aſſumed his form, and under that ſafe diſguiſe eaſily enjoyed his deſires. It is ſaid he was ſo enamoured, that he prolonged the darkneſs for three days and three nights ſucceſſively. Hercules was the fruit of this extraordinary amour, and at the ſame time Alcmena bore twins to her huſband, Laodamia, and Iphiclus, who was remarkable for his extraordinary ſwiftneſs.

This intrigue of Jupiter, as uſual, ſoon came to the ears of his jealous wife, who from that moment meditated the deſtruction of Hercules. A favourable occaſion offered to her reſentment. Archippe, the wife of Sthenelus, king of Mycene, being pregnant at the ſame time with Alcmena, Jupiter had ordained, that the child firſt born ſhould have the ſuperiority, or command over the other. Juno cauſed Archippe to be delivered, at the end of ſeven months, of a ſon, called Euryſtheus, and to retard the labour of Alcmena, in the form of an old woman ſhe ſat at the gate of Amphitryon's palace with her legs acroſs, and her fingers interwoven. By this ſecret enchantment, that princeſs was ſeven days and nights in extreme pains, till Galanthis, one of her attendants, ſeeing Juno in this ſuſpicious poſture, and conjecturing

(2) The Egyptian Hercules is reckoned the eldeſt of theſe who ſignalized himſelf in the giants war, and was one of the principal divinities of that country.

ing the cause, ran hastily out with the news that her mistress was delivered. The goddess starting up at the news, Alcmena was that moment freed of her burthen; but Juno was so incensed at Galanthis, that she changed her into a weesel.

During his infancy, Juno sent two serpents to destroy him, in his cradle, but the undaunted child strangled them with both his hands. After this, as he grew up, he discovered an uncommon stature and strength of body (3), as well as heroic ardour of mind. These great qualities of nature were improved by suitable care, his education being intrusted to the greatest masters (4); so that it is no wonder if, with such considerable advantages, he made such a shining figure in the world.

His extraordinary virtues were early put to the trial, and the tasks imposed on him by Eurystheus, on account of the danger and difficulty which attended their execution, received the name of the Labours of Hercules, and are commonly reckoned to be twelve in number.

1. The first labour, or triumph of Hercules, was the death of the Nemæan lion. It is said this furious animal, by Juno's direction, fell from the orb of the Moon, and was invulnerable. It infested the Nemæan woods, between Philus and Cleone, and did infinite mischief. The hero attacked it both with his arrows and club, but in vain, till perceiving his error, he first strangled, and then tore it in pieces with his hands. The skin he preserved, and constantly wore, as a token of his victory.

2. His next enterprize was against a formidable serpent, or monster, which harboured in the fens of Lerna, and infected the region of Argos with his poisonous exhalations. The number of heads assigned

---

(3) Some say when he arrived at manhood he was four cubits high, and had three rows of teeth.

(4) Linus, the son of Apollo, instructed him in philosophy; Eurytus taught him archery; Eumolpus, music, particularly the art of touching the lyre; from Harpalychus, the son of Mercury, he learnt wrestling and the gymnastic exercises; Castor shewed him the art of managing his weapons; and to complete all, Chiron initiated him in the principles of astronomy and medicine.

ed this creature is various (5); but all authors agree, that when one was cut off, another succeeded in its place, unless the wound was immediately cauterised. Hercules, not discouraged, attacked this dragon, and having caused Iolaus to cut down wood sufficient for flaming brands, as he cut off the heads, applied them to the wounds, and by that means obtained the conquest, and destroyed the Hydra. Some explain this fable, by supposing Lerna a marsh, much troubled with snakes, and other poisonous animals, which Hercules and his companions destroyed, by setting fire to the reeds. Others imagine he only drained this fen, which was before unpassable. Others make Lerna, a fort or castle of robbers, under a leader called Hydra, whom Hercules extirpated. However this be, in consideration of the service of Iolaus on this occasion, when he grew decrepid with old age, his master, by his prayers, obtained a renewal of his youth.

3. The next task imposed on him by Eurystheus, was to bring him alive a huge wild-boar, which ravaged the forest of Erymanthus, and had been sent to Phocis by Diana, to punish Oneus for neglecting her sacrifices (6). In his way he defeated the Centaurs, who had provoked him by insulting Pholus his host. After this he seized the fierce animal in a thicket, surrounded with snow, and, pursuant to his injunction, carried him bound to Eurystheus, who had like to have fainted at the sight.

4. This monarch, after such experience of the force and valour of Hercules, was resolve to try his agility: for this end he was commanded to take a hind which frequented mount Mænalus, and had brazen feet and golden horns. As she was sacred to Diana, Hercules durst not wound her, and it was not easy to run her down: this chase cost him a whole year's foot-speed. At last, being tired out, the hind took to the recesses of mount Artemesius, but was in her way overtaken, as she crossed the river Ladon, and brought to Mycene.

5. Near

---

(5) Some make the heads of the Lernæan Hydra to be seven; others nine; others fifty.

(6) This story has a near resemblance with the boar of Calydon, mentioned in the article of Diana.

5. Near the lake Stymphalus, in Arcadia, harboured certain birds of prey, with wings, beaks, and talons of iron, who preyed on human flesh, and devoured all that passed that way. These Euryftheus sent Hercules to destroy. Some say he killed them with his arrows (7); others, that Pallas lent him some brazen rattles made by Vulcan, the found of which frightened them to the island of Aretia. Some suppose the birds called Stymphalides, a gang of desperate banditti, who had their haunts near that lake.

6. His next expedition was against the Cretan bull. Minos, king of that island, being formidable at sea, had forgot to pay Neptune the worship due to him. The deity, to punish his neglect, sent a furious bull, whose nostrils breathed fire, to destroy the country. Hercules brought this terrible animal bound to Euryftheus, who, on account of his being sacred, let him loose in the territory of Marathon, where he was afterwards slain by Theseus. Some reduce the story to this, that Hercules only was sent to Crete, to procure Euryftheus a bull for breeding out of.

7. Diomede, king of Thrace, the son of Mars and Cyrene, was a tyrant possessed of a stud of horses, so wild and fierce, that they breathed fire, and were constantly fed with human flesh, their master killing all strangers he could meet with for provender for his cattle. Hercules having vanquished him, gave him as a prey to them, and killing some, brought the rest to Euryftheus.

8. The next employment of Hercules seems a little too mean for a hero, but he was obliged to obey a severe task-master, who was so sensible of his own injustice in these injunctions, that he did not care to trust himself in the power of the person he commanded (8). Augeas, king of Elis, had a stable intolerable, from the stench arising from the dung and filth it contained, which is not very suprising, if it be true, that it sheltered three thousand oxen, and had not been cleaned for thirty years. This place Euryftheus ordered Hercules to clear in one day, and Augeas promised

(7) There is an ancient gem expressive of this. See Ogle's antiquities.

(8) It is said Euryftheus never would suffer Hercules to enter Mycene, but notified his commands to him over the walls, by Capreas, an herald.

promised him, if he performed it, to give him a tenth part of the cattle. Hercules, by turning the course of the river Alpheus through it, executed his design; which Augeas seeing, refused to stand by his engagement. The hero, to reward his perfidy, slew him with his arrows, and gave his kingdom to Phyleus, his son, who had shewed his abhorrence of his father's treachery. Some add, that, from the spoils taken at Elis, Hercules instituted the Olympic games of Jupiter, celebrated every fifth year, and which afterwards gave rise to the Grecian æra.

9. Eurystheus, desirous to present his daughter Admeta with the belt or girdle worn by Hippolyta, queen of the Amazons, Hercules was sent on this expedition; he was but slenderly provided, having but one ship; but valour like his was never destitute of resources in distress. In his way he defeated and killed Mygdon and Amycus, two brothers, who opposed his passage, and subduing Bebrycia, gave it to Lycus, one of his companions, who changed its name to Heraclea, in memory of his benefactor. On his approach to Themiscyra, he learnt that the Amazons had collected all their forces to meet him. The first engagement was warm on both sides, several of the bravest of these viragoes were killed, and others made prisoners. The victory was followed by the total extermination of that female nation, and Hippolyta, their queen, was by the conqueror given to Theseus, as a reward for his valour. Her belt he brought to Eurystheus.

10. His succeeding exploit was against Geryon, king of Spain, who had three bodies, and was the son of Chrysaoris and Calirrhoe. This monarch had a breed of oxen, of a purple colour, who devoured all strangers cast to them, and were guarded by a dog with two heads, a dragon with seven, besides a very watchful and severe keeper. Hercules killed both the monarch and his guards, and carried the oxen to Gadira, or Cadiz, from whence he brought them to Eurystheus. It was during this expedition, that our hero, as eternal monuments of his glory, erected two pillars at Calpe and Abyle, upon the utmost limits of Africa and Europe. Some give a more simple turn to the whole, by saying Geryon was a king of Spain, who governed by means of three sons famous for valour and prudence, and that Hercules

cules having raised an army of mercenary troops in Crete, first overcame them, and subdued that country.

11. The next task enjoined him by Eurystheus, was to fetch him the golden apples of the Hesperides (9), which were guarded by a dragon with a hundred heads. The injunction was not easy, since Hercules was even ignorant of the place where they grew. The nymphs of Eridanus, whom he consulted, advised him to go to Prometheus (1), who gave him the information and direction he wanted, after which he vanquished the dragon, and brought the precious fruit to his master.

12. The last command of Eurystheus was for him to go down to hell, and bring away Cerberus, Pluto's mastiff. Hercules, having sacrificed to the gods, entered the infernal regions, by a cavity of mount Tænarus, and on the banks of Acheron found a white poplar-tree, of which he made him a wreath, and the tree was ever after consecrated to him; passing that river he discovered Theseus and Pirithous chained to a stone. The former he released, but left the latter confined. Mænetius, Pluto's cowherd, endeavouring to save his master's dog, was crushed to death. Cerberus, for refuge, fled beneath Pluto's throne, from whence the hero dragged him out, and brought him upon earth by way of Træzene. At sight of the day, the monster vomited a poisonous matter, from whence sprung the herb aconite, or wolf's-bane; but being presented to Eurystheus, he ordered him to be dismissed, and suffered him to return to hell.

It would be almost endless to enumerate all the actions of this celebrated hero of antiquity, and therefore we shall only touch on the principal. He delivered Creon, king of Thebes, from an unjust tribute imposed on him by Erginus and the Myniæ, for which service that prince gave him his daughter Megara, by whom he had several sons; but Juno

striving

(9) Juno, on her marriage with Jupiter, gave him these trees, which bore golden fruit, and were kept by the nymphs Ægle, Arethusa, and Hesperethusa, daughters of Hesperus, who were called the Hesperides.

(1) Or, as others say, to Nereus, who eluded his enquiry, by assuming various shapes.

striking him with frenzy, he slew these children, and on recovering his senses, became so shocked at his cruelty, that he abstained from all human society for some time. In his return from the expedition against the Amazons, Laomedon, king of Troy, by the promise of some fine horses, engaged him to deliver his daughter Hesione, exposed to a vast sea monster sent by Neptune; but when he had freed the princess, the deceitful monarch retracted his word. Upon this Hercules took the city, killed Laomedon, and gave Hesione to Telamon, who first scaled the walls (2). After this he slew Timolus and Telegonos, the sons of Proccus, two celebrated wrestlers, who put to death all whom they overcame. He also killed Serpedon, son of Neptune, a notorious pirate.

During his African expedition, he vanquished Cycnus, king of Thessaly, the son of Mars and Cleobulina, a savage prince, who had vowed to erect his father a temple with the heads or skulls of the strangers he destroyed. In Libya, he encountered the famous Antæus, the son of Earth, a giant of immense stature, who forced all whom he met to wrestle with him, and so strangled them. He challenged Hercules, who flung him thrice, and thought each time he had killed him; but on his touching the ground he renewed his strength. Hercules being apprised of this, held him up in the air, and squeezed him in such a manner, that he soon expired (3). In his progress from Libya to Egypt, Busiris, a cruel prince, laid an ambuscade to surprize him, but was himself, and his son Amphiadamus, sacrificed by the victor on the altars he had profaned. In Arabia, he beheaded Emathion, the son of Tithonus, for his want of hospitality; after which, crossing mount Caucasus, he delivered Prometheus. In Calydon, he wrestled with Achelous, for no less a prize than Deianira, daughter to king Oeneus. The contest was long dubious, for his antagonist had the faculty of assuming all shapes; but as he took that of a bull, Hercules tore off one of his horns, so that he was forced to submit, and

(2) This princess redeemed her brother Priamus; who was afterwards king of Troy.

(3. This is finely expressed in a double antique statue belonging to the Earl of Portsmouth, at Hurstbourne, in Hampshire.

and to redeem it, by giving the conqueror the horn of Amalthæa, the daughter of Harmodius; which Hercules filled with a variety of fruits, and confecrated to Jupiter. Some explain the fable thus; Achelous is a winding river of Greece, whose stream was so rapid, that it overflowed the banks, roaring like a bull. Hercules forced it into two channels; that is, he broke off one of the horns, and so restored plenty to the country

This hero reduced the isle of Coos, and put to death Eurylus, king of it, with his sons, on account of their injustice and cruelty; but the princess Chalchiope, the daughter, he married, by whom he had a son named Thessalus, who gave his name to Thessaly. He subdued Pyracmos, king of Euboea, who had, without a cause, made war on the Boeotians. In his way to the Hesperides, he was opposed by Albion, and Brigio, two giants, who put him in great hazard, his arrows being spent. Jupiter, on his prayer, overwhelmed them with a shower of stones, whence the place was called the stony field. It lies in the Gallia Narbonensis. Hercules did great service in Gaul, by destroying robbers, suppressing tyrants and oppressors, and other actions truly worthy the character of a hero; after which, it is said, he built the city Alesia, and made it the capital of the Celtæ, or Gauls. He also opened his way through the Alps into Italy, and by the coasts of Liguria and Tuscany, arrived on the banks of the Tyber, and slew the furious robber Cacus, who from his den on mount Aventine, infested that country. Being denied the rites of hospitality, he killed Theodama, the father of Hylas, but took the latter with him, and treated him kindly.

Hercules, however intent on fame and glory, was, like other heroes, but too susceptible of love. We find an instance of this in Omphale, queen of Lydia, who gained such an ascendant over him, that he was not ashamed to assume a female dress, to spin amongst her women, and submit to be corrected by her according to her caprice.

His favourite wife was Deianira, before-mentioned, and whose jealousy was the fatal occasion of his death. Travelling with this princess through Ætolia, they had occasion to pass a river, swelled by the sudden rains. Nessus, the centaur, offered Hercules his service to carry over his consort, who accepting it,

crossed

crossed over before them. The monster, seeing the opportunity favourable, offered violence to Deianira, upon which her husband, from the opposite bank, pierced him with one of those dreadful arrows, which being dipped in the blood of the Lernæan Hydra, gave a wound incurable by art. Nessus expiring, gave the princess his garment all bloody, as a sure remedy to recover her husband, if ever he should prove unfaithful. Some years after, Hercules having subdued Oechalia, fell in love with Iole, a fair captive, whom he brought to Euboea, where, having erected an altar to sacrifice to Jove for his victory, he dispatched Lycus to Deianira, to carry her the news, and inform her of his approach. This princess, from the report of the messenger, suspecting her husband's fidelity, sent him as a present the coat of Nessus, which he no sooner put on, but he fell into a delirious fever, attended with the most excruciating torments. Unable to support his pains, he retired to mount Oeta, and erecting a pile of wood, to which he set fire, threw himself into the flames, and was consumed (4). Lycus, his unhappy friend and companion, in his agony, he first hurled into the river Thermopolis, where he became a rock; his arrows he bequeathed to Philoctetes, who buried his remains in the river Dyra.

So perished this great hero of antiquity, the terror of oppressors, the friend of liberty and mankind, for whose happiness (as Tully observes) he braved the greatest dangers, and surmounted the most arduous toils, going through the whole earth with no other view than the establishing peace, justice, concord, and freedom. Nothing can be added to heighten a character so glorious as this.

Hercules left several children; by Deianira he had an only daughter, called Macaria; by Melita, who gave her name to the isle of Malta, he had Hylus: Afar, Lydus, and Scythes, were his sons, who are said to have left their appellation to Africa, Lydia, and Scythia; besides which, he is said to have had fifty sons by the fifty daughters of Thestius. However,

(4) There is at Wilton, the seat of the Earl of Pembroke, amidst a multitude of other valuable curiosities, a small marble statue of Lycus, supporting the dying Hercules, of inimitable workmanship, in which the chissel appears to be infinitely superior to the pencil.

ever, his offspring were fo numerous, that above thirty of his defcendants bore his name, whofe actions being all attributed to him, produced the confufion we find in his hiftory.

Euryftheus, after his death, was fo afraid of thefe Heraclidæ, that by his ill ufage he forced them to fly to Athens, and then fent an embafly to that city to deliver them up, with menaces of a war in cafe of refufal. Iolaus, the friend of Hercules, who was then in the fhades, was fo concerned for his mafter's pofterity, that he got leave from Pluto to return to earth, and kill the tyrant, after which he willingly returned to hell.

Hercules, who was alfo called Alcides, was, after his death, by his father Jupiter deified, and with great folemnity married to Hebe his half fifter, the goddefs of youth. At firft facrifices were only offered to him as a hero; but Phæftius coming into Sycionia altered that method. Both the Greeks and Romans honoured him as a god, and erected temples to him in that quality. His victims were bulls or lambs, on account of his preferving the flocks from wolves, i. e. delivering men from tyrants and robbers. He was called alfo Melius, from his taking the Hefperian fruit, for which reafon apples were ufed (5) in his facrifices. Mehercule, or by Hercules, was, amongft the Romans, an oath only ufed by the men.

Many perfons were fond of affuming this celebrated name. Hence Diodorus reckons up three; Cicero fix; others to the number of forty-three. But the Greeks afcribed to the Theban Hercules the actions of all the reft. But the foundation of all was laid in the Phœnician or Egyptian Hercules; for the Egyptians did not borrow the name from the Grecians, but rather the Grecians, efpecially thofe who gave it to the fon of Amphitryon from the Egyptians; principally, becaufe Amphitryon and Alcmena, the parents of the Grecian Hercules, were both of Egyptian defcent (6). The name too is of Phœnician extraction (7), a name given to the difcoverers of new countries, and the planters of colonies there; who frequently fignalized themfelves no

lefs

(5) From μελος, an apple.
(6) Herodotus in Euterpo.
(7) Harokel, a merchant.

less by civilizing the inhabitants and freeing them from the wild beasts that infested them, than by the commerce which they established; which no doubt was the source of ancient heroism and war (8). And however the Phœnician and Egyptian hero of this name may have been distinguished by a multitude of authors; I am fully persuaded, after the most diligent enquiry, that they were indeed one and the same person: of whose history let us take a short review.

About the year of the world 2131, the person distinguished by the name of Hercules Assis (9), succeeded Janias as king of Lower Egypt, being the last of the Hycsos, or shepherd-kings from Canaan; who had held the country 259 years. He continued the war with the kings of Upper Egypt 49 years, and then by agreement withdrew, with his subjects, to the number of 240,000. In his retreat he is said to have founded first the city of Jerusalem (1), and afterwards that of Tyre, where he was called Melcarthus (2). From Egypt he brought the computation of 365 days to the year, and settled it in his own kingdom, where it continued many ages. In his voyages he visited Africa, where he conquered Antæus, Italy, France, Spain as far as Cadiz, where he slew Geryon; and proceeded thence even to the British isles; settling colonies, and raising pillars wherever he came, as the standing monuments of himself, and of the patriarchal religion which he planted; for pillars placed on eminences in circular order, were the temples of those early times, and as yet we find no footsteps of idolatry, either in Egypt or Phœnicia. To his arrival in these islands (and not in Liguria) must be applied whatever is related of his encounter with Albion and Bergion, and of his being assisted, when his weapons were spent, by a shower of stones from heaven. Albion is the name given afterwards to this country; and by the miraculous shower of stones no more is intended, than that the inhabitants were at last reconciled to him on account of the divine religion

---

(8) Banier's Mythology, vol. iv. p. 72.

(9) Assis, the valiant; so that Hercules Assis, is the heroic merchant.

(1) Manetho apud Josephum, l. 1. contra Apion.

(2) Or king of the city, from Melek, king, and Cartha, city.

gion which he taught, and the great number of these open temples of stone erected by him. He is said to have been attended by Apher, the grandson of Abraham, whose daughter he married, and by whom he had a son named Dodorus (3). To him the Phœnicians were indebted for the gainful trade of tin, which gave name to these islands.(4). He found out also the purple dye, and seems to have been the first who applied the loadstone to the purposes of navigation, thence called Lapis Heraclius. He is supposed to have been drowned at last; and became afterwards one of the first objects of idolatry amongst his countrymen. The solemnities were performed to him in the night, as to one, who after all his great fatigues and labours, had at length gained a time and place of rest. Manetho calls him Arcles.

Hercules is usually depicted in a standing attitude, having the skin of the Nemæan lion thrown over his shoulders, and leaning on his club, which is his inseparable attribute. The judgment of this hero, or his preference of Virtue to Vice, who both solicit him to embrace their party, makes one of the finest pictures of antiquity. The choice he made did no dishonour to his memory.

It may not be amiss to add the explanation of the fable of the Hesperides, as given by a late ingenious author (5), and which sufficiently shews how the most important and useful truths, represented under the plainest symbols, became disguised or disfigured by error and fiction. The Phœnicians were the first navigators in the world, and their trade to Hesperia and Spain was one of the noblest branches of their commerce. From hence they brought back exquisite wines, rich ore of gold and silver, and that fine wool to which they gave so precious a purple dye. From the coast of Mauritania they drew the best corn, and, by the way of the Red Sea, they exchanged iron ware and tools of small value for ivory, ebony, and gold dust. But, as the voyage was long, the adventurers were

(3) Josephus, from Polyhistor and Cledemus. Idem in Antiq. l. 1. Shindler's Lexicon. See Stukely's Abury and Stonehenge; and Cooke's Enquiry into the Patriarchal Religion.
(4) Britannia is from Barat-anac, the land of tin.
(5) La Pluche's history of the heavens, vol. II. 150.

were obliged to associate and get their cargoes ready in winter, so as to set out early in spring. The public sign, exposed on these occasions, was a tree with golden fruit, to denote the riches arising from this commerce. The dragon which guarded the tree, signified the danger and difficulty of the voyage. The capricorn, or sometimes one horn placed at the root, expressed the month or season; and the three months of winter, during which they prepared for the expedition, were represented by three nymphs, who were supposed to be proprietors of the tree, and had the name of Hesperides (6); which fully shewed the meaning of this emblematical groupe, from whence the Greeks, mistaking its design and use, composed the romance of the Hesperian gardens.

CHAP. XLV.

OF HEBE AND GANYMEDE.

HEBE, the goddess of youth, was, according to Homer, the daughter of Jupiter and Juno. But the generality of writers relate her birth thus: Juno being invited to an entertainment by Apollo, eat very eagerly some wild lettuces, upon which she conceived, and instantly brought forth this goddess. Jove was so pleased with her beauty, that he made her his cup-bearer, in the discharge of which office she always appeared crowned with flowers. Unluckily at a festival of the gods in Ethiopia, Hebe being in waiting, slipped her foot, and got so indecent a fall, that Jupiter was obliged to remove her from her usual attendance. To repair this disgrace, as well as the loss of her post, Jupiter, upon Hercules being advanced to the skies, married him to Hebe, and their nuptials were celebrated with all the pomp becoming a celestial wedding. By this union she had a son named Anicetus, and a daughter called Alexiare.

Hebe was held in high veneration amongst the Sicyonians, who erected a temple to her by the name of

(6) From Esper, the good share or best lot. See 2 Samuel ii. 19.

of Dia. She had another at Corinth, which was a sanctuary for fugitives; and the Athenians consecrated an altar in common to her and Hercules.

Ganymede, who succeeded to her office, was the son of Tros, king of Phrygia or Troy, and a prince of such wisdom and personal beauty, that Jupiter, by the advice of the gods, resolved to remove him from earth to the skies. The eagle dispatched on this commission, found him just leaving his flock of sheep, to hunt on mount Ida, and seizing him in his talons, brought him unhurt to the heavens, where he entered on his new office of filling nectar to Jupiter; though others say, he was turned into that constellation, or sign of the Zodiac, which goes by the name of Aquarius (7).

The mythologists make Hebe signify that mild temperature of the air, which awakens to life the trees, plants, and flowers, and cloaths the earth in vegetable beauty; for which cause she is called the goddess of perpetual youth. But when she slips or falls, that is, when the flowers fade, and the autumnal leaves drop, Ganymede, or the winter, takes her place.

CHAP. XLVI.

OF CASTOR AND POLLUX.

WE have already, under the article of Jupiter, mentioned his amours with Leda, the wife of Tyndarus, king of Sparta, in the form of a swan, on which account he placed that figure amongst the constellations. Leda brought forth two eggs, each containing twins. From that impregnated by Jupiter proceeded Pollux and Helena, both immortal; from the other Castor and Clytemnestra, who being begot by Tyndarus, were both mortal. They went, however, all by the common name of Tyndaridæ, and were born and educated in Paphnus, an island belonging to Lacædemon, though the Messinians disputed this honour with the Spartans. The two brothers, however,

(7) The winter being attended with frequent rains, it is not improbable that Ganymede should be the sign Aquarius.

however, differing in their nature and temper (8), had entered into an inviolable friendship, which lasted for life. Jove soon after sent Mercury to remove them to Pellene, for their further improvement. As Jason was then preparing for his expedition to Colchis, in search of the golden fleece, and the noblest youths of Greece crowded to become adventurers with him, our two brothers offered their services, and behaved, during the voyage, with a courage worthy of their birth. Being obliged to water on the coast of Babrycia, Amycus, son of Neptune, king of that country, challenged all the Argonauts to box with him, Pollux accepted the bravado and killed him.

After their return from Colchis, the two brothers were very active in clearing the seas of Greece from pirates. Theseus, in the mean time, had stolen their sister Helena; to recover whom, they took Athens by storm, but spared all the inhabitants, except Æthra, mother to Theseus, whom they carried away captive. For this clemency they obtained the title of Dioscuri (9); yet love soon plunged them in the same error they had sought to punish in the person of Theseus. Leucippus and Arsinoe had two beautiful daughters, called Phœbe and Talayra. These virgins were contracted to Lynceus and Ida, the sons of Aphareus. The two brothers, without regard to these engagements, carried them off by force. Their lovers flew to their relief, and met the ravishers with their prize near mount Taygetus. A smart conflict ensued, in which Castor was killed by Lynceus, who, in return, fell by the hands of Pollux. This immortal brother had been wounded by Ida, if Jupiter had not struck him with his thunder. Pollux, however, was so touched with his loss, that he earnestly begged of this deity to make Castor immortal; but that request being impossible to grant, he obtained leave to share his own immortality with his brother; so that they are said to live and die alternately every day (1).

They

(8) This particular we learn from Horace:
Castor gaudet equis: ovo prognatus eodem
Pugnis: quot capitum vivunt totidem studiorum
—————millia. Horat.
(9) The sons of Jupiter.
(1) Virgil alludes to this;
Si fratrem Pollux alterna morte redemit
——— Itque reditque viam. VIRG. Æneid VI.

They were buried in the country of Lacedæmon, and forty years after their deceafe tranflated to the fkies, where they form a conftellation called Gemini, (one of the figns of the Zodiac) one of which ftars rifes as the other fets. A dance of the martial kind was invented to their honour, called the Pyrhic or Caftorean dance.

Caftor and Pollux were efteemed as deities propitious to navigation: the reafon was this: when the Argonauts weighed from Sigæum (2), they were overtaken with a tempeft, during which Orpheus offered vows for the fafety of the fhip; immediately two lambent flames were difcovered over the heads of Caftor and Pollux, which appearance was fucceeded with fo great a calm, as gave the crew a notion of their divinity. In fucceeding times thefe fires, often feen by the mariners, were always taken as a good or favourable omen. When one was feen alone, it was reckoned to forbode fome evil, and was called Helena (3).

The Chephalenfes (or inhabitants of Cephalonia) placed thefe two deities amongft the Dii Magni. The victims offered them were white lambs. The Romans paid them particular honours for their affiftance in an engagement with the Latins, in which they appeared on their fide, mounted on white horfes, and turned the fcale of victory in their favour. For this a temple was erected to them in the Forum. Amongft the Romans, Æcaftor was an oath peculiar to the women, but Ædepol was ufed indifcriminately by both fexes.

Caftor and Pollux were reprefented as two beautiful youths, completely armed, and riding on white horfes, with ftars over their helmets. Thefe deities were unknown to the Egyptians or Phœnicians.

CHAP. XLVII.

OF PERSEUS AND BELLEROPHON.

THIS hero was the fon of Jupiter and Danae, whofe amour has been already mentioned, and is inimitably

(2) This cape lies near Troy.
(3) The firft Helena carried off by Thefeus.

mitably described by Horace (4). Acrisius her father, on hearing of his daughter's disgrace, caused her and the infant to be shut up in a chest and cast into the sea, which threw them on the isle of Seriphus, governed by king Polydectes, whose brother Dictys being a fishing, took them up, and used them kindly. When Perseus, for so he was called, was grown up, Polydectes, who was enamoured of his mother, finding he would be an obstacle to their courtship, contrived to send him on an exploit he judged would be fatal to him : this was to bring him the head of Medusa, one of the Gorgons. This inchantress lived near the Tritonian lake, and turned all who beheld her into a stone. Perseus in this expedition was favoured by the gods ; Mercury equipped him with a scymeter, and the wings from his heels ; Pallas lent him a shield, which reflected objects like a mirror ; and Pluto granted him his helmet, which gave him the privilege of being invisible. In this manner he flew to Tartesses in Spain, where, directed by his mirror, he cut off Medusa's head, and putting it in a bag lent him by the nymphs, brought it to Pallas. From the blood arose the winged horse Pegasus, and all sorts of serpents. After this the hero passed into Mauritania, where his interview with Atlas has been already spoken of under its proper article (5).

In his return to Greece (others say, at his first setting out) he visited Ethiopia, and mounted on Pegasus, delivered Andromeda, daughter of Cephus, king of that country, who was exposed to a sea monster. After his death this princess, and her mother Cassiope, or Cassiopeia, were placed amongst the celestial constellations.

Perseus was not only famous for arms, but literature, if it be true that he founded an academy on mount Helicon. Yet he had the misfortune inadvertently to commit the crime of parricide ; for being reconciled to his grandfather Acrisius, and playing with him at the discus or quoits, a game he had invented, his quoit bruised the old king in the foot, which turned to a mortification, and carried him off. Perseus interred him, with great solemnity, at the gates of Argos. Perseus himself was buried

(4) Horat. Lib. III. Ode XVI.
(5) See the article of Atlas.

ried in the way between Argos and Mycenæ, had divine honours decreed him, and was placed amongst the stars.

Bellerophon, the son of Glaucus, king of Ephyra, and grandson of Sisyphus, was born at Corinth. Happening accidently to kill his brother, he fled to Prætus, king of Argos, who gave him an hospitable reception; but Sthenobæa, his queen, falling enamoured with the beautiful stranger, whom no entreaties could prevail on to injure his benefactor, accused him to her husband, who, unwilling to take violent measures, sent him into Lycia, with letters to Jobates, his father-in-law (6), desiring him to punish the crime. This prince, at the receipt of the order, was celebrating a festival of nine days, which prevented Bellerophon's fate. In the mean time he sent him to subdue the Solymi and Amazons, which he performed with success. Jobates next employed him to destroy the chimæra (7), a very uncommon monster. Minerva, or, as others say, Neptune, compassionating his innocence, exposed to such repeated dangers, furnished him with the horse Pegasus, by whose help he came off victorious. Jobates, on his return, convinced of his truth and integrity, and charmed with his virtues, gave him his daughter Philonoe, and associated him in his throne. Sthenobæa hearing how her malice was disappointed, put an end to her life. But, like other princes, Bellerophon grew foolish with too much prosperity, and, by the assistance of Pegasus, resolved to ascend the skies; Jupiter, to check his presumption, struck him blind in the flight, and he fell back to the earth, where he wandered till his death, in misery and contempt. Pegasus, however, made a shift to get into heaven, where Jupiter placed him amongst the constellations.

Let us once more try to give some explanation of these two fables. The subjects of Cyrus, who before this time had been known by the name of Cuthæans and Elamites, henceforward began to be distinguished by that of the Persians (8), or horsemen.

For

---

(6) King, in his history, makes Jobates his son-in-law.
(7) The chimæra was a monster with the forepart like a lion, the middle like a goat, and the tail like a serpent.
(8) Persim, horsemen.

For it was he who first inured them to equestrian exercises, and even made it scandalous for one of them to be seen on foot. Perses, or Perseus, then is a horseman, one who had learned the art of horsemanship from the Phœnicians, who attended Cadmus into Greece. The wings at his heels, with which he is said to have been supplied by Mercury, were the spurs he wore; by the assistance of which he made such speed. The Pegasus was no more than a reined steed (9). His rider, Bellerophon, is the captain of the archers or lancemen (1). The chimæra, having the form of a lion before, a dragon behind, and a goat between, is but the innocent representative of three captains of the Solymi, (a colony of the Phœnicians in Pisidia) whose names, in the language of that people, happened to signify these three creatures (2). And the very place in the country of the Argives, where Bellerophon mounted his horse and set forward, the Greeks called Kenthippe (3). From such trifling grounds, the industrious Greeks, according to their custom, wove this wondrous tale.

CHAP. XLVIII.

OF JASON, AND THE GOLDEN FLEECE.

THIS ancient Greek hero was the son of Æson, king of Thessaly and Alcimede; and by the father's side allied to Æolus. Pelias, his uncle, who was left his guardian, sought to destroy him; but he was conveyed by his father's friends to a cave, where Chiron instructed him in physic; whence he took the name of Jason (4). Arriving at years of maturity, he returned to his uncle, who, probably with no favourable

(9) From Pega, a bridle, and Sus, a horse.
(1) From Bal, a lord or captain, and Harovin, archers or lancemen.
(2) Ary, a lion; Tsoban, a dragon; and Azal or Urzil, a kid.
(3) From κεντέω, to stimulate or spur, and ἵππος, an horse. See Bockart's Hierozoicon, l. 2, c. 6, p. 99.
(4) Or Healer, his former name being Diomede.

favourable intention to him, firſt inſpired him with the notion of the Colchian expedition, and agreeably flattered his ambition with the view of ſo tempting a prize as the Golden Fleece.

Athamas, king of Thebes, by his firſt wife had Helle and Phrixus. Ino, his ſecond, fell in love with Phrixus, her ſon-in-law; but being rejected in her advances, ſhe took the opportunity of a great famine to indulge her revenge, by perſuading her huſband, that the gods could not be appeaſed, till he ſacrificed his ſon and daughter. But as they ſtood at the altar, Nephele, their mother (5), inviſibly carried them off, giving them a golden ram ſhe had got from Mercury, to bear them through the air; however, in paſſing the Streights between Aſia and Europe, Helle fell into the ſea, which from thence was called Helleſpont. Phrixus continued his courſe to Colchis, where Æta, king of the country, entertained him hoſpitably: after which he offered up his ram to Jupiter (6), and conſecrated the ſkin or hide in the grove of Mars. It was called the Golden Fleece from its colour (7), and guarded by bulls breathing fire, and a watchful dragon that never ſlept, as a pledge of the utmoſt importance.

Jaſon being determined on the voyage, built a veſſel at Iolchos, in Theſſaly, for the expedition (8). The fame of this deſign ſoon drew the braveſt and moſt diſtinguiſhed youth of Greece to become adventurers with him, though authors are not agreed as to the names or number of the Argonauts, for ſo they were called (9). The firſt place which Jaſon touched at was the iſle of Lemnos, where he continued ſome time with Hipſipile, the queen, who bore him twins. He next viſited Phineus, king of Paphlagonia; from whom,

(5) Nephele, in Greek, ſignifies a cloud.
(6) Who placed it amongſt the conſtellations.
(7) Some make the fleece of a purple colour, others white.
(8) Argos, a famous ſhipwright, was the builder, whence ſhe was called Argo.
(9) Some make the number forty-nine, others more. The principal were Ancæus, Idmon, Orpheus, Augias, Calais, Zethus, Caſtor, Pollux; Tiphys was their pilot, and Lynceus, remarkable for his quick ſight, their look-out in caſe of danger. It is ſaid Hercules was with them.

horn, as he had the gift of prophecy, he received some informations of service to him in his enterprize. After this, safely passing the Cyanean rocks (1), he entered the Euxine, and landing on the banks of the Phasis, repaired to the court of king Æta, and demanded the Golden Fleece. The monarch granted his request, provided he could overcome the difficulties which lay in his way (2), and which appeared not easily surmountable. Jason was more obliged to love than valour for his conquest. Medea, daughter to Æta, by her enchantments, laid the dragon asleep, taught him to subdue the bulls, and so by night he carried off the prize, taking with him the princess, to whose aid he was chiefly indebted for his success (3).

Æta, enraged at the trick put upon him, pursued the fugitives; and, it is said, that to elude his fury, Medea tore in pieces her younger brother, Absyrtes, and scattered the limbs in his way, to stop his progress (4). After this Jason returned safely to Greece, and soon heard that Pelias had destroyed all his friends, and made himself master of the kingdom. To revenge this action, Medea sails home before him, and introducing herself to the daughters of Pelias, under the character of a priestess of Diana, shewed them several surprizing instances of her magical power. She proposed making their father young again, and to convince them of the possibility of it, she cut an old ram in pieces, and seething it in a cauldron, produced a young lamb. The daughters, serving Pelias in the same manner, killed him (5), and fled the country. Jason, having notice of this, arrived in Thessaly, and took possession of the kingdom; but afterwards he generously restored it to Acastus, son of Pelias,

(1) Cyanean rocks, called the Symplegades, were so called because they floated, and often crushed ships together. The Argonauts escaped this danger, by sending out a pigeon, and lying by till they saw her fly through.
(2) Such as killing the brazen-footed bulls, and the dragon.
(3) Ovid, lib. VII. 159.
(4) Others say, that Æta, to obstruct their return, stationed a fleet at the mouth of the Euxine sea, and so obliged Jason to come home by the west of Europe.
(5) Some authors relate this story differently, and say that this experiment was tried by Medea on Æson, Jason's father. See Ovid in the place cited.

Pelias, who had accompanied him in the Colchian expedition, and with Medea went and settled at Corinth.

Here Jason finding himself censured for cohabiting with a sorceress and a stranger, quitted her, and married Crusa, daughter to Creon, king of the country. Medea seemingly approved the match, but meditated a severe revenge. She first privately killed the two children she had by him, and then sent the bride a present of a robe and a gold crown tinged in naptha, which set fire to her and the whole palace. The enchantress then ascending her car (6), drawn by dragons, escaped through the air to Athens, where she married king Ægeus, by whom she had a son named Medus. But attempting to poison Theseus, his eldest son, and the design being revealed, she with her son Medus fled to Asia, where he left his name to Media (7).

Jason had several temples erected to him, particularly one at Athens, by Parmenio, of polished marble. The place where he was chiefly worshipped was at Abdera, in Thrace.

If we seek for the real truth of the Argonautic expedition, we shall find it to be this: the value of the royal treasury at Colchis had been greatly cried up; and the pillage of it was the thing aimed at by the Argonautic expedition. The word Gaza, in the Colchian language (the same, according to Herodotus, with the Egyptian) signifies a fleece as well as a treasure. This gave occasion to the circumstance of the Golden Fleece. The word Sor is also wall and a bull; Nachash, brass and a serpent. So this treasure being secured by a double wall and brass doors, they formed hence a romantic story of its being a Golden Fleece, guarded by two bulls and a dragon (8). The mariner's compass is supposed (9) to have made a part of this treasure, (and, if so, this was of itself a curiosity of infinite value) whence the ships of Phrixus and Jason, which carried it, are said to have been oracular, and to have given responses.

CHAP.

(6) Given her by Phœbus, or the Sun.
(7) A region of Persia.
(8) Bochart in Phaleg. l. 4. c. 31. p. 287.
(9) Stukely's Stonehenge.

CHAP. XLIX.

OF THESEUS AND ACHILLES.

WITH thefe two great men, we fhall clofe the lift of demi-gods and heroes.

Thefeus was fon to Ægeus, king of Athens and Æthra. In his youth he had an early paffion for glory, and propofed Hercules for his model. Sciron, a notorious robber, who infefted the roads between Megara and Corinth, was by him thrown down a precipice, as he was accuftomed to treat fuch as fell into his hands. Procruftes, a famous tyrant of Attica, he faftened to a bended pine, which being loofed, tore him afunder (1).

His firft diftinguifhing adventure was the deftruction of the Cretan minotaur. Minos, king of that ifland, had made war on Ægeus, becaufe the Athenians had bafely killed his fon, for carrying away the prize from them. Being victorious, he impofed this fevere condition on the vanquifhed, that they fhould annually fend feven of their nobleft youths, chofen by lot, into Crete, to be devoured by the minotaur (2). The fourth year of this tribute, the choice fell on Thefeus, fon to Ægeus, or, as others fay, he entreated to be fent himfelf. However this be, on the arrival of Thefeus at the court of Minos, Ariadne, his daughter, fell deeply in love with him, and gave him a clue, by which he got out of the labyrinth. This done, he failed with his fair deliverer for the ifle of Naxos, where he ungratefully left her (3), and where Bacchus found her, and took her for his miftrefs.

The

---

(1) He was a tyrant of Attica, who feized all ftrangers, and meafured them by his bed; if they were too long for it, he cut them fhorter; if too fhort, he ftretched them till they died.

(2) Pafiphæ, wife to Minos, king of Crete, and daughter of the Sun, inftigated by Venus, conceived a brutal paffion for a bull. To gratify her, Dædalus contrived an artificial cow, in which placing her, fhe had her defire. The fruit of this beaftial amour was the minotaur, who was kept in a labyrinth made by the fame Dædalus, and fed with human flefh.

(3) For this ftory fee the article of Bacchus.

The return of Theseus, through his own neglect, became fatal to his father. The good king, at his departure, had charged him, as he failed out with black fails, to return with the fame in cafe he mifcarried, otherwife to change them to white. Impatiently he every day went to the top of a rock that overlooked the ocean, to fee what fhips appeared in view. At laft his fon's veffel is difcovered, but with the fable omens he dreaded; fo that through defpair he threw himfelf into the fea, which ftill retains his name (4). The Athenians decreed Ægeus divine honours, and facrificed to him as a marine deity, the adopted fon of Neptune.

Thefeus performed after this feveral confiderable actions: he killed the minotaur, he overcame the Centaurs, fubdued the Thebans, and defeated the Amazons. He affifted his friend Pirithous, in his enterprize to the infernal world, to carry off Proferpine; but in this expedition he failed, being imprifoned or fettered by Pluto, till releafed by Hercules. No doubt, was the ftory of Thefeus divefted of the marvellous, it would make a confiderable figure (5).

Thefeus had feveral wives; his firft was Helena, daughter of Tyndarus, whom he carried off; the fecond Hippolyta, queen of the Amazons, given him by Hercules; the laft was Phædra, fifter to Ariadne, whofe lewdnefs fufficiently punifhed him for his infidelity to her fifter. This princefs felt an inceftuous flame for her fon-in-law, Hippolitus (6), a youth of uncommon virtue and chaftity. On his repulfing her folicitations, her love turned to hatred, and fhe accufed him to his father, for an attempt to ravifh her. Thefeus, now grown old and uxorious, too eafily gave ear to the accufation. The prince, informed of his danger, fled in his chariot; but his horfes being frighted by the Phocæ, or fea calves, threw him out of his feat, and his feet being intangled, he was dragged through the woods, and torn in pieces (7). Phædra, tormented with

(4) The Ægean fea.
(5) He firft walled Athens, and inftituted laws; together with that democratic form of government which lafted till the time of Pififtratus.
(6) Son of Hippolyta, queen of the Amazons.
(7) Some fay Æfculapius reftored him to life, and that he came into Italy, where he changed his name to Virbius, i. e. twice a man.

with remorse, laid violent hands on herself; and soon after Theseus, being exiled from Athens, ended an illustrious life in obscurity.

To explain the story of the minotaur: it is said, that Pasiphæ fell in love with a young nobleman of the court, named Taurus; that Dædalus lent his house for the better carrying on of their intrigue, during a long illness of Minos; and that the queen in due time was delivered of two children, one of which resembled Minos, the other Taurus, whence the minotaur: and the Athenians have aggravated the story, from their extreme prejudice to Minos.

But what became of the Athenian youth, the tax of whom was three times paid? The Cretan king had instituted funeral games in honour of Androgeos, wherein those unhappy slaves were assigned as the prize of the conqueror. The first who bore away all the prizes was Taures, of an insolent and tyrannical disposition, and particularly severe to the Athenians delivered up to him; which contributed not a little to the fable. These wretches grew old in servitude, and were obliged to earn their living by the most painful drudgery under Taurus, the subject of Minos; and may therefore with some propriety be said to have been devoured by him. But it is certain that they neither fought at those games, nor were destroyed by the cruelty of a monster which never existed (8).

Of the same stamp is the tale of the Centaurs. The Thessalians pretty early distinguished themselves from the rest of Greece, who fought only on foot or in chariots, by their application to horsemanship. To acquire the more agility in this exercise, they were wont to fight with bulls, whom they pierced with darts or javelins; whence they obtained the name of Centaurs (9) and Hippocentaurs (1). As these horsemen became formidable by their depredations, the equivocation, which appeared in the name, made them to be accounted monsters, compounded of two natures. The poets catched at this idea, which gave the story the air of the marvellous; and they who made oranges to pass for golden apples,

shepher-

---

(8) Abbé Banier's Mythology, vol. 3, p. 500.
(9) From κεντεω, to prick or lance, and Ταυρος, a bull.
(1) From Ἱππος, an horse.

shepherdesses for nymphs, shepherds in disguise for satyrs, and ships with sails for winged dragons, would make no difficulty in calling horsemen Centaurs (2).

Achilles was the offspring of a goddess. Thetis bore him to Peleus(3), and was so fond of him, that she took herself the charge of his education. By day she fed him with ambrosia, and by night covered him with celestial fire, to render him immortal (4). She also dipped him in the waters of Styx, by which his whole body became invulnerable, except that part of his heel by which she held him. She afterwards intrusted him to the care of the Centaur Chiron, (the master of so many heroes) who fed him with honey and the marrow of lions and wild boars, to give him that strength and force necessary for martial toil.

When the Greeks undertook the siege of Troy, Chalcas, the priest of Apollo, foretold the city could never be taken, unless Achilles was present. Thetis, his mother, who knew what would be his fate if he went there, had concealed him in female disguise in the palace of Lycomedes, king of the isle of Scyros. Ulysses, who had engaged to bring him to the Greek camp, having discovered the place of his retreat, used the following artifice: under the appearance of a merchant, he is introduced to the daughters of Lycomedes, and while they were studiously intent on viewing his toys, Achilles employed himself in examining an helmet and some other armour, which the cunning politician had purposely thrown in his way. Thus was Achilles prevailed on to go to Troy, after Thetis furnished him with a suit of impenetrable armour made by Vulcan (5). His actions before Troy, as well as his character, are so finely described by Homer, that it would be doing them injustice to repeat them here. It is sufficient to say he could not escape his fate, being treacherously killed by
H 5   Paris

(2) See the Abbe Banier's Mythology, vol. 3, p. 536.
(3) King of Thessaly.
(4) See the story of Triptolemus, under the article of Ceres. Upon Peleus discovering this, Thetis parted from him.
(5) The description of this shield in Homer is one of that poet's master-pieces.

Paris (6), who with an arrow wounded him in the only part that was vulnerable. The Greeks, after the capture of Troy, endeavoured to appease his manes, by facrificing Polyxena. The oracle at Dodona decreed him divine honours, and ordered annual victims to be offered at his tomb. In purfuance of this, the Theffalians brought hither yearly two bulls, one black, the other white, crowned with wreaths of flowers, and water from the river Sperchius.

CHAP L.

OF CADMUS, EUROPA, AMPHION, AND ARION.

AGENOR, king of Phœnicia, by the nymph Melia, had a daughter called Europa, one of the moft beautiful princeffes of her age. She could hardly then be fuppofed to efcape the notice of Jupiter, whofe gallantries extended to all parts of the world. To feduce her, he affumed the form of a white bull, and appeared in the meadows, where fhe was walking with her attendants. Pleafed with the beauty and gentlenefs of the animal, fhe ventured on his back, and immediately the god triumphantly bore her off to Crete (7); where laying afide his difguife, he made the bull a conftellation in the Zodiac, and, to honour his new miftrefs, gave her name to the fourth part of the world.

In the mean time Agenor, difconfolate for his daughter's lofs, fent his fons, Cadmus and Thafus, with different fleets, in search of her (8). Thafus fettled in an ifland of the Ægean fea, to which he gave his name (9). Cadmus enquiring of the Delphic oracle for a fettlement, was anfwered, that he fhould follow the direction of a cow, and build a city where fhe laid down. Arriving among the Phocenfes, here one of Pelagon's cows met him, and conducted him through

(6) The cafe was thus: Achilles enamoured with Polyxena, defired her of Priam, who confented to the match. The nuptials were to be folemnized in the temple of Apollo, where Paris had privately concealed himfelf, and took the opportunity to kill Achilles.

(7) Ovid, Lib. II. 835.

(8) With an injunction not to return without her under pain of banifhment.

(9) It was before called Plate.

through Bœotia, to the place where Thebes was afterwards built. As he was about to sacrifice his guide to Pallas, he sent two of his company to the fountain Dirce, for water, who were killed by a dragon. Cadmus soon revenged their death by slaying the monster; but sowing his teeth, according to Pallas's advice, there sprung up a number of men armed, who assaulted him to revenge their father's death. It seems the goddess of wisdom had only a mind to frighten him; for on his casting a stone amongst them, these upstart warriors turned their weapons on each other with such animosity, that only five survived the combat, who proved very useful to Cadmus, in founding his new city. After this, to recompense his toils, the gods gave Cadmus Harmonia or Hermione, the daughter of Mars and Venus, and honoured his nuptials with peculiar presents and marks of favour. But their posterity proving unfortunate, they quitted Thebes to Pentheus, and went to govern the Eclellenses, where, in an advanced age, they were turned to serpents (1), or, others say, sent to the Elysian Fields in a chariot drawn by serpents. The Sidonians decreed divine honours to Europa, and coined money in memory of her, with the figure of a woman crossing the sea on a bull.

The Greeks were indebted to Cadmus, for the invention of brass, and the first use of arms. In the phœnician tongue the *two words*, which the Greeks translated *serpent's teeth*, signified as well spears of brass (2). The ambiguity of *another word* helped on the fable (3), which from the difference of pronunciation signified either the number *five*, or *one ready for action;* and so the same sentence, which, with the Phœnicians, intended only that *he commanded a disciplined body of men armed with spears of brass*, was rendered by these miracle-mongers, *he made an army of five men out of the teeth of a serpent* (4). Cadmus being an Hivite, a name of near affinity with that of a serpent, gave further occasion to that part of it, which says that his men sprung from a serpent, and that himself and his wife were changed into this animal. Thus industrious were the Greeks to involve the most simple facts in the most mysterious confusion.

The

(1) Ovid, Lib. IV. 562.
(2) Sheni Nachash.
(3) Chemesh.
(4) Bochart de Coloniis Phœnicium, cap. 19.

The Phœnicians with Cadmus, expelled their country by Joshua, first introduced among the Greeks the practice of consecrating statues to the gods; and the use of letters; thence called Phœnician or Cadmæan letters. For the Greek characters are manifestly taken from the Samaritan or Phœnician alphabet. Cadmus and Og, or Ogyges, are the same: whence any thing very ancient was termed Ogygian by the Thebans. The Gophyræi, settled at Athens, were Phœnicians that came with him, and preserved the memory of him by the name of Ogyges; as from his name Cadmus, or Cadem (5), was their famous place of learning, and thence every other named Academia (6).

Amphion, the son of Jupiter and Antiope, was instructed in the lyre by Mercury, and became so great a proficient, that he is reported to have raised the walls of Thebes by the power of his harmony. He married Niobe, whose insult to Diana occasioned the loss of their children. The unhappy father, in despair, attempted to destroy the temple of Apollo, but was punished with the loss of his sight and skill, and thrown into the infernal regions.

Arion was a native of Methymna, and both a skilful musician and a good Dithyrambic poet. He lived in the time of Periander, king of Corinth. After passing some time in Italy and Sicily, and acquiring an easy fortune by his profession, he sailed from Tarentum in a Corinthian vessel homeward-bound. When they were got to sea, the avaritious crew agreed to throw Arion over-board, in order to share his money. Having in vain used all his eloquence to soften them, he played a farewell air (called Lex Orthia), and crowned with a garland, with a harp in his hand, plunged into the sea, where a dolphin, charmed with his melody, received him, and bore him safe to Tænarus, near Corinth. Having informed Periander of his story, the king was incredulous, till the ship arrived, when the mariners, being seized and confronted with Arion, owned the fact, and suffered the punishment due to their perfidy. For this action the dolphin was made a constellation.

CHAP.

(5) Signifying the East. He was so called because he came from thence.
(6) Stillingfleet's Origines sacræ.

CHAP. LI.

OF ÆOLUS AND BOREAS

IN the multiplication of fabulous deities, the ancients not only affigned each element, and part of nature its tutelar god, but even idolized the paffions. No wonder then if we fee a god or chief of the winds too, controuling all the reft. This province was naturally affigned to that which was the moft violent and uncontroulable itfelf. For this imaginary deity they borrowed a name from the Phoenicians, and called him Æolus (7), the fon of Jupiter, by Acafta or Sigefia, the daughter of Hippotus. He reigned in the Liparæan ifles, near Sicily, from whence perhaps the fable took its original (8); but his refidence was at Strongyle, now called Strombolo (9). Here he held thefe unruly powers enchained in a vaft cave, to prevent their committing the like devaftation they had been guilty of before they were put under his direction (1).

According to fome authors, the Æolian or Liparean ifles were uninhabited, till Liparus, the fon of Aufonis, fettled a colony here, and gave one of them his name. Æolus, the fon of Hippotus, who married his daughter, peopled the reft, and fucceeded him in the throne. He ruled his fubjects with equity and mildnefs, was a hofpitable good prince, and being fkilled in Aftronomy, by means of the reflux of the tides which is remarkable near thofe iflands, as well as by obferving the nature of the volcanos with which they abound, he was able to foretell the winds that fhould blow from fuch a quarter (2).

We are indebted to Virgil for a fine poetical defcription of this god, when Juno vifits his cave to defire his affiftance to deftroy Æneas in his voyage to Italy.

Boreas

(7) From Aol or Alol, a ftorm, whirlpool or tempeft.
(8) Thefe iflands being greatly fubject to winds and ftorms.
(9) Famous for its volcano, though fome place his refidence at Regio in Calabria.
(1) They had disjoined Italy from Sicily, and by difuniting Europe from Africa, opened a paffage for the ocean to form the Mediterranean fea.
(2) It is faid that before a foutherly wind blows, Lipara is covered with a thick cloud; but when it changes to the north, the volcano emits clear flame, with a remarkable noife.

Boreas was of uncertain parentage; but his ufual refidence was in Thrace (3). When Xerxes, king of Perfia, croffed the Hellefpont with his numerous armada, to invade Greece, the Athenians invoked his affiftance, and he fcattered and deftroyed the greateft part of their fleet. This deity, notwithftanding his rage, was not inflexible to love. He debauched Chloris, the daughter of Arcturus, by whom he had Hyrpace, and carried her to mount Niphates, (called the bed of Boreas) but fince known by the name of Caucafus: but his favourite miftrefs was Orithya, the daughter of Erictheus, king of Athens. By this princefs he had two fons, Zetes and Calais, who attended Jafon in the Colchic expedition, delivered Phineus from the Harpies (4), and were afterwards killed by Hercules: as alfo four daughters, Upis, Laxo, Hecaerge, and Cleopatra. Perhaps the north wind, or Boreas alone, was deified, becaufe, of the regular winds, it is the moft tempeftuous and raging that blows.

CHAP. LII.

OF MOMUS AND MORPHEUS.

MOMUS was the god of pleafantry and wit, or rather the jefter of the celeftial affembly; for, like other great monarchs, it was but reafonable that Jupiter fhould have his fool. We have an inftance of his farcaftic humour in the conteft between Neptune, Minerva, and Vulcan, for fkill. The firft had made a bull; the fecond a houfe; and the third a man; Momus found fault with them all: he difliked the bull, becaufe his horns were not placed before his eyes, that he might give a furer blow; he condemned Minerva's houfe, becaufe it was immoveable, and fo could not be taken away if placed in a bad neighbourhood. With regard to Vulcan's man, he

(3) Probably becaufe this country is much fubject to the cold northerly winds.

(4) Some fay out of envy for their fwiftnefs; others, becaufe their father had by a tempeft deftroyed the ifle of Cos.

he said he ought to have made a window in his breast. Hesiod makes Momus (5) the son of Somnus and Nox.

Morpheus (6) was the god of dreams, and the son of Somnus, whom Ovid calls the most placid of all the deities. Mr. Addison observes, that he is still represented by the ancient statuaries under the figure of a boy asleep, with a bundle of poppy in his hand: and black marble, from the relation which it bears to night, has with great propriety been made use of.

CHAP. LIII.

OF ORION.

THE origin, or birth of Orion, borders a little on the marvellous. Hyricus, a citizen of Tanagra, in Bœotia, was so hospitable to strangers, that Jupiter, Neptune, and Mercury, were resolved, under the character of benighted travellers, to know the truth. Their entertainment was so agreeable, that, discovering their quality, they offered the old man whatever he should ask; his request was a son (7). The gods, to gratify his wish, called for an ox hide, in which having deposited their urine, they bid him keep it under ground for ten months; at the expiration of which time, he found it produced a boy, who was at first called Urion, to express his origin; but after, for decency's sake, his name was changed to Orion.

He was a remarkable hunter, and kept a fleet pack of hounds. Neptune gave him the power of walking on the surface of the waters, with the same speed that Iphiclus did (8) over the ears of corn. This faculty seemed needless, if it be true that Orion was so tall, that the deepest sea could not cover his shoulders.

(5) From Μωμῷ, cavilling or finding fault.
(6) From Μορφη, a form or vision.
(7) His wife having left him childless, whom on her death-bed he promised never to marry again.
(8) Brother to Hercules. See the article of that god.

shoulders. As a proof of this, he crossed from the continent of Greece to the isle of Chios, where attempting to vitiate Ærope, the wife of king Oenopion, that monarch deprived him of his eye-sight (9). From Chios he proceeded and found his way to Lesbos, where Vulcan received him kindly, and gave him a guide to the palace of the sun, who restored him to sight. He then made war on Oenopion, who concealed himself under ground to escape his vengeance; so that frustrated of his design he went to Crete, where he pursued his favourite exercise of hunting. But having by some means offended Diana (1), that goddess put him to death (2); but afterwards relenting, prevailed on Jupiter to raise him to the skies, where he forms a constellation (3). remarkable for predicting rain and tempestuous weather.

CHAP. LIV.

OF THE MARINE DEITIES, OCEANUS, NEREUS, TRITON, INO, PALEMON, AND GLAUCUS.

As the ancient theogany took care to people the heavens and air with deities, so the sea naturally came in for its share, nor was it just to leave the extended realms of water without protection and guardianship. Neptune, though monarch of the deeps, could not be present every where, and it was proper to assign him deputies, who might relieve him of some part of the weight of government.

Nereus son of Oceanus, settled himself in the Ægean sea, and was regarded as a prophet. He had the faculty of assuming what form he pleased. By his

(9) His pursuit of the Pleiades has been mentioned under the article of Atlas.

(1) Either for attempting her chastity, or for boasting his superior skill in the chace; others say, for endeavouring to debauch Opis, one of her nymphs.

(2) Either by her arrows, or as others say, raising a scorpion, which gave him a mortal wound.

(3) Virgil calls it Nimbosus Orion, on account of the showers which attend his rising. Æneid I. 535. Lib. IV. 52.

his wife Doris he had fifty nymphs, called Nereids (4), who conftantly attended on Neptune, and when he went abroad furrounded his chariot.

Triton was the fon of Neptune and Amphitrite (5), and was his father's herald. He fometimes delighted in mifchief, for he carried off the cattle from the Tanagrian fields, and deftroyed the fmall coafting veffels; fo that to appeafe his refentment, thofe people offered him libations of new wine. Of this he drank fo freely that he fell afleep, and tumbling from an eminence, one of the natives cut off his head. He left a daughter called Triftia, by whom Mars had a fon named Menalippus.

This god is reprefented of a human form, from the waift upwards, with blue eyes, a large mouth, and hair matted like wild parfley. His fhoulders were covered with a purple fkin, variegated with fmall fcales, his feet refembling the fore feet of a horfe, and his lower parts turned like a dolphin with a forked tail. Sometimes he is drawn in a car with horfes of a fky colour. His trumpet is a large conch, or fea fhell. Ovid (6) has given two very beautiful defcriptions of him. There were indeed many Tritons, who compofed the numerous equipage of Neptune, and were reckoned as deities propitious to navigation.

Ino was the daughter of Cadmus and Harmonia, and married to Athamas king of Thebes. This prince having the misfortune to lofe his fenfes, killed his fon Learchus in one of his mad fits, upon which his queen, to fave Melicertes, her remaining boy, leaped with him from the rock Molyris into the fea. Neptune received them with open arms, and gave them a place amongft the marine gods, only changing their names, Ino being called Leucothea, and Melicertes, Palemon (7); for this we are indebted to the

fertile

(4) By which are meant the rivers which empty themfelves in the ocean.

(5) Some fay of Neptune and Cæleno, others of Nereus or Oceanus.

(6) Ovid Met. Lib. I.

(7) The Romans called him Portunus; and painted him with a key in his hand, to denote him a guardian of harbours. To Ino they gave the name of Matuta, being reputed the goddefs that ufhers in the morning.

fertile invention of the Greeks, Melicertes being no other than Melcarthus or Hercules of Tyre, who, from having been drowned in it, was called a god of the sea, and from his many voyages, the guardian of harbours.

Glaucus was a fisherman, whose deification happened in a comical manner. His parentage and country (8) are variously reported: but he was an excellent swimmer, and a skilful fisherman. Having one day taken a large draught in his nets, he observed with surprize, that the fishes on tasting a certain herb jumped into the sea again. Upon trying the experiment upon himself, he followed them, and became a sea god. Some ascribe to Glaucus the gift of prophecy. Ovid has not forgot his transformation amongst his metamorphoses (9). Virgil has given an elegant list of the sea deities in his fifth Æneid (1).

CHAP. LV.

OF PROTEUS AND PHORCYS, WITH THE GRÆÆ AND GORGONS, SCYLLA AND CHARYBDIS.

PROTEUS, the son of Neptune, by the nymph Phænice, was by his father appointed keeper of the Phocæ, or sea-calves. His residence was at Alexandria, in Egypt, from whence in a journey he made to Phlegra (2), he married the nymph Torone, who bore him Tmolous and Telegonus, both killed by Hercules for their cruelty to strangers. Their father Proteus, who left them on account of their inhospitable temper, it is said, was not much concerned at their death. By Torone he had also three daughters, Cabera, Ratia, and Idothea. Proteus had the art of assuming all forms (3); as also the gift of prophecy or divination;

(8) Some make him the son of Mercury, others of Neptune, others of Anthadon; on account of his skill in swimming he was called Pontius.
(9) Ovid, Lib. XIII. 899.
(1) Æneid, Lib. V. 822.
(2) A town in Campania.
(3) See Ovid, Lib. VIII. 730.

divination; Orpheus calls him the univerfal principle of nature.

Hiftorians make Proteus king of Carpathus (4) who on account of his great character for wifdom and equity, was chofen king of Egypt, and deified after his death. According to Herodotus, Paris and Helena in their flight from Sparta, were received at his court, where Helen continued all the time of the Trojan fiege, after which he reftored her honourably to Menelaus.

Proteus is ufually reprefented in a chariot drawn by horfes, in the form of Tritons.

His half brother Phorcys, or Phorcus, was the fon of Neptune, by the nymph Thefea (5). He married his fifter Ceto, by whom he had the Phorcydes and Gorgons, Thoofa (6) and Scylla. He was vanquifhed by Atlas, who threw him into the fea, where his father raifed him to the rank of a fea god.

The Gorgons were in all four fifters, of whom Medufa was the chief. They had hair like fnakes, tufks like wild boars, brazen hands and golden wings. On the death of their fifter, they purfued Perfeus, who faved himfelf by putting on the helmet lent him by Pluto, and which rendered him invifible.

The Grææ were their fifters, and are reprefented as three old women, who lived in Scythia, and had but one eye and tooth in common amongft them, which they ufed as they had occafion, and afterwards laid up in a coffer. For the prefervation of this valuable legend we are indebted to Palæphatus.

Scylla (7), another daughter of Phorcys, by her familiarity with Glaucus, excited the jealoufy of Circe, daughter of the Sun, who by magic fpells, or poifon, fo infected the fountain in which fhe bathed, that fhe became a monfter (8), upon which, through defpair at

(4) An ifland in the Ægean fea, between Rhodes and Crete, now called Scarpanto.

(5) Others call him the fon of Pontus and Terra.

(6) By whom Neptune had the Cyclops Polyphemus.

(7) Some make her the daughter of Phronis and Hecate, and fay that her misfortune was owing to the jealoufy of Amphitrite, for her cohabiting with Neptune.

(8) Authors difagree as to her form; fome fay fhe retained her beauty from the neck downwards, but had fix dogs heads;

at the lofs of her beauty, fhe threw herfelf into the fea, and was changed into a rock (9), which became infamous for the multitude of fhipwrecks it occafioned. Thofe who would fee a beautiful defcription of Scylla will find it in Virgil (1).

Care muft be taken not to confound this Scylla with another of the fame name, and daughtter of Nifus, king of Megara. Minos had befieged this monarch in his capital, but the oracle had pronounced Nyfus invincible, while he preferved a purple lock of hair which grew on his head. Scylla, who was fecretly in love with Minos, betrayed both her father and country into his hands, by cutting off the lock; but the conqueror detefting her treachery, banifhed her ~~his~~ fight. Unable to bear the treatment fhe fo juftly merited, fhe caft herfelf into the fea, and was changed into a lark (2). Her father, transformed into a hawk, ftill purfues her for her ingratitude and perfidy.

Charybdis was a female robber, who, it is faid, ftole Hercules's oxen, and was by Jupiter, on that account, changed into a whirlpool (3), which is very dangerous to failors, and lying oppofite to the rock Scylla, occafioned the proverb of running into one danger to avoid another (4).

CHAP. LVI.

OF PAN AND FAUNUS; OF THE NYMPHS, AND THE GODDESSES FERONIA AND PALES.

IT is now time to revifit the earth again, and fee the numerous train of the inferior deities, appropriated

heads; others maintain, that her upper parts continued entire, but that fhe had below, the body of a wolf, and the tail of a ferpent.

(9) It lies between Sicily and Italy, and the noife of the waves beating on it, gave rife to the fable of the barking of dogs and howling of wolves, afcribed to the monfter.

(1) Virgil makes her changed to a rock, which confounds her with the other Scylla. Æneid, Lib. III. 424.

(2) Ovid, Lib. VIII. 142.

(3 An eddy, or whirlpool, on the coaft of Sicily, as you enter the fair of Meffina. See Virgil, Æneid III. 420.

4. *Incidit in Scyllam qui vult vitare Charybdim.*

ated to the forests, woods, and those recesses of nature whose prospect fills the imagination with a kind of religious awe or dread.

Pan the principal of these, is said to be the son of Mercury and Penelope (5), the wife of Ulysses, whom, while she kept her father's flocks on mount Taygetus, he deflowered in the form of a white goat. As soon as born, his father carried him in a goat skin to heaven, where he charmed all the gods with his pipe; so that they associated him with Mercury in the post of their messenger. After this he was educated on mount Mænalus, in Arcadia, by Sinoe and the other nymphs, who, attracted by his music, followed him as their conductor.

Pan, though devoted to the pleasures of a rural life, distinguished himself by his valour. In the giants war he entangled Typhon in his nets as we have already observed: he attended Bacchus in his Indian expedition with a body of Satyrs, who did good service. When the Gauls invaded Greece, and were about to pillage the temple of Delphos, he struck them with such a sudden consternation by night, that they fled without any one to pursue them (6). He also aided the Athenians in a sea fight, gained by Miltiades over the Persian fleet, for which they dedicated a grotto to his honour under the citadel.

This deity was of a very amorous constitution. In a contest with Cupid, being overcome, that little god punished him with a passion for the nymph Syrinx, who treated him with disdain. But being closely pursued by him, and stopped in her flight by the river Ladan, she invoked the Naiades, who changed her into a tuft of reeds, which the disappointed lover grasped in his arms. Contemplating a transformation so unfavourable to his desires, he observed the reeds tremble with the wind, and emit a murmuring sound. Improving this hint, he cut some of them, and formed the pipe for which he became so famous. His other amours were the more successful. He charmed Luna, or the moon, in the shape

---

(5) Some say of Penelope and all her lovers, whence he was called Παν.

(6) Hence the expression of a panic, for a sudden fear and terror.

shape of a beautiful ram. In the difguife of a fhepherd, he became fervant to the father of Dryope (7), in order to gain accefs to his miftrefs. By the nymph Echo (8) he had a daughter, called Irynge, a famous forcerefs, who fupplied Medea with her philtrum; but Pan afterwards flighting her, fhe retired to the receffes of the hills, where fhe pined with grief, till fhe dwindled to a fhadow, and had nothing left but a voice (9): others afcribe the change of Echo to another caufe.

Pan was properly the god of fhepherds and hunters, and, as he was a mountain deity, the flocks and herds were under his immediate protection and care. He was likewife honoured by the fifhermen, efpecially thofe who inhabited the promontories wafhed by the fea.

He was chiefly efteemed in Arcadia, his native country, where the fhepherds offered him milk and honey in wooden bowls. If fuccefsful in hunting, they allotted him part of the fpoil; but, if otherwife, they whipped his image heartily. At Molpeus, a town near the city Licofura, he had a temple by the title of Nomius, becaufe he perfected the harmony of his pipe on the Nomian mountains.

The Romans adopted him amongft their deities by the names of Lupercus and Lycæus. His feftivals, called Lupercalia, and celebrated in February, were inftituted by Evander, who being exiled Arcadia, fled for refuge to Faunus, king of the Latins, and was by him allowed to fettle near mount Palatine (1), Romulus made fome addition to thefe ceremonies, in which the Luperci, or priefts of Pan, ran naked through the city, ftriking thofe they met with things made of goat fkins, particularly the women, who fancied that it helped their eafy conception, or fpeedy delivery.

Pan

(7) Dryope rejected his fuit, but was afterwards changed into the lotus tree. See Ovid's Met. lib. IX. 325.

(8) Some fay that Echo fell in love with Narciffus, and was flighted by him.

(9) It is reported, that Juno punifhed Echo in this manner for her loquacity, becaufe when Jupiter was engaged in any new amour, he fent this nymph to amufe his jealous fpoufe with her chat.

(1) Where he had a temple afterwards.

Pan is reprefented with a fmiling ruddy face, and thick beard covering his breaſt, two horns on his head, a ſtar on his breaſt, with the nofe, feet, and tail of a goat. He is cloathed in a fpotted ſkin, having a fhepherd's crook in one hand, and his pipe of unequal reeds in the other, and is crowned with pine, that tree being confecrated to his fervice.

Pan, however, faid to be the offspring of Penelope, was indeed one of the moſt ancient, being of the firſt eight of the Egyptian gods, and was looked upon as the fymbol of nature. His horns, fay the mythologiſts, reprefent the rays of the fun; and the vivacity and ruddinefs of his complexion, the brightnefs of the heavens; the ſtar on his breaſt, the firmament; and his feet and legs overgrown with hair, denote the inferior part of the world, the earth, the trees and plants (2).

Faunus was the fon of Picus, king of the Latins, who was cotemporary with Orpheus. He reigned in Italy at the time that Pandion ruled Athens, and introduced both religion and hufbandry into Latium. He deified his father, and his wife Fauna or Fatua (3). He had the gift of prophecy. His fon Stercutius was alfo honoured on account of his fhewing how to improve land, by dunging or manuring it. The Faunalia were kept in December with feaſting and much mirth, and the victims offered were goats.

The Fauni, or children of Faunus, were vifionary beings much like the Satyrs, and were ufually crowned with pine. Both Faunus and they were deities only regarded in Italy, and wholly unknown to the Greeks.

The Fauni were the hufbandmen, the Satyrs the vine-dreffers, and the Sylvani thofe who cut wood in the foreſts; who, as was ufual in thofe early times, being dreffed in the ſkins of beaſts, gave rife to thofe fabulous deities.

The terreſtrial nymphs were divided into feveral claffes. The heathen theology took care that no part of nature fhould remain uninformed or unprotected.

The

(2) Abbé Banier's Mythology, vol. I. p. 540.

(3) Some add fhe was his fifter and a prieſtefs. He whipped her to death with myrtle rods for being drunk, and then made her a goddefs; for which reafon no myrtle was ufed in her temples; the veffels were covered, and the wine offered was called milk.

The Oreades, or Orefteades, prefided over the mountains (4). Of thefe Diana had a thoufand ready to attend her at her pleafure. It is faid, they firft reclaimed men from eating or devouring each other, and taught the ufe of vegetable food. Meliffa, one of thefe, was the inventrefs of honey (5). The Napeæ were the tutelar guardians of vallies and flowery meads. The Dryades inhabited the forefts and woods, refiding in their particular trees, with which they were thought to be coeval, as feveral inftances prove (6). The oak was generally their choice, either from its ftrength or duration. Some were called Hamadryades, whofe exiftence was infeparably united to that of the tree they animated. The Naiades were the nymphs of brooks and rivers; the Limniades frequented the lakes, and the Ephydriades delighted in fprings and fountains. Thus all the face of nature became enlivened by the force of imagination, and the poets did not fail to improve fo ample a field for defcription. The mythologifts deftroy all this fine landfcape, by making the nymphs only fignify the univerfal moifture which is diffufed through all nature.

There were alfo celeftial nymphs of a higher rank, who attended the Dii Majores. Jupiter boafts of his in Ovid (7). The Mufes were the nymphs or attendants of Apollo, as the Bafforides, or Mænades, belonged to Bacchus. Juno had fourteen who waited on her (8) perfon; and Neptune had no lefs than fifty Nereides at his beck, on which account he was called Nymphagater, or the captain of the nymphs (9).

The ufual facrifices to thefe deities were goats; but more commonly milk, oil, honey, and wine. The nymphs were always reprefented as young and beautiful virgins, and dreffed in fuch a manner as was fuitable to the character afcribed to them.

To the train of Pan we may join two rural goddeffes, of whom the firft is Feronia, or the goddefs of

(4) Some make them five only, and call them the daughters of Hecatæus; but Homer ftiles them the offspring of Jupiter.

(5) Whence the bees are called Meliffæ.

(6) Arcas preferving a decayed oak, by watering the roots, was rewarded, by marrying the nymph who refided in it.

(7) Ovid Metam. lib. I.

(8) Virgil, Æneid I. 75.

(9) See Hefiod and Pindar.

of woods and orchards (1). The Lacedæmonians firſt introduced her worſhip into Italy under Evander, and built her a temple in a grove near mount Soracte. This edifice being ſet on fire, and extinguiſhed, the neighbours reſolved to remove her ſtatue, when the grove became green again of a ſudden (2). Strabo tells us, that her prieſts or votaries could walk barefoot over burning coals unhurt. Slaves received the cap of liberty in her temple, on which account they regarded her as their patroneſs.

Pales was the protecting deity of ſhepherds and paſturage. Her feſtival was obſerved by the country people in May, in the open fields, and the offerings were milk, and cakes of millet, in order to engage her to defend their flocks from wild beaſts and infectious diſeaſes. Theſe feaſts were called Palilia. Some make Pales the ſame with Veſta or Cybele. This goddeſs is repreſented as an old woman.

Both theſe deities were peculiar to the Romans, and wholly unknown in Greece.

CHAP. LVII.

OF PRIAPUS AND TERMINUS.

PRIAPUS was, as the generality of authors agree, the ſon of Bacchus and Venus (3). This goddeſs meeting him in his return from his Indian expedition, their amorous congreſs produced this child, who was born at Lampſacus (4), but ſo deformed, that his mother, aſhamed of him, abandoned him (5). Being grown up, the inhabitants of that place baniſhed him their territory, on account of his vices; but being viſited with an epidemical diſeaſe, upon conſulting
the

---

(1) From Fero, to bear or produce.
(2) This miracle is aſcribed to other deities.
(3) Some make him the ſon of Bacchus and Naïs; others ſay Chione was his mother.
(4) A city of Myſia, at the mouth of the Helleſpont.
(5) Some ſay that Juno being called to aſſiſt at the labour, out of hatred to Bacchus, the ſon of her rival Semele, ſpoilt the infant in the birth.

the oracle of Dodona, he was recalled (6). And temples were erected to him as the tutelar deity of vineyards and gardens, to defend them from thieves and birds deſtructive to the fruit.

Priapus had ſeveral names. He was called Aviſtupor, for the reaſon juſt mentioned. The title of Helleſpontiacus was given him, becauſe Lampſacus was ſeated on that ſtreight or arm of the ſea. It is uncertain how he came by the epithet of Bonus Deus, aſcribed to him by Phurnutius. Thoſe of Phallus and Faſcinum were aſſigned him on a very obſcene account, and indeed his whole figure conveyed ſuch an idea of uglineſs and lewdneſs, that the poets generally treat him with great contempt (7). The ſacrifice offered him was the aſs, either becauſe of the natural uncomelineſs of that animal, and its ſtrong propenſity to venery, or becauſe, as ſome ſay, Priapus attempting the chaſtity of Veſta when aſleep, ſhe was awakened by the braying of old Silenus's aſs, and ſo eſcaped the injury deſigned her.

This deity is uſually repreſented naked and obſcene, with a ſtern countenance, matted hair, and carrying a wooden ſword (8) or ſickle in his hand. His body ended in a ſhapeleſs trunk or block of timber.

Some of the mythologiſts make his birth allude to that radical moiſture, which ſupports all vegetable productions, and which is produced by Bacchus and Venus, that is, the ſolar heat, and the water, or liquid matter, whence Venus is ſaid to ſpring. The worſhip of this infamous deity was taken from the Syrians of Lampſacus.

With Priapus we may aſſociate Terminus, a very ancient deity amongſt the Romans, whoſe worſhip was firſt inſtituted by Numa Pompilius, who erected him a temple on the Tarpeian Hill (9). This deity was thought to preſide over the ſtones or landmarks, called Termini, which were held ſo ſacred, that it was ſacrilege to move them, and the criminal becoming devoted to the gods, it was lawful for any man to kill him.

The

---

(6) Others ſay, that the women of Lampſacus prevailed on their huſbands to recall him.
(7) Horat. ſatyr VIII.
(8) Virgil, Georg. IV.
(9) Which wa open at op.

The feasts called Terminalia, were celebrated annually about the end of February, when the ancient Termini, or landmarks, were carefully visited and crowned with garlands. At first the sacrifices to these rural deities were very simple, such as wheat cakes, and the first fruits of the field, with milk (1); but in later times the victims were lambs, and sows that gave suck, whose blood was sprinkled upon the stones.

The Roman Termini were square stones, or posts, much resembling our mile stones (2).

CHAP. LVIII.

OF FLORA.

THE poets make this goddess the same with Chloris, the wife of Zephyrus (3), mentioned by Ovid; but the historians agree that she was a celebrated Roman courtezan, who having amassed a considerable fortune by her profession, made the Roman people her heirs, on condition that certain games, called Floralia, might be annually celebrated on her birthday. The senate, to give a gloss to so infamous a prostitution of religion, pretended this festival was designed in honour of Flora, a certain Sabine goddess who presided over flowers. These sports were held in the Campus Martius, and proclaimed by sound of trumpet. No women appeared at them, but the most immodest of the sex (4). Yet when Cato, during his censorship, came to behold them, they suspended the ceremonies through shame, till he thought fit to withdraw; such an influence had the virtue of one man over a corrupt and dissolute multitude.

Flora's image, in the temple of Castor and Pollux, was dressed in a close habit, holding in her hands the flowers of peas and beans; for, at the celebration of her rites, the aediles scattered these and other pulse amongst the people (5). The modern poets and painters

---

(1) To shew that no force or violence should be used in settling mutual boundaries.
(2) Ovid Fasti, lib. II.
(3) Ovid Fasti.
(4) Juvenal, sat. VI.
(5) See Valerius Maximus, lib. II.

painters have set off her charms in a more lavish manner, and not without reason, since no part of nature affords such innocent and exquisite entertainment to the sight and smell, as the variety which adorns, and the odours which embalm, the floral world.

CHAP. LIX.

OF POMONA AND VERTUMNUS.

THE goddess Pomona was a Latian nymph, whom that nation honoured as a tutelar deity of orchards and fruit-trees. Vertumnus (the Proteus of the Roman ritual) (6) was the god of tradesmen, and, from the power he had of assuming any shape, was believed to preside over the thoughts of mankind. His festivals, called Vertumnalia, were celebrated in October.

Vertumnus's courtship makes one of the most elegant and entertaining stories in Ovid (7). Under the disguise of an old woman he visited the gardens of Pomona, whom he found employed in looking after her plantations. He artfully praises the beauty of her fruit, and commends the care which produced it. Thence, from the view of the vine, supported by the elm, he insinuates to her the necessity and pleasure of a married life. The goddess heard all this eloquence with an indifferent ear. Her heart remained untouched, till, throwing off his disguise, the god assumed his youthful beauty, and by his form soon gained the goddess's consent.

Some imagine Vertumnus an emblem of the year, which though it assumes different dresses, according to the different seasons, is at no time so agreeable as in autumn, when the harvest is crowned, and the richest fruits appear in their full perfection and lustre. The historians say, that this god was an ancient Tuscan prince, who first taught his subjects to plant orchards, and to graft and prune fruit-trees; whence he is said to have married Pomona.

Both these deities were unknown to the Greeks, and only honoured by the Romans.

CHAP.

(6) Because of the turns or fluctuations to which trade is subject.
(7) Ovid, lib. XIV. 622.

CHAP. LX.

OF THE LARES AND PENATES, AND GENII.

THE Lares were the offspring of Mercury. The nymph Lara having offended Jupiter, by disclosing some of his intrigues to Juno, that deity ordered her tongue to be cut out, and banished her to the infernal mansions. Mercury, who was appointed to conduct her into exile, ravished her by the way, and she brought forth the Lares (8).

These deities not only presided over the highways, and the conservation of the public safety, but also over private houses, in most of which the Romans had a particular place called Lararium, where were deposited the images of their domestic gods, the statues of their ancestors, and the Lares.

Their festival, called Compitalia, was celebrated in January, in the open streets and roads. At first boys were sacrificed to them, but that savage custom was soon disused, and images of wool and straw (9), with the first fruits of the earth, wine, incense, and garlands of flowers, were the offerings. When the Roman youth laid aside the bulla, an ornament they constantly wore (1) till fourteen years of age, they consecrated or hung it up to the Lares, who were regarded as infernal as well as domestic deities.

The ancients supposed, according to some authors, that the souls of men after death became a kind of demons, called Lemures (2). These they subdivided into two classes, the one benevolent and friendly to mankind, which they termed Lares; the other, who being wicked during life, retained a malicious disposition in their disembodied state, they stiled Larvæ.

The Lares were represented as young boys with dogs skins about their bodies (3), and with their heads

(8) Ovid Fast. lib. II.
(9) They hung up as many images as there were persons of all sexes and ages in the family, and a woollen ball for every servant.
(1) The Bulla was a golden ornament shaped like a heart, but hollow.
(2) So called, from Remus, brother of Romulus, whose ghost haunted his brother. The Lamuralia was celebrated in the middle of May, during which it was unlawful to marry.
(3) Some say the images were like dogs.

heads covered, which was a sign of that freedom and liberty which men ought to enjoy in their own houses. They had always the image of a dog near them, to denote their fidelity in preserving the places allotted to their charge, on which account this animal was peculiarly consecrated to them. Some confound these with the Penates and Genii.

CHAP. LXI.

OF THE PENATES.

THE Penates (4) were the deities who presided over new born infants. The ancient Hetrusci called them Consentes, or Complices, though others make of them four of the Dii Majores (5). But there were three classes or ranks of them: those who presided over empires and states (6); who had the protection of cities; who took the care or guardianship of private families, and were called the lesser Penates (7).

These domestic gods were placed in the utmost recess of the house, thence called Penetrale (8). Dardanus brought them from Samothracia to Troy, whence, on the destruction of that city, Æneas transported them to Italy. They were reckoned so sacred, that the expression of driving a man from his Penates (9), was used to signify his being proscribed, or expelled his country.

Dionysius, of Halicarnassus, lib. 1, says, that he had seen them at Rome, under the figure of two young men sitting, with spears in their hands.

CHAP.

---

(4) So called, from Penus, within, either because they preside over lives, or were placed in the innermost parts of the house.

(5) Viz. Jupiter, Juno, Minerva, and Vesta. Some drop Vesta: Others make them only two, Neptune and Apollo: Others Cælum and Terra.

(6) Virgil, Æneid III. 148.

(7) Æneid VIII. 543.

(8) See Horace, lib. IV. ode 4, 26.

(9) Virgil, Æneid IV. 21.

Taken from the Isiac or Bembine Table now in the Bodleian Library.

CHAP. LXII.

OF THE GENII.

SOME do not diftinguifh between thefe and the Penates, or Lares; but they were very different. The ancients affigned to every thing its guardian or peculiar genius; cities, groves, fountains, hills, were all provided with keepers of this kind, and to each man they allotted no lefs than two, one good, the other bad (1), who attended him from the cradle to the grave. The Greeks called them Dæmons. They were named Præftites, from their fuperintending human affairs.

The facrifices offered thefe divinities were wine (2) and flowers, to which they joined incenfe, parched wheat, and falt. Sometimes the victim was a fwine (3), though animal offerings were not ufual to them. The Genii were reprefented under various figures, fuch as thofe of boys, girls, old men, and even ferpents. Thefe images were crowned with plane-tree leaves, a tree confecrated to the Genii.

By Genius, is meant the active power or force of nature, from whence the nuptial bed is ftiled genial, and the fame epithet given to all occafions wherein focial joys and pleafures are felt. Hence alfo the expreffions of indulging our Genius, that is, living happily, or according to our inclinations; confulting our Genius, for examining how far our capacity extends; and the term of a great Genius, for an exalted or comprehenfive mind. The later Romans, in the degenerate days of the ftate, introduced the fervile flattery of fwearing by the Genii of their Emperors, and the tyrant Caligula put feveral to death for refufing to take the oath.

CHAP. LXIII.

OF ISIS, OSIRIS, AND ORUS.

THESE three have been much fpoken of already as having given rife to almoft all the different divinities

of

---

(1) Horace, lib. II. epift. 2.
(2) Perfius, fat. VI.
(3) Some affert no blood was fuffered to be fpilt in their facrifices.

of Greece and Rome. Ifis is faid to have been the fifter of Ofiris (4), the daughter of Saturn, and a native of Egypt. She married her brother, and fhared his throne. They governed with great equity and wifdom, civilizing their fubjects, and inftructing them in hufbandry and other ufeful arts. Thefe inftructions were delivered in verfe, and were called the poems of Ifis (5).

Ofiris, having conferred the greateft benefits on his own fubjects, made the neceffary difpofition of his affairs, committing the regency to Ifis, and fet out with a body of forces in order to civilize the reft of mankind. This he performed more by the power of perfuafion, and the foothing arts of mufic and poetry, than by the terror of his arms. He marched firft into Ethiopia; thence to Arabia and India. Having traverfed Afia, he croffed the Hellefpont, and fpent fome time in Europe. Returning to Egypt, he was flain by his brother Typhon; of whom we have fpoken fufficiently in the chapter of the giants.

When the news of this reached Coptus, where Ifis then was, fhe cut her hair, and in deep mourning went every where in fearch of the dead body; which fhe found at length, and concealed at Butus. But Typhon hunting by moonlight, found it there, and tore it into many pieces, which he fcattered abroad. Ifis then traverfed the lakes and watry places in a boat made of the papyrus, feeking the mangled limbs of Ofiris: where fhe found one, there fhe buried it. Hence the many tombs afcribed to Ofiris. Thus Plutarch. But Diodorus fays, that fhe joined the fragments, embalmed and buried them at Memphis; prevailing on the Egyptian priefts to promote his deification, in confideration of a third part of the kingdom given to them.

Ifis afterwards, with the affiftance of her fon Orus, vanquifhed Typhon, reigned happily over Egypt to her death, and was alfo buried at Memphis. At Bufiris, a moft fuperb temple was raifed to her. She was fucceeded by her fon Orus, who completed the reign of the gods and demi-gods in Egypt.

To do the greater honour to thefe their favourites, the Egyptians made them to reprefent the objects

(4) Diodor. Sic. l. 1.
(5) Plato de Leg. dialog.

Taken from the Isiac or Bembine Table now in the Bodleian L...

objects of their idolatrous worship. The attributes of Isis, indeed, when exposed as the public sign of their feasts, differed according to the different purposes to which they applied the figure. But at other times this goddess was represented with a flowing veil, having the earth under her feet, her head crowned with towers (like the Phrygian mother) the emblem of height and stability; and sometimes with upright horns, equally expressive of dominion and power; next to these the crescent, then the sun, and above all expanded wings. She has also wings and a quiver on her shoulders; her left-hand holds a cornucopia, her right a throne charged with the cap and scepter of Osiris, and sometimes a flaming torch; and her right arm is entwined by a serpent. The imagination of the reader will presently conceive this to be the symbol of the æther, the natural parent and spirit of the universe, comprehending and pervading the whole creation. As such, she is easily confounded with nature, which is defined by Balbus in Cicero (6) to be *That which contains and sustains the whole world.* In Herodotus, she is the same with Ceres; in Diodorus, with Luna, Ceres and Juno; in Plutarch, with Minerva, Proserpine, Luna, Thetys. By Apuleius, she is called the Mother of the Gods, and is the same with Minerva, Venus, Diana, Proserpine, Ceres, Juno, Bellona, Hecate, Rhamnusia; hence termed sometimes Μυριώνυμος, or *The Goddess of a thousand names.* Being a female figure, and thus principally honoured, she was denominated Isis (7.

So likewise in Herodotus, Osiris and Bacchus are the same; in Diodorus, Sol, Osiris, Serapis, Dionysius, Pluto, Ammon, Jupiter, Pan; in Plutarch, Sol, Osiris, Pluto, Bacchus, Serapis, Apis, Oceanus, Sirius. Hence we see him in gems with a radiated crown and a basket on his head, having the horns of Ammon; and in his hand a trident entwined by a serpent. He is the great emblem of the solar body.

Orus is the symbol of light, as the name imports (8), and is generally figured as a winged boy, standing between

(6) *Natura est quæ contineat mundum omnem eumque tueatur.* De Nat. Deor. l. 2.

(7) Or Isha, the woman. κατ ἐξοχὴν.

(8) From Aor, light.

between Ofiris and Ifis. He is the Herws of the Greeks, and the Cupid of the Romans; the fon of Ofiris and Ifis, whofe paffion for each other is faid to have commenced in the womb, where they embraced; and Orus was the fruit of this early conjunction. The whole containing this fimple truth, *That light has began to flow from the body of the fun, from its firft exiftence, through the midft of æther.* But thefe themfelves were but natural emblems. Plutarch therefore refers us higher, affirming that Ofiris fignifies the active principle, or the moft holy being; Ifis, the wifdom or rule of his operation; Orus, the firft production of his power (9), the model or plan by which he produced every thing, or the archetype of the world (1).

EXPLANATION OF THE THREE PLATES OF ISIS, OSIRIS, AND ORUS.

Thefe three following plates, viz. of ISIS, OSIRIS, and ORUS, were taken originally from the Bembine or Ifiac table in the Bodleian library. This table or altar-plate is of brafs, full of hieroglyphics inlaid in filver and enamel, which conftitute an epitome of the whole Egyptian theology. It has been defcribed, copied, and elaborately explained by the learned Jefuit, Athanafius Kircher, in his Ædipus Ægyptiacus, vol. 3, p. 80, & feq. Romæ, 1654. 7. Hor. Apoll.

IN this of Ifis, the top cornice over her abounds with flames, diffufed like rifing ferpents, indicating light and life fupernal and diftant from the contagion of grofs matter. In thofe underneath, is the circle with expanded wings, the emblem of æther. The architraves

---

(9) De Ifid. & Ofirid. p. 354. See Ramfay's Theology of the Pagans.

(1) The bull Apis was the fubftitute of Ofiris; the name of the latter Sor, or Sur, fignifying a bull, and Apis, the moft mighty. But the bull Apis had particular marks, and they added, that the Apis was animated by the foul of Ofiris. The Greeks gave the article and the termination to the word Ofiris; fo difguifing it, that the Egyptians knew it not again.

architraves are supported by two columns, with alternate square divisions of black and white, crowned with the head of Isis. At some distance, on the outsides, are two pilasters, decorated with flowers, from which rise two aspics, symbols of warmth and moisture conjoined, the secondary cause of life. In the midst of this magnificent throne, is the goddess seated, to denote stability and power. From the navel to the foot her habit is composed of wings, representing the velocity and sublimity of the æther, diffusing itself universally. Thence upwards to the breast, she is full of paps, shewing the body of the world, or the universal machine, to be thence nourished and supported. The collars round her neck are the celestial orbs. The great variety of created beings, is aptly signified by the party-coloured feathers of the African hen, which cover her head in a flying attitude. The basket on the back of this bird is the emblem of plenty, from which, on each side, springs a leaf of the Egyptian peach; and two horns, which point out the crescent moon, inclosing a circle marked with the figure of the scarabæus or beetle, representing the sun. The gesture of her left hand is commanding and monitory: her right holds a sceptre of the flowering lotus. Her seat is adorned with the figure of a dog sitting; to intimate her dominion, according to Diodorus, refulgent in the dog star. Within the table, beneath the throne, is the body of a lion with the head of an hawk, at his fore-feet a canopus, supporting upright wings; emblems of earth, fire, water, and air. Over the back of the lion-hawk is the serpent transmitted through a circle with expanded wings, explained in the chapter of Mercury, page 87, of whose caduceus these are the attributes, and on his head a crescent, with the sun over that. By the small hieroglypic characters near the Isis, she is said to be *The spirit of the world, penetrating all things with the eye of Divine Providence; and the bond of the superior and inferior worlds.*

EXPLANATION OF THE PLATE OF OSIRIS.

OSIRIS is represented here seated on a tesselated throne, to express dominion and vicissitude of day and

and night, which depend upon him. He has the head of an hawk, a bird, from his strength of vision, by which he is said to look steady on the meridian sun, frequently depicted for the symbol of the solar orb. He is crowned with a mitre, full of small orbs, to intimate his superiority over all the globes. The gourd upon the mitre implies his action and influence upon moisture, which, and the Nile particularly, was termed by the Egyptians the efflux of Osiris. The lower part of his habit is made up of descending rays, and his body is surrounded with orbs. His right hand is extended in a commanding attitude, and his left holds a thyrsus or staff of the papyrus pointing out the principle of humidity, and the fertility thence flowing, under his direction.

EXPLANATION OF THE FIGURE OF ORUS.

THE figure of Orus, which is the emblem of the solar efflux, is juvenile, as perpetually renewed and renewing youth and vigour. He stands to denote the unabated activity of light, and is habited in a sort of network, composed of globules of light pushing and intersecting each other every way. He holds a staff crossed, expressing his power in the four elements; and on it the head of the hoop, a transient bird, to represent the continual change of things which he produces by those elements. This staff, the symbol of his rule, is further adorned with a gnomon and trumpet, indicating season and symmetry, harmony and order. At his back is a triangle with a globe fixed to it; shewing the regular being of the world to depend upon him. The sides of the portal, which he stands in, are decorated with the celestial bodies, and on the top of it is the circle with expanded wings. The hieroglyphics, engraven on the base, call him, *The Parent of vegetable Nature; the Guardian of Moisture; Protector of the Nile; Averter of Evils; Governor of the Worlds; the many-figured God; the Author of Plenty.*

CHAP.

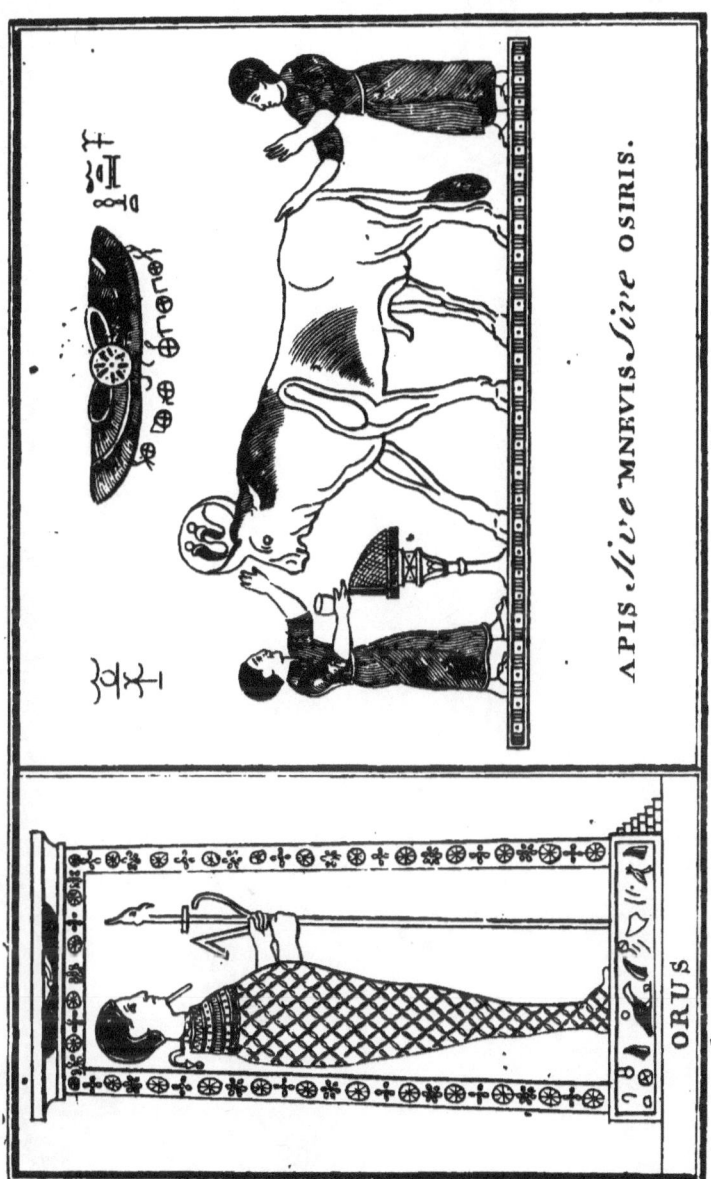

APIS sive MNEVIS sive OSIRIS.

ORUS

Taken from the Isiac or Bembine Table now in the Bodleian Library.

CHAP. LXIV.

OF THE CABIRI.

BOCHART says, that the Cabiri were the Gods of the Phœnicians, and observes justly that Cabir signifies, both in the Hebrew and Arabic tongue, Great or Mighty; so that Cabiri, in the plural, are THE GREAT or MIGHTY ONES. He that ministered in holy things went by the appellation of Cohes, a manifest corruption of the Hebrew Cohen, priest or intercessor.

They are spoken of by the names of Axieros, Axiocherfos and Axiocherfa; as three distinct persons: and in them our author thinks that he has found Ceres, Proserpine and Pluto; the Abbe Pluche, Osiris, Orus, and Isis; others, Jupiter, Ceres, and Bacchus. To these, the Scholiast upon Apollonius, has added a fourth, Casmilus or Cadmilus; the same, says he, is Hermes, or Mercury, whom Varro declares to be only a minister attendant on the Cabiri.

Several authors have confined the appellation of Cabiri to Jupiter, Minerva, and Juno. Nor is it at all improbable that these should have been so called in after ages, when the world in general had forsaken the worship of the Creator for that of the creature, and understood by these terms those things which must indeed be allowed the most proper and significant emblems of the divine personalities (2); the solar fire being meant by Jupiter (3); by Minerva, darting from the head of him, the light thence springing; and by Juno, the æther (including the air), the natural representative of the SACRED SPIRIT. These are indeed the same with the Egyptian Osiris, Orus, and Isis.

But in earlier times it was judged an act of irreverence to pronounce their names; which was the case of the tetragrammaton with the Jews. They were therefore only spoken of by the general denomination of Dioskouroi, or sprung from Jove; a title afterwards conferred upon Castor and Pollux.

Even

---

(2) *Sic Homines novere Deos, quos arduus Æther.*
  Occulit, & colitur pro jovibus Jovis.   OVID.

(3) Macrob. l. 1. c. 23. Plato in Phæd. Orpheus, &c.

Even children were initiated into these mysteries, and thought by their parents to be afterwards secure from dangers of any kind. Such as were permitted to partake of the ceremonies, were wont to assemble in a wood or grove, which was held sacred and became a sanctuary. By the initiation men were believed to become more holy, just and pure; and it is said that none ever duly performed the ceremonies, without being amply rewarded for his piety.

As to what is said of a man's being sacrificed in these mysteries upon some extraordinary occasion, I cannot find the assertion to be well grounded. Julius Firmicus intimates, that the Cabiri were three brothers, one of whom was slain by the other two, and then deified; and speaks of his worshippers, as holding up their bloody hands to the once-bleeding; which may refer either to their hands being imbrued in the blood of the ordinary victims, or to the warlike disposition of that conquering people (Macedonians). But, if the thing be fact, it must have proceeded from an assurance that such a sacrifice was one day or other to promote the happiness of mankind (4).

CHAP. LXV.

OF THE INFERIOR DEITIES ATTENDING MANKIND FROM THEIR BIRTH TO THEIR DECEASE.

IT would be a task almost endless to enter into a minute detail of the inferior deities acknowledged by the Greeks and Romans. The names of these visionary beings occur so seldom in the classic authors, that it is sufficient barely to mark their denominations.

During pregnancy, the tutelar powers were the god Pilumnus (5), and the goddesses Intercidonia (6), and

(4) This was also the leading opinion of the British Druids: *Pr. vita hominis nisi vita hominis reddatur, non posse aliter deorum immort. ... numen placcari arbitrantur.* Cæs. Comm. l. 6. c. 15.

(5) Either from Pilum, a pestle, or from Pello, to drive away, because he procured a safe delivery.

(6) She taught the art of cutting wood with a hatchet to make fires.

and Deverra (7). The signification of these names seems to point out the necessity of warmth and cleanliness to persons in this condition.

Besides the superior goddesses Juno-Lucina, Diana-Ilythia, and Latona, who all presided at the birth, there were the goddesses Egeria (8), Prosa (9), and Manageneta (1), who with the Dii Nixii (2), had all the care of women in labour.

To children, Janus performed the office of doorkeeper or midwife, and in this quality was assisted by the goddess Opis, or Ops (3); Cunia rocked the cradle, while Carmenta sung their destiny; Levana lifted them from the ground (4), and Vegitanus took care of them when they cried; Rumina (5) watched them while they sucked; Potina furnished them with drink, and Educa with food or nourishment; Ossilago knit their bones, and Carna (6) strengthened their constitutions; Nundina (7) was the goddess of children's purification; Statilinus or Statanus, instructed them to walk, and kept them from falling; Fabulinus learnt them to prattle; the goddess Paventia preserved them from frights (8), and Camæna learnt them to sing.

Nor was the infant, when grown to riper years, left without his protectors; Juventas was the god of youth; Agenoria excited men to action; and the goddesses Stimula and Strenua inspired courage and vivacity; Horta (9) inspired the love of fame or glory;

and

(7) The inventress of brooms.
(8) From casting out the birth.
(9) Aulus Gellius, chap. xix.
(1) Ælian.
(2) From Enitor, to struggle. See Ausonius, Idyll. 12.
(3) Some make her the same with Rhea or Vesta.
(4) Amongst the Romans the midwife always laid the child on the ground, and the father, or somebody he appointed, lifted it up; hence the expression of Tollere Liberos, to educate children.
(5) The goddess had a temple at Rome, and her offerings were milk.
(6) On the kalends of June sacrifices were offered to Carna, of bacon and bean-flour cakes; whence they were called Fabariæ.
(7) Boys were named always on the 9th day after the birth, girls on the 8th.
(8) From Pavorem vertendo.
(9) She had a temple at Rome, which always stood open.

and Sentia gave them the sentiments of probity and justice; Quies was the goddess of repose or ease (1); and Indolena, or laziness, was deified by the name of Murcia (2); Vacuna protected the idle; Adeona and Abeona, secured people in going abroad and returning (3); and Vibilia if they wandered, was so kind to put them in the right way again; Fessonia refreshed the weary and fatigued; and Meditrina healed the sickly (4); Vitula was the patroness of mirth and frolic (5); Volupia, the goddess who bestowed pleasure (6); Orbona was addressed, that parents might not lose their offspring; Pellonia averted mischiefs and dangers; and Numeria taught people to cast and keep accounts; Angerona (7) cured the anguish or sorrows of the mind; Hæres-Martia secured heirs to the estates they expected; and Stata, or Statua-Mater, secured the forum, or marketplace from fire; even the thieves had a protectress in Laverna (8); Averruncus prevented sudden misfortunes; and Consus was always disposed to give good advice to such as wanted it; Volumnus inspired men with a disposition to do well; and Honorus raised them to preferment and honours.

Nor was the marriage-state without its peculiar defenders. Five deities were esteemed so necessary, that no marriages were solemnized without asking their favours; these were Jupiter-perfectus, or the Adult, Juno, Venus, Suadela (9), and Diana.

Jugatinus tied the nuptial knot; Domiducus ushered the bride home; Domitius took care to keep her there, and preventing her gadding abroad; Manturna

(1) She had a temple without the walls.
(2) Murcia had her temple on mount Aventine.
(3) From Abeo, to go away, and Adeo, to come.
(4) The festival of this goddess was in September, when the Romans drank new wine mixed with old by way of physic.
(5) From Vitulo, to leap or dance.
(6) From Voluptas.
(7) In a great murrain which destroyed their cattle, the Romans invoked this goddess, and she removed the plague.
(8) The image was a head without a body. Horace mentions her, lib. I. epist. XVI. 60. she had a temple without the walls, which gave the name to the Porto Lavernalis.
(9) The goddess of eloquence or persuasion, who had always a great hand in the success of courtship.

turna preserved the conjugal union entire; Virginensis (1) loosed the bridel zone or girdle; Viriplaca was a propitious goddess ready to reconcile the married couple in case of any accidental difference; Matura was the patroness of matrons, no maidservant being sufferred to enter her temple; Meno and Februo (2) were the goddesses who regulated the female Catamenia; the goddess Vacuna (3) is mentioned by Horace (4) as having her temple at Rome; the Rustics celebrated her festival in December, after the harvest was got in (5).

The ancients assigned the particular parts of the body to peculiar deities; the head was sacred to Jupiter, the breast to Neptune, the waist to Mars, the forehead to Genius, the eyebrows to Juno, the eyes to Cupid, the ears to Memory, the right hand to Fides or Veritas, the back to Pluto, the reins to Venus, the knees to Misericordia, or Mercy, the legs to Mercury, the feet to Thetis, and the fingers to Minerva (6).

The goddess who presided over funerals was Libitina (7), whose temple at Rome the undertakers furnished with all the necessaries for the interment of the poor or rich; all dead bodies were carried through the Porto Libitina, and the Rationes Libitinæ, mentioned by Suetonius, very nearly answer our bills of mortality.

CHAP.

(1) She was also called Cinxia Juno.
(2) From Februo, to purge.
(3) She was an old Sabine deity. Some make her the same with Ceres; but Varro imagines her to be the goddess of victory, the fruits of which are ease and repose.
(4) Horace, Lib. I. Epist. 10, 49.
(5) Ovid Fast. Lib. VI.
(6) From this distribution arose, perhaps the scheme of our modern astrologers, who assign the different parts of the body to the cælestial constellations, or signs of the Zodiac; as the head to Aries, the neck to Taurus, the shoulders to Gemini, the heart to Cancer, the breast to Leo, the belly to Virgo, the reins to Libra, the secrets to Scorpio, the thighs to Sagittarius, the knees to Capricorn, the legs to Aquarius, and the feet to Pisces.
(7) Some confound this goddess with Proserpine, others with Venus.

CHAP. LXVI.

OF THE INFERIOR RURAL DEITIES.

THE Romans were not content with the great variety of gods, which filled their ritual. They were daily inventing new deities of an inferior order, to anfwer the demands of fuperftition, and increafe the kalendar. Rufina thus became the name of a goddefs, who prefided over the country in general. Collina had the charge of the hills, and Vallona the infpection of the vallies; Hippona was the guardian of ftables and horfes; and Bubona took care of oxen; Sein, or Segetia, watched the feed till it fprouted; and Runcina weeded the young corn; Sarritor was the god of fowing, and Occator of harrowing; Robigus kept the blights or Mildew away (8); Stercutius manured or dunged the ground; Nodotus, or Nodofus, took care to ftrengthen or knit the ftalks of the corn; Volufia watched the blade; Patelina unfolded the ear; Lactucina filled it; and Matura brought it to due ripenefs; Heftilina produced a plentiful crop; and Tutelina took care to reap and get it fafe in; Pilumnus kneaded the bread; and Fornax baked it (9); Mellona was the goddefs of honey; but the truth is, thefe fanciful deities are fo little mentioned in authors, that we may call them the refufe or fcum of the gods.

CHAP. LXVII.

OF THEMIS, ASTREA, AND NEMESIS.

THEMIS was the daughter of Cælum and Terra and the goddefs of laws, ceremonies and oracles. Jupiter confulted her in the giants war, and afterwards efpoufed her; fhe inftructed Deucalion how to re-people the world after the deluge, and was rather indeed a moral than an hiftorical deity, as fhe fignifies

(8) His feftival, called Robigalia, was celebrated in the beginning of May.
(9) Ovid Fefti. Lib. VI,

signifies that power which rewards virtue and punishes vice.

To Jupiter, Themis, besides a numerous offspring, already spoken of, bore the goddess Astræa, who resided on earth during the golden age, and inspired mankind with the principles of justice and equity; but as the world grew corrupted she returned to heaven (1), and became that constellation in the Zodiac which is called Virgo. This goddess is represented with her eyes bound or blinded, having a sword in one hand, and in the other a pair of balances equally poised.

Nemesis was the daughter of Jupiter and Necessity (2). She had the title of Adrastea, because Adrastus, king of Argos, first raised an altar to her. She had a magnificent temple at Rhamnus in Attica, with a statue. She is represented with a stern aspect, having in one hand a whip, in the other a pair of scales.

CHAP. LXVIII.

OF THE GODDESS FORTUNA, OR FORTUNE AND THE OTHER VIRTUES AND VICES DEIFIED BY THE ANCIENTS.

FORTUNE was thought to have so great a share in human affairs, that it is no wonder that the Romans made her a goddess. Juvenal, however, is not a little severe upon his countrymen (3) for this choice; and Horace expresses, if not an absolute contempt for (4), yet at best a very mean opinion of this deity. But whatever sentiments the philosophers or poets might entertain of her, they did not lessen her in the sight of the vulgar, who paid her much veneration.

This goddess had a variety of epithets: she was termed Regia and Aurea, from an image of her usually kept in the apartment of the Cæsars. In the capital she was worshipped by the title of Bona, but her

(1) Terras Astrea reliquit.
(2) Others say of Oceanus and Nox.
(3) Satyr X.
(4) Lib. I. Ode XXXIV. 14.

her temple at the Esquilia was consecrated by the name of Mala. She was called Conservatrix, Manens and Felix, in ancient inscriptions, to denote the happiness she bestows. Domitian consecrated her a chapel by the stile of Redux, and in some ancient monuments she is called Stata. The names of Barbata and Pan were given her by Servius Tullius, who dedicated a shrine to her (5); she was also termed Cæca, not unjustly, on account of the injudicious distribution of her favours. She was honoured at Rome by the title of Fortuna Equestris (6). In a temple she had near that of Venus, she bore the appellations of Mascula and Virilis. At other times she was named Mammosa (7), Primogenia (8), and Privata, or Propria (9). In the quality of Fortuna Virgo, coats of young children were offered to her before they put them on; and she was stiled Viscata, or Viscosa (1), on account of her alluring or attracting people by her deceitful kindness.

The principal temple of this goddess was at Præneste, whence she was called Prænestina. She is usually represented blind, standing on a wheel in a moving attitude, and holding a cornucopia, from whence she powers wealth, and all the emblems of prosperity. Horace has given a very masterly picture of her in an ode to Mæcenas (2).

She is sometimes figured in a flying attitude, with broad wings, sounding a trumpet, and her flying robe wrought all over with eyes, ears and tongues, to denote the surprize, attention and discourse she excites

---

(5) He also called her Obsequens, from her favouring his wishes. Horace called her Sæva on a quite contrary account.

(6) This temple was erected in pursuance of a vow of the prætor Q. Fulvius Flaccus, for a victory he obtained in Spain by means of his cavalry.

(7) Either from her having large breasts, or the plenty she supplies.

(8) From her giving birth to the city and empire.

(9) From her favouring particular persons. These two last appellations were given her by Servius Tullius, a very great admirer of her divinity.

(1) From Viscus, birdlime. Hence Seneca says, *Beneficia sunt viscosa*, obligations are catching.

(2) Horace, Lib. III. Ode XXIX. 49.

excites. Virgil (3) has given an inimitable defcription of her, nor does Ovid fall much fhort of him (4).

Peace is a bleffing fo univerfally efteemed, that it is no wonder if fhe was deified. The Athenians (according to Plutarch) erected her an altar with her ftatue, attended by that of Plutus, the god of riches, to fhow that fhe was the fource of plenty. At Rome fhe had a magnificent temple in the Forum (5), which was confumed by fire in the reign of Commodus.

On medals, this goddefs is reprefented before an altar, fetting fire with a torch in her left hand to a pile of arms, and with the other holding an olive branch. Behind her, on a column, appears the image of a naked body or man extending his arms in a rejoicing pofture (6). The poets generally introduce her in company with the moft fhining virtues (7). And Virgil reprefents her as the common wifh of mankind (8). Claudian has compofed her panegyric in a very diftinguifhed manner. Sometimes fhe appears like a matron holding a bunch or ears of corn, and crowned with olive or rofes.

The goddefs Concordia, or Concord, was another divinity of the Romans. At the requeft of his mother Livia, widow of Auguftus, a temple was dedicated to her by Tiberius at Rome. She had feveral other magnificent temples; in one of thefe were depofited the rich fpoils of the temple of Jerufalem.

Virtue and Honour had their temples at Rome. That to Virtue was erected by M. Marcellus (9), and was the only paffage to the temple of Honour, to fhew that worthy actions were the true foundation of lafting fame. The facrifices to Honour were performed by the priefts bareheaded.

Virtue was reprefented like an elderly matron fitting on a fquare ftone; in ancient medals they appear

(3) Virgil, Æneid I.
(4) Ovid, Metam. 42, 63.
(5) Begun by Claudius, and finifhed by Vefpafian.
(6) The legend of this medal, which was ftruck by Vefpafian on the conqueft of Judæa, is *Pici Orbis Terrarum*. On a medal of his fon Titus, fhe is feen with a palm in one hand and a fceptre in the other, the infcription *Pax Æternæ*.
(7) Horace, Carmen Sec. 57.
(8) Æneid XI. 362.
(9) Son of Auguftus.

pear jointly: however, upon some of Gordian and Numenian, she is found in the figure of an old man with a beard.

Fides, or Faith, had a temple near the capitol, founded by Numa Pompilius. No animals were offered, or blood spilt in the sacrifices; during the performance of her rites, her priests were cloathed in white vestments, and their heads and hands covered with linen cloth; to shew that fidelity ought to be secret. Her symbol was a white dog, and a figure where two women are joining hands represents the goddess.

Hope is another of the passions deified by the Romans. She had a temple in the herb-market, which was consumed by lightning. On medals she appears in a standing attitude, with her left hand holding up lightly her loose robes, and leaning on her elbow; in her right she has a plate, in which is placed a ciborium, or cup, fashioned like a flower, with this inscription, Spes, P. R. the hope of the Roman people (1). In the modern statues and paintings, her characteristic is a golden anchor.

Piety, or filial Affection, had a chapel at Rome, consecrated by the Duumvir Attilius and Glabrio on a remarkable occasion: " A man being sentenced to
" hard imprisonment, his daughter, who was then a
" nurse, daily visited him, and was strictly searched
" by the goaler, to see she brought no food to the
" prisoner. At last a discovery was made, that she
" supported him with her milk. This instance of
" piety gained her father's freedom. They were
" both afterwards supported at the public expence,
" and the place was consecrated to this goddess (2)."

Pudicitia, or Chastity, was honoured at Rome under two names. Into the temple of Pudicitia Patricia, none were admitted but ladies of noble birth. Virginia, the daughter of Aulus, having married a Plebeian, so offended these, that they excluded her their assemblies: upon which Virginia called a meeting of the plebeian matrons, dedicated a chapel to this goddess by the name of Pudicitia Plebeia (3).

Her

---

(1) The reverse is a head of Adrian.
(2) Pliny's Nat. Hist. lib. VII. cap. 36.
(3) All matrons who married but once, were honoured with the Corona Pudicitiæ, or crown of chastity.

Her speech on this occasion was truly great: "I de-
"dicate," says she, "this altar to Pudicitia Plebeia,
"and desire you will adore Chastity as much as the
"men do Honour; and I wish that this temple may
"be frequented by purer votaries (if possible) than
"that of Pudicitia Patricia." In both of these temples no matron was permitted to sacrifice unless she
had an unblemished character, and was but once
married. In medals this deity is represented under
the figure of a woman veiled, pointing with the fore-
finger of her right-hand to her face, to signify that
she had no reason to blush.

Mercy, or Clemency, had an altar at Athens,
erected by the kindred of Hercules. At Rome was a
temple dedicated to the Clemency of Cæsar (4). Both
the Romans and Greeks gave the name of Asylum to
the temples each had erected to this goddess.

Truth, according to Plutarch, was the daughter of
Saturn and Time, and the mother of Virtue, and
was represented as a beautiful young virgin of a
proper stature, modestly clad in a robe, whose white-
ness resembled that of snow. Democritus, to give an
idea of the difficulty of her being found, says that
she is concealed in the bottom of a well.

Liberty was so much the delight of the Romans,
that it was but natural for them to imagine her a
goddess, and to consecrate to her temples and altars.
She was represented in the form of a virgin cloathed
in white, holding a sceptre in her right hand, and a
cap in her left.

Good Sense, or Understanding [mens], was honoured with an altar in the Capitol, by M. Æmilius;
and Attilius the prætor erected her chapel.

Faustitas, or the public Felicity and Welfare, had
many altars, and was adored both by the Greeks and
Romans: the former honoured this goddess under the
names of Endaimonia and Macaria. The Athenians
consulting an oracle on the success of a battle, were
informed, that they should win the victory if one of
the children of Hercules would submit to a voluntary
death: on this Macaria, one of his daughters, killed
herself, and the Athenians becoming victorious, paid
her adoration under the name of Felicity. She was
represented in painting as a lady cloathed in a purple
vestment

---

(4) This temple was built by a decree of the senate, after
the death of Julius Cæsar.

vestment trimmed with silver, sitting on an imperial throne, and holding in one hand a caduceus, and in the other a cornucopia.

Victory was honoured by several nations as a goddess. According to Hesiod, she was the daughter of Styx and Pallas: she was painted by the ancients in the form of a woman clad in cloth of gold, and is represented on some medals with wings, flying through the air, holding a palm in one hand, and a laurel crown in the other; in others she is to be seen standing upon a globe, with the same crown and branch of palm.

The goddess Salus, or Health, had a temple at Rome near the gate, from thence called Porto Salutaris; and as the blessings she bestows are known to all, so no doubt but she had a great number of votaries. She was represented by a woman sitting on a throne, and holding a globe in her hand. Near her stood an altar, with a snake entwined round it. In this temple was performed the Augurium Salutis, a ceremony which Augustus revived from desuetude. It was a day set apart annually, for enquiring of the gods by divination, whether they would allow the people to pray for peace? On this day the Roman armies were forbid to march or engage. It is worthy of remark, that the priests of this temple had arrogated to themselves the sole privilege of offering supplications for the health of every individual, as well as for the state.

The Good Genius was adored by the Greeks, and, according to Pausanius, had a temple in the road leading to mount Mænalus. At the close of supper a cup was always offered him of wine and water, and called the grace-cup.

Wealth has such an influence on the affairs of life, that it has in all ages been the object of public worship, or of secret idolatry. Thus the Romans deified both Plutus and Pecunia, or Money. Menander wittily observes on this subject, " That if you can " possess this deity, you may ask and have what you " please; even the gods themselves shall be at your " devotion."

Silence was, amongst the Romans, both a male and female deity, by the names of Harpocrates and Angerona; but the latter seems only to have been a female imitation of the former, whom they borrowed from the Egyptians. He was the son of Isis, begotten by Osiris after his death, and on that account said to have been

a weakly

a weakly child. His ftatue was placed at fome fmall diftance from thofe of Ofiris, Orus, and Ifis, with his finger on his mouth; intimating to the worfhippers, that not a word was to be faid that thofe deities had once been mortal. The Greeks and Romans appropriated to themfelves this fymbol of Silence, but in general were ignorant of its original intention.

Nor were thefe the only vifionary deities erected by the heathens. Fear, Hope, Difeafes, Calamities, and even Vices, were honoured with a view of averting their vifitation, or allaying their noxious influences. Thus Febris, or the Fever, had her altars at Rome. Hoftilius Tullus vowed a temple to the goddeffes Terror and Palenefs. M. Marcellinus, after efcaping a ftorm near Sicily, built a chapel to the god Tempeftas, without the gate of Capena. And Poverty and Art were both deified by the people of Gadara, becaufe Neceffity is the mother of invention. Envy was a goddefs, whofe perfon and abode are inimitably defcribed by Ovid (5).

Calumny had an altar erected to her by the Athenians. We have a very remarkable picture of this mifchievous goddefs, as drawn by the hand of the great Apelles. Credulity, reprefented by a man with large open ears, invites this deity to him, extending his hand to receive her. Ignorance and Sufpicion ftand juft behind him. Calumny, the principal figure of the piece, appears advancing, her countenance ruffled with paffion, holding in her left hand a lighted torch, and with her right dragging along a youth, who lifts up his hands as fupplicating the gods. Juft before her goes Envy, pale and fquinting. On her right fide are Fraud and Confpiracy. Behind her follows Repentance, with her cloaths torn, and looking backwards on Truth, who flowly clofes up the rear (6). Contumely and Impudence were alfo honoured by the Athenians under the figure of partridges, efteemed a very bold bird. Difcord is reprefented as a goddefs by Petronius Arbiter, whofe defcription of her is worthy fo mafterly a pencil; and Virgil has given us a picture of Fury, a deity much of the fame ftamp.—It is now time to clofe the particular account, and to proceed to a confideration at large of the Heathen Theology.

(5) Metam. lib. II. 762.
(6) Lucian.

A
DISSERTATION

ON THE

THEOLOGY OF THE HEATHENS.

THE religion of mankind was at firſt one, like the object of it. But when the latter was changed, the mode and ceremonial of worſhip continued ſtill the ſame; for idolatry, that WORST of things, was but in its origin, the corruption of true religon, which is the BEST! We are not therefore to wonder, if we ſee the ſame uſage of temples, altars, prieſts, ſacrifices, firſt fruits, &c. common to the patriarchs and unbelievers. We even behold, in theſe, and many other inſtances, the ſame religious cuſtoms amongſt the heathens, which it pleaſed the Divine Being to enforce the continuance of by the Moſaic diſpenſation; a convincing argument that they muſt have been uncorrupt and innocent in their original.

Nor did mankind in general loſe ſight of the original object ſo ſoon, or ſo totally, as is commonly apprehended. Since we find amongſt the eaſtern nations, and indeed amongſt ſeveral of the Greeks and Romans, the moſt exalted notions of the Supreme Being, the Creator of heaven and earth.

According to the Egyptians (1), Eicton, or the firſt God, exiſted in his ſolatcry unity before all beings. He is the fountain and original of every thing, that either has underſtanding, or is to be underſtood. He is the firſt principle of all things, ſelf-ſufficient, incomprehenſible, and the father of all eſſences. Hermes ſays, likewiſe, that this Supreme God has conſtituted another God, called Emeph, to be head over all ſpirits, whether etherial, empyrean, or celeſtial; and that this ſecond God, whom he ſtiles the Guide, is a wiſdom that transforms and converts into itſelf all ſpiritual beings. He makes nothing ſuperior to this god-guide, except the firſt intelligent, and firſt intelligible, who ought to be adored in ſilence. He adds,

(1) Pamblicus de Myſt. Egypt. Ed. Lngd. 1552. p. 153, 4.

adds, that the spirit which produceth all things has different names, according to his different properties and operations; that he is called in the Egyptian language Amoun, as he is wise; Ptha, as he is the life of all things; and Osiris, as he is the author of all good (2).

Let us proceed to the Greeks, amongst whom Orpheus claims the first place in right of his antiquity, and to whose theological sentiments the preference is always given by the early writers in favour of Christianity.

" There is one unknown Being, exalted above, and
" prior to all beings (3), the author of all things, even
" of the æther, and of every thing that is below the
" æther: this exalted being is LIFE, LIGHT, and
" WISDOM; which three names express only one and
" the same power, which drew all beings, visible and
" invisible, out of nothing."

Thus also the divine Plato: " That which (4) gives
" truth and reality to things unknown, and endues
" the knower with the power of understanding; this
" call thou the idea of the GOOD ONE, the source of
" wisdom and truth." But GOD is every where distinguished throughout the works of this illustrious philosopher, as the BEAUTIFUL, the GOOD, the JUST ONE.

Would you see the being and the providence of GOD demonstrated from the order and administration of the world? You will no where find it more convincingly than in the reasoning of Balbus in Cicero; and from which observations you must of necessity draw the same conclusion which he does, that (5) " All
" things in the world are wonderfully directed by a
" divine mind and counsel, to the safety and conservation of the whole."

These

(2) See Ramsay's Theology, annexed to Cyrus, 4to ed. p. 14 and 17.
(3) Suid. de Orph. p. 350, and Cedrenus, p. 47.
(4) Τουτο τοι υν το την αηθειαν περεχεν τοις γιγνωσκομενοις καί τω γιγνωσκοντι· την δυναμιν αποδιδον, την τυ Αγαθυ ιδεαν, φαθι ειναι. De Repub. lib. 6.
(5) *Sic undique omni ratione concluditur mente consilioque divino omnia in hoc mundo ad salutem omnium conservationemque admirabiliter administrari.* De Nat. Deor. l. 2. c. 53.

These sentiments are also the result of Seneca's enquiries: "By Jove, says he (6), the wise men amongst "the ancients did not mean such an one as we see in "the Capitol and other temples, but the Guardian "and Ruler of the universe, a MIND and SPIRIT, the "master and artificer of this mundane fabric, whom "every title suits. Would you call him Fate? you "will not err; for he it is on whom all things depend; the CAUSE OF CAUSES. Would you call "him Providence? you are in the right? for by his "wisdom is the world directed; hence it moves "unshaken, and performs its every office. Would "you call him Nature? 'tis not amiss; since from "him all things proceed, and by his spirit we live; "or the World? tis well; for he is All in all, and "existing by his own power."

Innumerable are the instances which might be brought from the ancients to this purpose. But these may suffice. And from an attentive consideration of these it will appear, that the philosophers endeavoured to establish a particular system with relation to the origin of idolatry, which tends very much to lessen the supposed absurdity of it. They maintained (7) that the idea which the wise men of antiquity had formed to themselves of GOD, was that of a Being superior to whatever exists; of a SPIRIT present in all the bounds of the universe, who animates all, who is the principal of generation, and communicates fertility to every being; of a FLAME, lively, pure, and always active; of an INTELLIGENCE, infinitely wise, whose providence continually watches and extends over all; in a word, an idea of a Being, to whom they had given different names answering to his superior excellence; yet such as always bore the stamp of that supreme right of possession, which is only inherent in the absolute Lord, and in him from whom all things flow.

It is, however, too fatally to be denied, that as the corruption of the heart of man dilated and enlarged itself, a disrelish of spiritual things gradually came on, and the mind grew more devoted to sensible objects. Of all created things within his prospect, the Sun was the most glorious and the most likely to engage

(6) Natural. Quæst. l. c. 45.
(7) See Banier's Mythology, vol. I. p. 171.

engage his attention firſt, and next his wonder and his worſhip. Accordingly it had been conſidered from the beginning as the great or primary emblem of the divinity, being not only the moſt beautiful of all bodies in its appearance, but the moſt beneficent in its effects; the regulator of the ſeaſons, and the natural parent of light and fertility. Hence Plato (8) calls it " The offspring of the GOOD ONE, which the " GOOD ONE produced analogous to himſelf." It is termed by others (9) " The eye of Jove," and the " mind of Jove, of heaven, of the world." In fine, whoever will be at the pains to conſult Macrobius, may ſee that the figures of all the heathen deities were but ſo many different expreſſions of the qualities and attributes of the Sun, or of the ſeaſons which depended on and were governed by him; to whom his votaries aſcribed omnipotence, and whom in their invocations they ſaluted as " The power, " the light, and the ſpirit of the world (1)."

The Solar Body, before writing, could not more properly be repreſented than by the figure of a circle; a ſymble ſo plain and inoffenſive, that one would think, it ſhould not eaſily be perverted to the uſes of idolatry. It was accordingly ſubſtituted in hieroglyphics as the artificial (its principal the Sun being the great natural) emblem of the divinity, and became the figure of all the open temples; the earlieſt places of religious worſhip. Theſe circles, or diſcs, are the ſun-images mentioned in ſcripture (2), and are at this day the ſymbols of royalty, glory, and divinity: and it may be worth while perhaps to remark that the word from which this is ſupplied (3), is uſed to ſignify idolatry in general, from the near relation which it bears to the original object of it (4), whoſe derivative it is.

When

(8) Τὸν τῦ Ἀγαθῦ ἔκγονον, ὅν τ' Ἀγαθὴν ἐγέννησεν ἀναλογον ἑαυτῷ. De Repub. l. 6.

(9) Apuleius de Mundo Macrobius Saturnal. l. 1. cap. 17. uſque ad finem cap. 23.

(1) *Potentiam ſolis ad omnium poteſtatum ſummitatem referri indicant theologi; qui in ſacris hoc breviſſima precatione demonſtrant dicentes.* Ἥλιε παντοκράτο, κοσμυ πνεῦμα, κοσμυ δύναμιν κοσμυ φῶς. Ibid. c. 23.

(2) Haminichem, ſun-images.

(3) Hamon, idolatry.

(4) Hamah, the ſun.

When religious worſhip began to be transferred from the divinity to his emblem, from the creator to the creature, then that particular day of the week, which had ever been kept ſacred to the creator of all things, began likewiſe to be ſet apart and dedicated to the honour of this luminary, was thence termed Sunday, and continued to be had in eſpecial reverence above all the reſt. Hence celebrated by one of the moſt ancient writers, as "An holy day, becauſe it "was the birth-day of Apollo, or the ſun (5)." Which indeed was ſo far true, that it was the commemoration of that day, on which the human eye was bleſſed with the proſpect of that glorious object. For it requires no extraordinary ſagacity, but only a little attention, however generally and unaccountably this point has been over-looked, to ſee and be convinced that the firſt Holy Seventh Day was the particular ſtated day of the Chriſtian ſabbath. It appears from the original account of it, that the work of the creation took up ſix days, and that the laſt created being was man; who was therefore in all probability formed on the evening of the ſixth day. That which immediately ſucceeded was the firſt of Adam's life as well as the firſt ſabbath. It was the firſt day of his firſt week, and month and year, i. e. the firſt in man's account of time. On the expiration of this firſt ſabbath, he began to number his ſecular days, as they advanced in order, till he had told ſix. The next was again his Holy Seventh; yet the firſt day of his ſecond week, for his weeks were aſcertained by the return of ſabbath. Thus obtained it duly in all ordinary and civil computations to be the firſt day of the week, at the ſame time that it was diſtinguiſhed, with a retroſpect to the work of creation, as an Holy Seventh Day. And remarkable it is, that the moſt ancient of the heathen writers, while they ſpeak of it as ſuch, have rendered the very ſame reaſon for it (6), which the Jewiſh legiſlator had before

(5) ——— εβδομον ιερον ημαρ.
Τῷ γὰρ Ἀπολλωνᾶ χρυσάορα γείνατο Λητώ. HESIOD.
(6) ———Ἑβδομον ἱερὸν ἦμάρ.   HESIOD.
Ἑβδόμη ἥν ἱερη,   HOMER.
Ἑβδομον ἠμαρ ἔην και τῷ τετέλεςο ἀπαντα.   HOMER.
Ἑβδοματη δ' ἠρι τετελεσμινα παντα τετυκται.   LIN.
Ἑβδομη ἐν πρωτοισι, και ἑβδύμη ἐς τηλείη.   CALLIM.

Vide Clemont. Alex. Storm. l. 5. p. 560, and Poli. Synnops. ad Geneſ. xi. 2.

before given, namely, that "On it all things were "ended or compleated." This then being of ancient or patriarchial ufage, was not confined to any particular nation or fet of men, like the Jewifh fabbath, but extended to all mankind, and was univerfally obferved as the birth-day of the world; but being at length abufed and defecrated to the purpofes of idolatry, it pleafed the divine Being, when he delivered his people from the bondage of the Ægyptians, to confecrate another day to his peculiar worfhip. This was the felf fame day in which he brought them forth with their armies from the land of Ægypt. Which was therefore to be a memorial of their deliverance (7), as long as their ftate and polity fhould laft, and a fign (8) and covenant that the Moft High God was their God.

But to refume our fubject; from which, we hope, the reader will excufe this little digreffion, if fuch it be. Another emblem of the divinity, in a manner univerfally received, was the Seraph, or fiery-flying Serpent, the Salutis Draco (9), the great fymbol of Light and Wifdom, of Life and Health. Why the figure of this animal was thus honoured, feveral reafons may be affigned; as, the annual renovation of its youth and beauty; its finuofity, which enabled it to put on various forms; the acutenefs of vifion, and extraordinary fagacity afcribed to it; and its colour, which is that of vivid flame, or burnifhed brafs. Its name of Seraph particularly is fo expreffive (1) of that blaze of brightnefs, which it feems to furnifh when reflecting the fplendor of the funbeams, that it has been transferred to a fuperior order of angels; and is once made ufe of to denote even the glorious appearance of the cherubim (2). This is the fame fymbol which was erected by Mofes in the wildernefs. But this alfo was at length proftituted to abominable purpofes, and made the attribute of all the Ægyptian deities (3).

Expanded

(7) Deuteronom. c. v. 15.
(8) Ezekiel. c. xx. 10, 11, 12, 13.
(9) Macrobius.
(1) Seraph, a flame or burning.
(2) Ifaiah vi.
(3) Orus Apollo; ad initium.

Expanded Wings made a third emblem of the divinity. This was the hieroglyphic substituted for the æther, which was considered as the natural symbol of the divine spirit, and, as such, succeeded to a share of idolatrous worship (4). In some of the original open temples, particularly in that wonderful one of Abiry in Wiltshire, the complex figure of the Circle, and Seraph, with expanded wings, was represented entire.

Such were the natural emblems of the divine Being, and so plain and simple their hieroglyphical representations; the original intent of which is explained to us by Kircher (5), from a piece of antiquity in the Phœnician language: "Jove," says this fragment, " is a figured Circle; from it is produced a Serpent: " the Circle shews the divine nature to be without " beginning or end; the Serpent his word, which " animates the world and makes it prolific; his " Wings the spirit of God, which gives motion to " the whole system."

The commencement of idolatry, avowed and aiming at some establishment, must bear date from the extraordinary project set on foot at Babel. The design, as appears from the original account of it (6), was to build a city and a tower, the citadel or commanding part of which was to be erected to these powers, which are there distinguished as the Shemim, or Heavens. The supposition of its being to reach unto the heavens is an addition of the translators. The confusion there spoken of, was the confusion of the

---

(4) Τίνα δη και σεμνύναν ποτέ λέγω θεὸν, ὦ Μέγιλλε και Κλεινία? χερὶν Οὐρανὸν; ὃν και δικαιότατον ὡς ξύμπαντες ἄλλοι δαίμονες; ἅμα και θεοί τιμᾶν τε και εὔχεσθαι διαφερόντως αὐτῷ. Τον δὲ και τῶν ἄλλων αἴτιον ἀγαθῶν πάντων ἡμῖν αὐτον γεγονέναι, πάντες ἄτομολ γοῖμεν Platon. Epinomis.

Zenoni & reliquis fere Stoicis Æther videtur summus Deus, mente præditus, qua omnia regantur. Ciceron Academ. Quæst. l. 4. c. 41.

Cleanthes autem, qui Zenonem audivit, tum ultimum & altissimum atque undique circumfusum, & extremum omnia cingentem, atque complexum ardorem, qui Æther nominatur; certissimum Deum judicat. Id. de Nat. Deor. l. 1. c. 14. See Chap. 62. of Isis, Osiris and Orus.

(5) Obel. Pamph. p. 403.

(6) Gen. xi. 4. The original runs strictly thus: *Let us erect to us a city and a tower, and the chief place of it to the heavens.*

the lip, or religious confession. The true believers on this occasion separated from the idolaters, whom they left behind in Assyria to proceed in their mad enterprize, and dispersed themselves in the adjoining countries, carrying with them the same language and the same patriarchal religion, where we find both for a considerable time after. The confusion of tongues, as it is called, was but the natural, and by no means the immediate consequence of this dispersion.

Next we find the solar body, and its natural symbol the fire, worshipped at Ur of the Chaldees, thence denominated. The same symbol was held in especial reverence afterwards by the Persians, but never worshipped, in the proper sense of the expression. The species of idolatry relating to the worship of the human figure was not introduced till long after; nor was the temple, which Ninus is said to have built, erected to his father Belus, as many have asserted, but to Bel or Baal-Shemim, the Lord of the Heavens, meaning the Sun.

Thus idolatry in Assyria was prior to the time of Abraham (7), but it was confined to that country; for neither in his time, nor for some time after, do we find any traces of it in Arabia, Phœnicia, or Egypt. We may rest assured that Ishmael, the father of the Arabians, and his brethren by Keturah, adored the GOD of their father, and established his worship in the east-country, whither they were sent (Gen. xviii. 19). In Phœnicia, we find Abimelech, the king of the Philistines, believing in GOD, favoured with a divine intercourse, and pleading to the heavenly vision the righteousness of his nation. Their behaviour with Isaac afterwards leaves no room to doubt that they continued then in the same faith (8). GOD himself declares to Abraham, that his children shall not possess that land *till the fourth generation after him*, because the *iniquity of its inhabitants was not yet full*. Whence it is but rational to conclude, *that till the fourth generation after*, or till about the time of Exodus, they had not, at least generally, swerved into idolatry. Sir Isaac Newton (9) imagines that they continued in the true religion till the death of Melchizedec; but that afterwards

---

(7) Joshua, xxiv. 2.
(8) Gen. xxvi. 28, 29, & seq.
(9) Chronology of ancient kingdoms amended, p. 188.

afterwards they began to embrace idolatry spreading thitherward from Chaldæa. They could not, however, in any short time after, have amongst them more than the beginnings of idolatry; though I presume, they sunk into it apace after the departure of Joseph's brethren with their families into Egypt. When the patriarch came into this last-mentioned country also, GOD is said to have sent judgments upon Pharoah's family, because of Abraham's wife; and the king of Egypt seems to have been no stranger to the true GOD, but to have had the fear of him before his eyes, and to have been influenced by it in all his actions (1). Abraham was entertained by him without the appearance of any indisposition towards him, or any the least sign of their having a different religion. Even the heathen writers give hints, that the Egyptians were at first worshippers of the true GOD. Plutarch testifies, that in Upper Egypt, the inhabitants paid no part of the taxes raised for the idolatrous worship; asserting themselves to own no mortal being for God (2), but professing to worship their GOD CNEPH only. Porphyry calls this Egyptian CNEPH, τον Δημιυργον, the Creator of the universe.

I cannot persuade myself that Joseph, when long after this he flourished at the head of the Egyptian ministry, had that people deserted the worship of the true GOD, would have married into the family he did, or that the zealous patriarch would have held so sacred and inviolable the lands and endowments of an idolatrous priesthood. With justice therefore has the great Grotius remarked (3) that in the age of Joseph no certain footsteps of idolatry are to be discerned in Egypt. I would give it to the reader as a conjecture highly probable, that idolatry was not established by law in any part of that country, till the disgrace of Moses at the court of Egypt, when he first retired to his brethren in Goshen; about forty years before the Exodus. This is countenanced by a passage of scripture, where it is said of the children of Israel, that *they sacrificed unto devils, not to* GOD; *to gods whom they knew not, to* new *gods that* came newly up, *whom their fathers feared not* (4).

So

(1) See Shuckford's Connection, vol. I. p. 281, and 312.
(2) De Iside & Osiride.
(3) Vide Poli Synopsin in Gen. 46, verf. ultim.
(4) Deuter. 32, 17.

So that Eufebius, Lactantius, Caffian, Lucian, with many of the Jewifh Rabbies, as well as Voffius; the Abbe Banier, and the moderns in general, appear to have been grofsly miftaken, in making either Phœnicia or Egypt the birth-place of idolatry. But this fymbolical and hieroglyphical divinity, proceeded from Affyria through Phœnicia to Egypt. But it was the Phœnician commerce which fpread it in the remoteft quarters of the world; and it is obferved, that in all the religions we know, even in the Eaft and Weft Indies, there is not one of them, whofe theology is not full of the like emblems.

It muft be confeffed that the multiplication of fymbols became at length an inexhauftible fund of idolatry. Thofe characters which, before the knowledge of letters, were innocent and even neceffary, being by that rendered in a fhort time ufelefs, generally neglected, underftood by few, and at laft grievoufly perverted, were the occafion of infinite errors. This may be well exemplified by a fhort account of the Zodiac (5).

The crab, an animal walking backwards or obliquely, feemed a proper emblem of the fun, who arriving at this fign begins his retrogradation (6). The wild goat on the contrary, whofe cuftom is to feed as he climbs, was chofen to denote the Sun, who on coming to this point of the heavens, quits the loweft part of his courfe to regain the higheft. The ram, the bull, and the two kids gave name to the three celeftial houfes, through which the Sun paffes in fpring. This diftinguifhed the different kinds of young cattle, produced in this feafon, as they naturally fucceeded each other: the lambs appearing firft, the calves next, and the kids laft. Two of thefe latter were chofen, on account of the peculiar fruitfulnefs of the goat, which generally bears twins. But thefe the Greeks difplaced, fubftituting the twin-brothers, Caftor and Pollux. The fury of the Lion juftly expreffed the heat of the Sun, on his leaving Cancer. The virgin crowned with ears of corn, was an emblem of the harveft, ufually ending about that time. Nothing could better denote the equality of days and nights under the autumnal equinox, than the balance Libra. The difeafes,

(5) See Abbe Pluche's Hift. of the Heavens, vol. I. p 10, & feq.
(6) Macrob. Saturn. l. 1. c. 17.

eases, consequent upon the fall of the leaf, were characterised by the Scorpion. The chase of wild beasts, annually observed at that time, was not improperly distinguished by Sagittarius, a man on horseback, armed with a bow and arrow. Aquarius represented the rains of winter; and the two Fishes bound together, or inclosed in a net, indicated the season for fishing, ever best at the approach of spring. What could be more simple and useful than this division of the Sun's annual course into twelve equal portions, expressed by so many visible signs, which served to regulate and describe the seasons and the business proper to each. These rude delineations of the celestial houses probably gave birth to painting. But then these images presented to the mind a meaning very different from the idea conveyed to the eye. And when this meaning was lost, the imagination was quickly at work to supply another more agreeable to its own corruption.

The kingdom of Egypt, on account of its peculiar situation, became the great school of this symbolical learning; and thence, in process of time, the grand mart of idolatry. It is not improbable that the priests might endeavour to stem the torrent of superstition that ensued from it, till finding all their strength ineffectual, they submitted to the times, and from views of avarice and ambition became public defenders of those errors, which secretly they condemned. For, it is certain, that while thus they complied with the popular language, they yet studied all they could collect of the ancient and real signification of the symbolical figures, taking care to require a profound secresy of all persons whom they instructed in this kind of knowledge. And for this reason sphinges were placed at the entrances of their temples, intimating to those who approached, that they were to look for a further meaning in what they should see; for that all was mysterious there.

Such was the origin of those initiations so much sought after in Egypt, Asia, and afterwards in Greece. Indeed these mysteries themselves were in the end most grosly abused: yet there is no question, but that in their primary institution they were intended to explain the natural and divine things couched under those representations. For they did not only unfold the nature

ture of things, though this seems to have had (7) the greatest share in them; but inculcated also the immortality of the soul, a future state of (8) rewards and punishments, the consequent necessity of virtue, and the other great truths of religion which had been handed down from the earliest ages.

Thus the ancient Eastern nations had a reserved meaning in all their emblematical figures; which it is frequently in our power, even at this distance of time, to make out. Much of the language spoken by them is still existing: by the means of which, matters of so remote antiquity may in a great measure be disengaged from that mysterious darkness, in which the ignorance of some ages, and the follies of others, have involved them. I shall be easily understood to speak this of the Hebrew tongue; so much of which, I say, is yet remaining to us, as will easily, by a comparison with other languages, manifest it to be an original: and all others, on examination, will discover how largely they have drank of this fountain. The names of animals, so intimately expressive of their properties, bespeak it to have been given by the great author of nature; and those of the first men (9), so nicely applied to their respective conditions and circumstances, leave no room to doubt that they were coæval with the persons themselves. The Greeks borrowed their idolatry from Phœnicia and Egypt, which indeed the innovating

---

(7) *Omitto Eleusinam sanctam illam & augustam,*
 Ubi initiantur gentes orarum ultimæ :
 Prætereo Samothraciam, eoque
 ——— *Quæ Lemni*
 Nocturno aditu occulta coluntur
 Sylvestribus sepibus densa :
Quibus explicatis, ad rationemque revocatis, rerum magis Naturæ cognoscitur quam Deorum. Cicero de Nat. Deor. l. 1. c. 42.

(8) Τελεταὶ δὲ μετέχοντες περὶ τὲ τῆς τὸ βίο τελυτῆς καὶ τὸ σύμπαντος αἰῶνος ἡδείας τὰς ἐλπίδας ἔχυσι. Isocr. in Panegyr.

Mihi cum multa eximia divinaque videntur Athenæ peperisse, atque in vita hominum attulisse, tum nihil melius illis mysteriis, quibus ex agresti immaniqui vita, exculta ad humanitatem & mitigati sumus: initiaque, ut appellantur, ita re vera principia vitæ cognovimus; neque solum cum lætitia vivendi rationem accepimus, sed etiam cum spe meliore moriendi. Cicero de legibus, l. 2. c. 14.

(9) See Origin of Languages by the late Dr. Gregory Sharpe.

ing spirit of that people improved in the most extravagant manner; and it is not possible to explain their religious antiquities without having recourse to the language of those countries from which they were transplanted. When therefore this is done without force or constraint, proposing an interpretation natural and easy; not to receive it were to reject the only means (in many cases) of information, which remain to us at this immense distance of time. The reader will consider this as an apology for the free use which is made of this tongue in the preceding sheets; where he will find a great number of strange *and otherwise* unaccountable stories, having their foundations solely in the different meanings of the same word: So that an account, in itself innocent and easy, by being perversely rendered, became frequently the source of idle wonder, and at length of idolatrous veneration. It is not from the fabulous Greeks themselves that we are to expect full satisfaction in these matters. Very few of them gave themselves the trouble to enquire into the meaning of their own ceremonies. Every thing that was but Egyptian was readily adopted, and the very names of the gods they worshipped were originally taken upon trust. For the Pelasgians, as Herodotus informs us (1), had formerly sacrificed and prayed to gods in general, without attributing either name or sirname to any deity, which in those times they had never heard of; but they called them gods, because they disposed and governed all actions and countries. After a long time the names of the other gods were brought among them from Egypt, and last of all that of Bacchus; upon which they consulted the oracle of Dodona, still accounted the most ancient, and then the only oracle in Greece, and having enquired whether they should receive these names from the barbarians, the oracle answered, they should. So from that time they invoked the gods in their sacrifices under distinct names; and the same were afterwards received by the Greeks from these Pelasgians. This, says my author, I had from the priestesses of Dodona.

It is said to the honour of Moses, that he was learned in all the wisdom of the Egyptians. Whence is it then that greater absurdities in religion have been ascribed to this wise people, than have been met

(1) In Euterpe.

met with amongst the most barbarous and uncivilized nations? This could only proceed from the travelling Greeks, who understood little of what they saw, and made the worst use of what they carried home; which, by their poets, was afterwards enlarged and diversified with all the wantonness of a licentious imagination. Thus that idolatry, which had its foundation in the vanity and corruption of the human heart, was chiefly indebted for its fabulous bulk amongst the Greeks, to the warm and plastic imagination of the poets; was still further improved by the boldness of the pencil, the fine expression of the chissel, and the licence of the stage.

When the human figure was first made the object of idolatrous veneration, may perhaps be difficult to determine. We read of graven images in the land of Canaan, in the time of Moses and Joshua. But these in all probability were extremely rough and inartificial, and perhaps nothing more than upright stones or standing pillars. Such as they were, however, Cadmus is said to have carried the use of them into Greece. I should imagine, that they were not worshipped in Egypt till long after; especially if that be true, which Clemens of Alexandria quotes Leo as affirming (2), in his treatise of the Egyptian gods, that their celebrated Isis lived not till the time of Lynceus, in the eleventh generation after Moses.

It has been generally allowed, that the persons whose memory was thus religiously preserved, were such as had been greatly distinguished for the invention of useful arts, and their beneficence to mankind (3). But to make this species of idolatry go down with the people, something more than a pretended deification seems to have been necessary; because, in order to secure this extravagant honour to their favourites, we find the Egyptians arraying their images with various ensigns and attributes; thus making them the representatives of such natural things as were adored already by the superstitious herd. Thus we find Osiris adorned with the emblems of the sun, Isis decked with those of the æther, and the golden

Seraph

(2 Stromat. l. 1. p. 322

(3 *Suscepit autem vita hominum, consuetudoque communis, ut beneficiis excellentes viros in cælum fama ac voluntate tollerent.*

Cicero de Nat. Deo. l. 2. c. 24.

Seraph inseparable from Orus (4). Granting therefore that there were such persons in the world, as Jupiter, Apollo, Bacchus, Isis, &c. yet we must allow the attributes given, and the ceremonies paid to them, to be solely applicable to the luminaries, or to the natural causes and effects, which, it is manifest, were represented by them.

Or it may be that mankind were not altogether so eager and so hasty in their corruptions; that the consecration of eminent and virtuous men was no more in the first place than a sort of canonization; and that the worship paid to them was only considered as a public testimony of their belief, that such persons were received into the abodes of the blessed, and numbered among the sons of God. This at least was the opinion of Cicero (5). For that the law commands those who were consecrated from amongst men, to be worshipped; it shews indeed, says he, that the souls of all men are immortal; but that those of the brave and the good are divine.

May we not therefore conclude, with regard to the ancient Egyptians particularly, that they were not ignorant of the ONE SUPREME BEING, who by his knowledge conceived the world, before he formed it by his will; but to comply with the growing corruptions of mankind, in which compliance they were extremely guilty, allowed them to adore (and in this no doubt they found their account) the different attributes of his essence, and the different effects of his goodness under the symbols of the heavenly powers, of renowned personages, and at last even of terrestrial bodies, as plants and animals; thus wilfully laying the foundation of the grossest superstition and idolatry.

How little the besotted Greeks had to say for themselves on this head, and how ignorant indeed they were of their own religious rites, has been remarked already. As these took their gods so fondly from the Egyptians, so did the Romans theirs chiefly from them. This appears at large in the preceding sheets.

It

(4) *Infantemque vident, exporrectumque draconem.* OVID.
See chap. 63, of Isis, Osiris, and Orus.

(5) *Quod autem ex hominum genere consecratos, sicut Herculem & ceteros, coli lex jubet, indicat omnium quidem animos immortales esse, sed fortium bonorumque divinos.* De Legibus, l. 2. c. xi.

It muſt be confeſſed at the ſame time, that as ſome of theſe laſt refer the whole multitude of their divinities to the ſun, the original object of idolatry, thence called the univerſal one (6). So did others of them to the GREAT AUTHOR OF NATURE, affirming, "Jupiter to be the ſoul of the world (7), who formed "the univerſe of the four elements, and fills and "moves it thus compacted." In the æther he is Jupiter; in the air, Juno; in the ſea, Neptune; in the lower parts of the ſea, Salacia; in the earth, Pluto; in hell, Proſerpine; in domeſtic fires, Veſta; in the working-furnace, Vulcan; in the heavenly bodies, the Sun, Moon, and Stars; amongſt diviners, Apollo; in trade, Mercury; in Janus, the Beginner; in boundaries, the Terminator; in time, Saturn; in war, Mars and Bellona; Bacchus in the vintage; Ceres in the harveſt; in the woods, Diana; in the ſciences, Minerva; and is himſelf, in fine, the whole multitude of vulgar gods and goddeſſes. Theſe are all the one Jupiter, whether they be conſidered, according to ſome, as parts of himſelf, or, according to others, as his virtues and attributes. This is exactly of a piece with the reaſoning of Seneca; who aſſerts that GOD may have names in number equal to his gifts (8).

Notwithſtanding this, we find on ſome occaſions, even among theſe, the monſtrous abſurdity of making new gods arrived to ſuch a pitch, that temples have been every now and then vowed and erected by magiſtrates and commanders, even to creatures of their own ſudden imagination; ſuch as the chance of war, or their own wiſhes or fears had raiſed. So that Pliny's obſervations (9), with ſome allowance for the latitude of expreſſion, may ſeem to have been not ill-

(6) *Diverſæ virtutes ſolis nomina Diis dederunt: unde ſapientum principes prodiderunt.* Macrob. Saturn. l. 1. c. 17.

(7) St. Auguſtin de civitate Dei, c. 11. Tome 5. p. 42, 43.

(8) *Jovem illum optimum ac maximum rite dices & tonantem & ſtatorem quot ſtant beneficio ejus omnia, ſtator ſtabilitorque eſt Quæcunque voles illi nomina proprie aptabis, vim aliquam effectumque cæleſtium rerum continentia. Tot appellationes ejus poſſunt eſſe, quot munera. Hunc & Liberum Patrem & Herculem, ac Mercurium noſtri putant. Quia omnium parens ſit: quia vis ejus invicta ſit. Quia ratio penes illum eſt, numeruſque, & ordo, & ſcientia, &c.* De Bene. l. 4. c. 7, 8.

(9) Nat. Hiſt. Lib. II. c. 7.

illfounded; that the extravagance of human paſſions and affections had made more gods than there were men.

Yet upon the whole, the hiſtory of religion is not ſo darkened with error, but that, through all theſe ſhades of folly, an attentive enquirer may ſtill diſcern the diſpenſations of GOD, from the firſt offence of man to this day, to have been regular and uniform, and directed to one great end, namely, his own ſupreme glory in the happineſs of his creatures.

Let us therefore adore this ever-gracious Being with humble ſincerity. Let us acknowledge his infinite mercies with a due ſenſe of our own demerits; and beware, above all things, that we attempt not to ſet up our own weak reaſon in oppoſition to the declared will and commandments of GOD. This has been the great ſtumbling-block in all ages: and from ſuch demeanour confuſion of every ſort muſt neceſſarily enſue.

OF

OF THE MYTHOLOGY OF THE HEATHENS.

WE shall now enter into the nature of the Pagan fables, their religious sentiments, and the manner of their worship. Here we shall find truth blended with error, and obscured with fiction, which has wrapt in clouds the most important doctrines, such as the creation of the world, the fall of man, the destruction of the human race by an universal deluge, the change produced in nature by that great event, the origin of natural and moral evil, and the final restitution of all things to their primitive glory and splendor.

Notwithstanding the great corruption which had crept into the worship of all nations, we have seen that the men of learning and reflection generally maintained honourable notions of the deity, and the obligations of moral virtue. As the Greeks and Romans had received their divinities from Phœnicia and Egypt, and by mistaking the manners, the customs and language of those nations, had made gods of the common symbols which they employed to teach the people to honour one God, the author of all good, to live in peace, to express the times and seasons for the performance of the common occurrences of life, and to expect a better state to come; so their religion became obscured by fables, and a variety of fictions, which, while the vulgar understood in a literal sense, their sages endeavoured to explain and reduce to ingenious allegories, and thereby to render the heathen worship consistent with all the natural notions of a supreme Deity, the wise governor of the world, and by accounting for the introduction of moral evil, to vindicate the rules of his providence, and to justify the ways of God to man.

Fables are indeed a very ancient method of conveying truth, and veils of so fine a texture as not wholly to conceal the beauties that lie beneath them.

" Thus "

"Thus," says Origen (1), "the Egyptian philoso-phers have sublime notions with regard to the Divine Nature, which they keep secret, and never discover to the people, but under the veil of fables and allegories, All the Eastern nations, the Persians, the Indians, the Syrians, conceal secret mysteries under their religious fables. The wise men of all nations (2) see into the true sense and meaning of them, whilst the vulgar go no further than the exterior symbol, and see only the bark that covers them."

This was frequently the case when foreign and distant nations adopted what they but imperfectly understood. Allegories became objects of faith. Thus could any thing give a more lively idea of the state of retribution, than the ceremonies with which the Egyptians buried their dead. The Greeks and Romans, struck with the ideas that were so strongly conveyed, took the type for the reality; the boat which was to convey the body to the place of burial, which was with the Egyptians an emblem of death, and was called Tranquillity, because it carried over none but the just, was represented by the Greeks and Romans as a boat to carry souls. Cerberus, an hieroglyphic, carved out of wood or stone, to express the lamentations bestowed on the virtuous, became an animated monster. The lake of Acherusia became a visionary river of Tartarus, and was called Acheron. The judges that decided the merit of the deceased, were represented as consigning the spirit to final happiness or misery, and the flowery field where the righteous alone were buried, into that place of joy which the elizout of the Egyptians was only designed as a faint representation of. Yet, notwithstanding the fables into which these mysteries were turned, this very important truth was still conveyed, that there would be a state of judgment, in which

---

(1) Origen contra Celsum, lib. 1. p. 11.

(2) "Those who are acquainted with these mysteries," says Isocrates, "insure to themselves very pleasing hopes against the hour of death, and which extend to a whole eternity." "These mysteries (says Epictetus) were established by the ancients, to regulate the lives of men, and to banish disorders from the world."

which the virtuous would be rewarded, and the vicious punished. The very prayer, or form of absolution, which was given by the Egyptian priests to the relations of the deceased, contained a useful lesson to the living, as it exhibited a concise system of those morals which were to entitle them to the Divine Favour, and to a decent burial in the plains, on the confines of the lake Acherusia. This prayer was preserved by Porphyry, who copied it from Euphantes, whose works are now lost, and is as follows:
" O Sun, thou first divinity! and ye celestial Gods
" who gave life to man! vouchsafe to receive me
" this day unto your holy tabernacles. I have endeavoured, to the best of my power, to render my
" life agreeable to you; I have behaved with the
" highest veneration towards the Gods, with whom
" I was acquainted in my infancy; I have never
" failed in my duty to those who brought me into
" being, nor in natural affection to the womb that
" bore me. My hands are pure from my neighbour's blood; I have maintained an inviolable
" regard to truth and fidelity; and may I not appeal
" to the silence of mankind, who have nothing to
" lay to my charge, as a sure and certain testimony
" of my integrity? If however, any personal and
" secret fault has escaped me, and I have offended in
" eating or in drinking, let these entrails bear all the
" blame." Here the entrails of the deceased were produced by the relations, and immediately thrown into the lake.

But however useful these ceremonies might be, as practised amongst the Egyptians, yet being considered as realities by the Greeks, and rendered more ridiculous by the absurdity of their fables, it is no wonder that they lost their efficacy, and became, as Juvenal informs us, disbelieved even by their children.

But it is not at all strange, that this should be the case with the Greeks, when the Egyptians themselves were fallen into idolatry, and those simple emblems, once so well known to this people, were become the medium of their prayers and adorations. Every thing had an air of mystery, and these mysteries were understood by none but the priests, or those to whom they were pleased to explain them, which was always done under the seal of secrecy. The vulgar were suffered to continue in their errors, since it might have

have been dangerous even for their priests to attempt to open their eyes, and to reduce their worship to the simplicity of the ancient practice.

Nothing has ever contributed more to disguise the truth, and to corrupt the worship of the Greeks and Romans, than the multitude of fictions introduced by their poets. It is this that has principally occasioned that jumble of images, that indecorum in characters, and that absurdity in their fictions, which are so justly condemned by their wisest philosophers.

It is the province of poetry to change the face of nature, to give life and activity to inanimate beings, substance and form to thought; to deify the passions, and to create a world of its own. The poet is not bound by the same laws as other men; he has a power that enables him to create and destroy at pleasure, and with the same ease he forms gods (3), heroes, men, and monsters. He makes quick transitions from reality to fiction; from fiction to reality, and from those gods which he believes to those of his own creating; and from hence arises a principal source of that confusion which has given such different interpretations to, and which renders it so difficult to explain the ancient mythology. The Greek and Roman poets have almost always preferred the marvellous and the sparkling to the simplicity of naked truth. If a princess died of grief for the loss of her husband or her child, she was changed into a rock or fountain; instead of saying that Cephalus rose with the sun, Aurora must be in love with the youth, and force him abroad. To represent the long life of Ioalus, the goddess of health must renew his age. Instead of saying that Endymion studied in the mountains of Caria the course of the moon, they tell us, that he had there an interview with Diana, and that her staying with her gallant was the cause of eclipses; but as these amours could not last for ever, they were obliged to invent a new fable, to account for them another way, and therefore they feigned that some sorceress of Thessaly, by her enchantments, drew down the moon to the earth. To account for the perpetual verdure of the laurel, they
talked

---

(3) The ancient heroes were supposed to be a middle kind of beings, that partook both of the nature of gods and men.

talked of the amours of Apollo and (4) Daphne. To exprefs the agility and fwiftnefs of Periclymnus, they affirmed that he was able to affume all fhapes, and at laft turned himfelf into an eagle. Amphion, by his oratory, prevailed on a barbarous people to build a city, and to dwell in fociety: he is therefore faid to raife up the walls of Thebes by the found of his lyre; and Orpheus to charm the lions and tigers, and to move the rocks and trees by his harmony, becaufe nothing could withftand his perfuafion, or refift the force of his eloquence.

Who would imagine that by the wings of Dedalus and Icarus, were fignified a fhip uuder fail? That all the changes of Achelous, were only frequent inundations? That by the combat of Hercules with the god of that river, was only meant a bank that was raifed to prevent its overflowing? That Hercules encountering the hydra of Lerna, fignified no more than a man's draining a marfhy country? or that Hercules feparating with his hands the two mountains Calpe and Abyla, when the ocean rufhed in with violence, and found a paffage into the Mediterranean, meant no more, perhaps, than that, in the time of one Hercules, the ocean, by the affiftance of an earthquake, broke a neck of land, and formed the ftraits of Gibraltar? Or that the fable of Pafiphæ contains nothing but an intrigue of the queen of Crete with a captain named Taurus?

Who could believe that Scylla and Charybdis were only two dangerous rocks near the ifland of Sicily, frequently fatal to mariners? That the frightful monfter which ravaged the plains of Troy, was the inundations of the fea; or that Hefione's being expofed to this monfter, meant no more than that fhe was to be given to him who put a ftop to thefe inundations?

Thus what Homer and Virgil afcribe to Minerva, is to be attributed to prudence and good conduct. It is no longer the exhalations that produce thunder, but Jupiter armed to affright mortals. If a mariner perceives a rifing ftorm, it is angry Neptune fwelling the waves. Echo ceafes to be a mere found, and becomes a nymph bewailing the lofs of her Narciffus.

Thus

(4) The laurel was called by the Greeks Daphne.

Thus by the cloud with which Minerva concealed Ulyffes, is meant the darknefs of the night, which fuffered him to enter the town of the Phœnicians without being difcovered; and when Priam is conducted by Mercury into the tent of Achilles, we are only to underftand, that he fet out to obtain Hector's body in the dark, with a prefent to appeafe his anger. If the delights of the country of the Lotophagi detain the companions of Ulyffes, we are told by Homer, that the fruits of that ifland made thofe who tafted them lofe all remembrance of their families, or their native country. This is an ingenious fiction intended to convey this important truth, that the love of pleafure debauches the mind, and banifhes from the heart every laudable affection. If they loiter at the court of Circe, and abandon themfelves to riot and debauchery, this pretended forcerefs, with great elegance and ftrength of expreffion, is faid to turn them into fwine.

If the poet, fays Lactantius, found it for his intereft to flatter or confole a prince for the lofs of his fon, it was but giving him a place amongft the ftars. Shepherds were all fatyrs or fauns; fhepherdreffes, nymphs or naiades; fhips, flying horfes; men on horfeback, centaurs; every lewd woman was a fyren or a harpy; oranges were apples of gold; and arrows and darts, lightning and bolts of thunder.

Rivers and fountains had their tutelary deities, and fometimes were reprefented as deities themfelves; the uniting their ftreams was called marriage, and brooks and canals were their children. If they would fpeak of the rainbow, that too muft be a goddefs dreffed in the richeft colours; and as they were at a lofs to account for the production of this phænomenon, it was called the daughter of Thaumas, a poetical perfonage, whofe name fignifies wonderful.

Sometimes a concern for the honour of the ladies became the fource of fables. If a princefs proved too frail to withftand the attempts of her lover; her flatterer, to fcreen her reputation, immediately called in the affiftance of fome enamoured god: this was eafily believed by the ignorant vulgar, for they could fuppofe none but a divine perfon could prefume to attempt one of her rank. Thus her reputation was unfullied, and, inftead of becoming infamous, fhe was honoured, and the hufband partook of her
glory

glory. Nor are the ftories of Rhea Sylvia (5), the mother of Rhemus and Romulus, and of Paulina (6), the only inftances to be found in hiftory of the credulity of hufbands and parents. From this fource and corruption of the priefts, were derived many of the fables relating to the amours of the gods.

At other times, the ftrangeft transformations fprung only from a fimilitude of names, and confifted in a play of words: the Cygnus was transformed into a fwan; Picus, into a woodpecker; Hicrafe, into a fpar-hawk; the Cecrops, into monkies; and Alopis, into a fox.

The ancient opinion, that the world was formed from Chaos, or a confufed concourfe of matter, which Hefiod calls the father of the gods, probably had its rife from a literal interpretation of the beginning of that fublime defcription, which Mofes gives us of the creation (7); where, before the formation of any part of the univerfe, it is faid, *The earth was without form, and void, and darknefs was upon the face of the deep;* as the latter part of the verfe, where the Spirit of God is reprefented as *moving or hovering over the waters*, might give the Egyptians, the Phœnicians, the Chaldeans, the Perfians, and the Indians, the idea which they mean to exprefs when they talk of the egg of the world.

L But

(5) Her uncle Amulius having found means to get into her apartments, Numitor, her father, fpread a report, that the twins of which fhe was delivered proceeded from the embraces of the god of war. Dion. de Halic. Ant. Rom. lib. I. Tit. Liv. liv. I.

(6) A young Roman knight, called Mundus, falling in love with Paulina, and finding all his endeavours to conquer her virtue prove fruitlefs, corrupted the priefts of Anubis, who perfuaded her to believe that the god was ftruck with her beauty, on which fhe was that very night led by her hufband to the temple. A few days after, feeing Mundus, whom fhe happened accidentally to meet, he let her into the fecret; Paulina, enraged and filled with indignation, carried her complaint before Tiberius, who ordered the ftatue of Anubis to be thrown into the Tiber, his priefts to be burnt alive, and Mundus to be fent into exile.

(7) Gen. i. 2.

But it was not sufficient for Hesiod to make a god of Chaos, to describe the order that sprang from this confusion; Chaos must have an offspring, and therefore, instead of saying like Moses, that darkness was upon the face of the deep, he says Chaos brought forth Gloominess and Night; and, to continue the genealogy, instead of saying with the inspired writer, *God divided the light from the darkness*, he expresses something like the same idea, by adding, that from Night sprang Air and Day. Moses says, *that God ordered the dry land to appear, and created the firmament which he called heaven:* Hesiod says, that the Earth begat Heaven, the high Mountains, and the Caves. He then informs us of the origin of the Ocean, who was the father of Springs and Rivers, of the birth of the Sun and Moon, and several other gods of the like kind.

It is very evident, that this whole account is nothing more than an allegorical history of the formation of all things, in which the various parts of nature are personated; but the hand of the great architect is wanting. Ovid treats this subject in a more intelligible manner, and with great beauty introduces the creator, whom he calls God, or Nature, forming the various parts with the utmost regularity and order. But in nothing does he come so near to Moses, as in the account he gives of the formation of man, which, as well as Moses, he makes the last work of the creation, and introduces Prometheus, or Council, forming him of clay, in the image of the gods.

A creature of a more exalted kind,
Was wanting yet, and then was man design'd;
Conscious of thought, of more capacious breast,
For empire form'd, and fit to rule the rest (8).

From this introduction it will not admit of a doubt, but that Ovid understood the story of Prometheus in the literal sense. And as to the circumstance which he omits, of his taking fire from heaven to animate the lumpish form; what is this, says a modern author, but *God's breathing into his nostrils the breath of life?*

And here it cannot be improper to mention a fable, which Plato puts into the mouth of Aristophanes(9):
" The

(8) Ovid, lib. 1.
(9) Plato in his Banquet

"The gods (says he) formed man at first of a round figure, with two bodies, two faces, four legs, four feet, and both sexes. These men were of such extraordinary strength, that they resolved to make war upon the gods: Jupiter, incensed at this enterprize, would have destroyed them as he had done the giants; but seeing that by this means he must have destroyed the whole human race, he contented himself with dividing them asunder; and, at the same time, ordered Apollo to stretch over the breast, and other parts of the body, the skin, as it is at present. These two parts of the body thus disjoined, want to be re-united; and this is the origin of love."

Ovid mentions only the formation of man, without taking the least notice of Eve, in which he evidently copies the account given us by Moses, who omits mentioning this in his general history of the creation. And the hint of this fable was probably taken from this circumstance, where the scripture says (1), *God created man*, and then adds, *male and female created he them;* and the circumstance of their being cut asunder, the closing up the flesh, and the reason given for conjugal love, from Eve's being made of a rib taken out of Adam's side, and his saying upon this, *She is bone of my bone, and flesh of my flesh; therefore shall a man leave his father and mother, and cleave unto his wife* (2).

Hence it seems at least probable, that the writings of Moses were not unknown to the Greeks, which makes it the more likely, that these writings, or a more ancient tradition, gave rise to the different representations the Pagans have given us of an original state of innocence, which was an object of faith amongst all civilized nations. This has been painted in the most beautiful colours, by the heathen poets, under the distinction of the golden age, or the reign of Saturn.

In several things, indeed, both Moses and the heathen philosophers agree: they equally assert, that man was created in a state of innocence, and consequently in a state of happiness, but that debasing his nature, and alienating himself from God, he became guilty,

(1) Gen. i. 27.
(2) Gen. ii. 21, 22, 23, 24.

guilty, subject to pain, diseases, and death, and to all those afflictions which are necessary to awaken his mind, and to call him to his duty; that we are strangers here, that this is a state of trial, and that it is as much our interest as duty to fit ourselves, by a course of virtue and piety, for a nobler and more exalted state of existence. The Egyptians (3) and Persians (4) had other schemes, wherein the same important truths were conveyed, tho' according to the genius of those countries, they were wrapped up in allegories. Plutarch has given us his sentiments on the same subject, and they are too just and rational to be omitted. "The world, at its birth, says he, "(5) received from its Creator all that is good; what"ever it has at present, that can be called wicked or "unhappy, is an indisposition foreign to its nature, "God cannot be the cause of evil, because he is "sovereignly good; matter cannot be the cause of "evil, because it has no active force; but evil comes "from a third principle, neither so perfect as God, "nor so imperfect as matter."

The notion of guardian angels has been contended for by many Christians, who alledge several passages of scripture that seem to favour this doctrine, while others have turned all that has been said of these genii into allegory; and assert, that by the two dœmons, the one good and the other bad, are meant the influences of conscience, and the strength of appetite.

It is very evident, however, that the Greeks had an idea of these beings, and that their existence was generally

(3) The Egyptians derive the source of natural and moral evil from a wicked spirit whom they call Typhon.

(4) The Persians deduce the origin of all the disorder and wickedness in the world from evil spirits, the chief of whom they call Ahrim or Arimanius. Light, say they, can produce nothing but light, and can never be the origin of evil; it produced several beings, all of them spiritual, luminous and powerful; but Arimanius, their chief, had an evil thought contrary to the light: he doubted, and by that doubting became dark; and from hence proceeded whatever is contrary to the light. They also tell us, that there will come a time when Arimanius shall be completely destroyed, when the earth will change its form, and when all mankind shall enjoy the same life, language and government. See Dr. Hyde's ancient religion of the Persians.

(5) Plutarch de Anim, form. p. 1015.

generally believed. Hence, according to Plutarch, came their fables of the Titans and Giants, and the engagements of Python againſt Apollo; which have ſo near a reſemblance to the fictions of Oſiris and Typhon. Theſe were beings ſuperior to men, and yet compoſed of a ſpiritual and corporeal nature; and conſequently capable of animal pleaſures and pains. The fictions relating to the giants, in Mr. Banier's opinion (6), took their riſe from a paſſage in Geneſis, where it is ſaid, that the (7) ſons of God, whom the ancients ſuppoſed to be guardian angels, became enamoured with the daughters of men, and that their children were mighty men, or giants, the word in the original ſignifying either giants, or men become monſtrous by their crimes; their heads inſtead of their guilt, were ſaid to reach to the clouds, while the wickedneſs of their lives might not improperly be termed fighting againſt God, and daring the thunder of heaven. But however this be, it will hardly be doubted but that this paſſage might give riſe to the amours of the gods and goddeſſes, and their various intrigues with mortals. As the frequent appearance of real angels to the patriarchs, and the hoſpitable reception they met with under the diſguiſe of travellers, might give room for the poets to form, upon the ſame plan, the tales of Baucis and Philemon, and to contraſt that beautiful picture of humble content, and of the peace that bleſſes the homely cottages of the innocent and good, with the ſtory of Lycaon; who wanting humanity, and being of a ſavage inhoſpitable temper, is, with great propriety, ſaid to change his form into one more ſuitable to the diſpoſition of his mind. The moral of this fable is, that humanity is the characteriſtic of man; and that a cruel ſoul in a human body is only a wolf in diſguiſe.

It is certain, that the traditions relating to the univerſal deluge, have been found in almoſt all nations; and though the deluge of Deucalion ſhould not appear to be the ſame as that of Noah, it cannot be doubted, but that ſome circumſtances have been
borrowed

(6) Banier, vol. I. 121, 122.
(7) Gen. vi. 2. By the ſons of God, is here undoubtedly meant the deſcendants of Seth, who had probably this title given them to diſtinguiſh them from the deſcendants of Cain, who were called the ſons of men.

borrowed from Noah's hiftory, and that thefe are the moft ftriking parts of the defcription. Lucian, fpeaking of the ancient people of Syria, the country where the deluge of Deucalion is fuppofed to have happened, fays (8) that " The Greeks affert in their " fables, that the firft men, being of an infolent and " cruel difpofition, inhuman, inhofpitable, and re- " gardlefs of their faith, were all deftroyed by a de- " luge; the earth (9) pouring forth vaft ftreams of " water, fwelled the rivers, which, together with " the rains, made the fea rife above its banks, and " overflow the land, fo that all was laid under water; " that Deucalion alone faved himfelf and family in " an ark, and two of each kind of wild and tame " animals, who, lofing their animofity, entered into " it of their own accord; that thus Deucalion floated " on the waters till they became affuaged, and then " repaired the human race."

We are alfo informed, that this veffel refted on a high mountain; and Plutarch even mentions the dove, and Abydenus fpeaks of a certain fowl being let out of the ark, which, finding no place of reft, returned twice into the veffel. We are told too, that Deucalion, a perfon of ftrict piety and virtue, offered facrifice to Jupiter, the faviour. Thus the facred writings inform us, that Noah offered facrifices of clean beafts, in token of gratitude to God, for having gracioufly preferved both him and his family.

Thus it appears, that idolatry and fables being once fet on foot, the people, who ftill retained con- fufed ideas of fome ancient truths, or the moft re- markable particulars of fome paft tranfactions, adapt- ed them to the prefent mode of thinking, or applied them to fuch fables as feemed to have any relation thereto. By this means truth and falfhood were blended together; and thus it happens, that we fre- quently find fome traces of hiftory intermingled with the moft ridiculous fictions, and remarkable tranfac- tions fometimes pretty exactly related, though at the fame time confounded with the groffeft abfurdities.

It is very evident, that the divifion of time into feven days, could only be a tradition conftantly pre- ferved,

(8) De Dea Syria.
(9) The fame thought is expreffed by Mofes, who fays, *The fountains of the great deep were broken up.*

ferved, and handed down from the moſt early ages. This appears to be the moſt ancient method of reckoning time, fince it was very early obſerved by the Egyptians. But of this we have ſaid enough in the preceding differtation, to which it properly belongs.

It appears from the account we have given of the theology of the ancients, that the Egyptians, Greeks, and Romans worſhipped only one Almighty, independent Being, the Father of gods and men, with a fupreme adoration; and that the ſeveral ſuperior deities publickly worſhipped, were only different names or attributes of the fame Gods. This is afferted not only by ſeveral of the Pagans, but even by St. Auſtin. Whether this diſtinction was maintained by the bulk of the people amongſt the Greeks and Romans, is not fo eafy to determine; it is probable, that they might imagine them diſtinct beings, ſubordinate to the ſupreme. However, there were others univerfally allowed to be of an inferior claſs, and thefe were the national and tutelary deities; among which laſt number we may reckon the good dæmons, or houſhold gods, which the Romans, upon conquering any nation or city, invited to take up their refidence amongſt them. Theſe were undoubtedly worſhipped with an inferior kind of adoration. Since the Stoic and Epicurean philofophers, who allowed their exiſtence, believed them to be mortal, and that they were to periſh in the general conflagration, in which they imagined the world was to be deſtroyed by fire. To this Pliny alludes, when deſcribing the darkneſs and horror that attended the eruption of Veſuvius, he fays, that ſome were lifting up their hands to the gods; but that the greater part imagined, that the laſt and eternal night was come, which was to deſtroy both the gods and the world together.

This diſtinction may be juſtified by the united teſtimony of the ancients; and indeed it in a great meaſure removes the abſurdity of the continually introducing what were called new gods; that is new mediators, and new methods or ceremonials to be added, on particular occaſions, to the ancient worſhip.

The idolatry of the Pagans, did not confiſt in paying a direct adoration to the ſtatues, but in making them

them the (1) medium of worſhip; and therefore, whether the ſeveral deities were reckoned to be inferior beings, or only different names or attributes of one ſupreme; yet their ſymbols, the ſun, moon, and ſtars, or the ſtatues erected to the honour of their gods, were never (except amongſt the loweſt and moſt ignorant of people) acknowledged as the ultimate objects of worſhip. In theſe ſtatues, however, the deity was ſuppoſed to reſide in a peculiar manner.

But even this was not always the caſe; it is very evident, that the ſtatues erected to the paſſions, the virtues, and the vices, were not of this claſs. The Romans had particular places for offering up particular petitions; they offered up their prayers for health in the temple of Sallus; they prayed for the preſervation of their liberties before the ſtatue of Liberty, and offered their ſacrifices to the Supreme before a figure expreſſive of their wants. Fever, in the opinion of the moſt ſtupid of the vulgar, could never be conſidered as a god, yet at the altar of Fever they beſought the Supreme to preſerve them from being infected with this diſorder, or to cure their friends who were already infected by it: and at the altar of Fear,

(1) The folly of repreſenting the infinite and omnipreſent ſpirit, by a ſenſible image, is obvious from a very ſmall degree of reflection; and from hence ariſes the crime of idolatry, or repreſenting him by the works of nature, or thoſe of men's hands, as it is a degradation of the deity, and an affront to the Being, whoſe glorious eſſence is unlimited and unconfined; from hence proceeds that exclamation of the prophet, *Whereunto ſhall you* LIKEN *me, ſaith the Lord,* &c.

When the Iſraelites made the golden calf, and cried out, *This is the God that brought us out of the land of* Egypt, they muſt be ſuppoſed to mean, *This repreſents the God that brought us out of the land of* Egypt. They had lately left a country fond of ſymbols, where they had been uſed to ſee one thing repreſented by another; and the ſun, the moſt glorious image of the deity, when he enters into Taurus, repreſented by a bull. Had they been ſo ſtupid as to imagine this calf, which they had juſt made, to be the god of their fathers; the god that had wrought ſo many miracles for them, even before they had given him exiſtence; their folly would be entirely inconſiſtent with the rational nature of man, and they muſt have been abſolutely incapable both of moral and civil government, and could only be accounted idiots or madmen.

Fear, they put up their supplications, that they might be preserved from the influence of a shameful pannic in the day of battle.

As this appears evidently to be the case, it is no wonder that the number of these kind of gods became very great. Some of these, by the parade of ceremonies that attended this method of devotion, were found to have a mighty effect on the minds of the vulgar: So that when any virtue began to lose ground, a temple, or, at least, an altar erected to its honour, was sure to raise it from its declining state, and to reinstate its influence on the heart of man.

This appears to be a true representation of the case, from the account which Dionysius of Halicarnassus gives (2) of the reasons which induced Numa Pompilius to introduce Faith into the number of the Roman divinities, and which, doubtless, gave rise to all the other deities of the same kind, that were afterwards introduced. "To engage his people to
" mutual faith and fidelity, says he, Numa had re-
" course to a method hitherto unknown to the most
" celebrated legislators; public contracts, he observ-
" ed, were seldom violated, from the regard paid to
" those who were witnesses to any engagement, while
" those made in private, though in their own nature
" no less indispensible than the other, were not so
" strictly observed; whence he concluded, that by
" deifying Faith, these contracts would be still more
" binding: besides, he thought it unreasonable, that
" while divine honours were paid to Justice, Nemesis
" and Themis, Faith, the most sacred and venerable
" thing in the world, should receive neither public
" nor private honour; he therefore built a temple to
" public Faith, and instituted sacrifices, the charge
" of which was defrayed by the public. This he did
" with the hope, that a veneration for this virtue
" being propagated through the city, would insensi-
" bly be communicated to each individual. His
" conjectures proved true, and Faith became so
" revered, that she had more force than even wit-
" nesses and oaths; so that it was the common me-
" thod, in cases of intricacy, for magistrates to re-
" fer the decision to the faith of the contending
" parties."

Thus

(2) Dion. Halic. l. 2. c. 75.

Thus it appears evident, that these kind of gods, and the temples erected to their honour, were founded not only on political, but on virtuous principles. This was undoubtedly the case, with respect to the Greeks as well as the Romans; for a proposal being made at Athens, to introduce the combats of the gladiators; first throw down, cried out an Athenian philosopher from the midst of the assembly, throw down the altar, erected by our ancestors above a thousand years ago to Mercy. Was not this to say, that they had no need of an altar to inspire a regard to mercy and compassion, when they wanted public spectacles to teach a savage cruelty and hardness of heart.

APPENDIX.

APPENDIX.

CONTAINING

An Account of the various Methods of Divination by Astrology, Prodigies, Magic, Augury, the Auspices and Oracles; with a short Account of Altars, sacred Groves and Sacrifices, Priests and Temples.

I. OF ASTROLOGY.

ASTROLOGY was doubtless the first method of divination, and probably prepared the mind of man for the other, no less absurd, ways of searching into futurity; and therefore a short view of the rise of this pretended science cannot be improper in this place, especially as the history of these absurdities is the best method of confuting them. And indeed, as this treatise is chiefly designed for the improvement of youth, nothing can be of greater service to them than to render them able to trace the origin of those pretended sciences, some of which have even still an influence on many weak and ignorant minds. But to proceed,

The Egyptians becoming ignorant of the astronomical hieroglyphics, by degrees, looked upon the names of the signs, as expressing certain powers with which they were invested, and as indications of their several offices. The Sun, on account of its splendor and enlivening influence, was imagined to be the great mover of nature; the Moon had the second rank of powers, and each sign and constellation a certain share in the government of the world; the Ram had a strong influence over the young of the flocks and herds; the Ballance could inspire nothing but inclinations to good order and justice; and the Scorpion excite only evil dispositions; and, in short, that each sign produced the good or evil intimated by its name. Thus, if the child happened to be born at the instant when the first star of the Ram rose above the Horizon, (when, in order to give this nonsense the air of a science, the star was supposed to have

have its greatest influence) he would be rich in cattle; and that he who should enter the world under the Crab, should meet with nothing but disappointment, and all his affairs should go backwards and downwards. The people were to be happy whose king entered the world under the sign of Libra; but completely wretched if he should light under the horrid sign Scorpion: the persons born under Capricorn, especially if the Sun at the same time ascended the Horizon, were sure to meet with success, and to rise upwards like the Wild Goat, and the Sun which then ascends for six months together; the Lion was to produce heroes; and the Virgin with her ear of corn to inspire chastity, and to unite virtue and abundance. Could any thing be more extravagant and ridiculous! " This way of arguing," says an ingenious modern author, " is nearly like that of a man, who should " imagine, that, in order to have good wine in his " cellar, he need do no more than hang a good cork " at the door."

The case was exactly the same with respect to the planets, whose influence is only founded on the wild supposition of their being the habitation of the pretended deities, whose names they bear, and the fabulous characters the poets have given them.

Thus to Saturn they gave languid and even destructive influences, for no other reason, but because they had been pleased to make this planet the residence of Saturn, who was painted with grey hairs and a scythe.

To Jupiter they gave the power of bestowing crowns, and distributing long life, wealth and grandeur, merely because it bears the name of the father of life.

Mars was supposed to inspire a strong inclination for war, because it was believed to be the residence of the God of war.

Venus had the power of rendering men voluptuous and fond of pleasure, because, they had been pleased to give it the name of one, who, by some, was thought to be the mother of pleasure.

Mercury, though almost always invisible, would never have been thought to superintend the prosperity of states, and the affairs of wit and commerce, had not men, without the least reason, given it the name of one who was supposed to be the inventor of civil polity.

According

According to the astrologers, the power of the ascending planet is greatly increased by that of an ascending sign; then the benign influences are all united, and fall together on the heads of all the happy infants which at that moment enter the world (1); yet can any thing be more contrary to experience, which shews us, that the characters and events, produced by persons born under the same aspect of the stars, are so far from being alike, that they are directly opposite.

Thus it is evident, that astrology is built upon no principles, that it is founded on fables, and on influences void of reality. Yet absurd as it is, and ever was, it obtained credit, and the more it spread, the greater injury was done to the cause of virtue. Instead of the exercise of prudence and wise precaution, it substituted superstitious forms and childish practices, it enervated the courage of the brave by apprehensions grounded on puns and quibbles, and encouraged the wicked by making them lay to the charge of a planet those evils which only proceeded from their own depravity.

But not content with these absurdities, which destroyed the very idea of liberty, they asserted that these

---

(1) " What completes the ridicule, says the Abbe la
" Pluche, to whom we are obliged for these judicious ob-
" servations, is, that what astronomers call the first degree
" of the Ram, of the Balance, or of Sagitarius, is no longer
" the first sign, which give fruitfulness to the flocks, inspires
" men with a love of justice, or forms the hero. It has
" been found that all the celestial signs have, by little receded
" from the vernal Equinox, and drawn back to the east:
" notwithstanding this, the point of the zodiac that cuts the
" equator is still called the first degree of the Ram, though
" the first star of the Ram be thirty degrees beyond it, and
" all the other signs in the same proportion. When there-
' fore any one is said to be born under the first degree of
" the Ram, it was in reality one of the degrees of Pisces
" that then came above the horizon; and when another is
" said to be born with a royal soul, and heroic disposition,
" because at his birth the planet Jupiter ascended the horizon,
" in conjunction with the first star of Sagittary; Jupiter was
" indeed at that time in conjunction with a star thirty degrees
" eastward of Sagittary, and in good truth it was the perni-
" cious Scorpion that presided at the birth of this happy, this
" incomparable child." Abbe Pluche's History of the Heavens, Vol. I. p. 255.

these stars, which had not the least connection with mankind, governed all the parts of the human body (2), and ridiculously affirmed, that the Ram presided over the head; the Bull over the gullet; the Twins over the breast; the Scorpion over the entrails; the Fishes over the feet, &c. By this means they pretended to account for the various disorders of the body; which was supposed to be in a good or bad disposition, according to the different aspects of the signs. To mention only one instance; they pretended that great caution ought to be used in taking a medicine under Taurus, or the bull, because as this animal chews his cud, the person would not be able to keep it in his stomach.

Nay, the influences of the planets were extended to the bowels of the earth, where they were supposed to produce metals. From hence it appears, that when superstition and folly are once on foot, there is no setting bounds to their progress. Gold, to be sure, must be the production of the Sun, and the conformity in point of colour, brightness, and value, was a sensible proof of it. By the same way of reasoning, the Moon produced all the silver to which it was related by colour; Mars all the iron, which ought to be the favourite metal of the God of War; Venus presided over copper, which she might well be supposed to produce, since it was found in plenty in the isle of Cyprus, which was supposed to be the favourite residence of this goddess. By the same fine way of reasoning, the other planets presided over the other metals. The languid Saturn was set over mines of lead;

(2) Each hour of the day had also one; the number seven, as being that of the planets, became of mighty consequence. The seven days in the week, a period of time handed down by tradition, happened to correspond with the number of the planets; and therefore they gave the name of a planet to each day; and from thence some days in the week were considered as more fortunate or unlucky than the rest: and hence seven times seven, called the climacterical period of hours, days or years, were thought extremely dangerous, and to have a surprizing effect on private persons, the fortune of princes, and the government of states. Thus the mind of man became distressed by imaginary evils, and the approach of these moments, in themselves as harmless as the rest of their lives, has, by the strength of imagination, brought on the most fatal effects.

lead; and Mercury, on account of his activity, had the superintendancy of quicksilver; while it was the province of Jupiter to preside over tin, as this was the only metal that was left him.

From hence the metals obtained the names of the planets; and from this opinion, that each planet engendered its own peculiar metal, they at length conceived an opinion, that as one planet was more powerful than another, the metal produced by the weakest was converted into another by the influence of a stronger planet. Lead, though a real metal, and as perfect in its kind as any of the rest, was considered as only a half metal, which, through the languid influences of old Saturn, was left imperfect; and therefore, under the aspect of Jupiter, it was converted into tin; under that of Venus, into copper; and at last into gold, under some particular aspects of the Sun. And from hence, at last arose the extravagant opinions of the alchymists, who, with wonderful sagacity, endeavoured to find out means for hastening these changes or transmutations, which, as they conceived, the planets performed too slowly; but, at last, the world was convinced that the art of the alchymist was as ineffectual as the influences of the planets, which, in a long succession of ages, had never been known to change a mine of lead to that of tin, or any other metal.

II. OF PRODIGIES.

WHOEVER reads the Roman historians (3), must be surprised at the number of prodigies which are constantly recorded, and which frequently filled the people with the most dreadful apprehensions. It must be confessed, that some of these seem altogether supernatural; while much the greater part only consist of some of the uncommon productions of nature, which superstition always attributed to a superior cause, and represented as the prognostication of some impending misfortunes.

Of this class may be reckoned the appearance of two suns, the nights illuminated by rays of light, the views

(3) Particularly Livy, Dionysius of Halicarnassus, Pliny, and Valerius Maximus.

views of fighting armies, swords and spears darting through the air; showers of milk, of blood, of stones, of ashes, or of fire; and the birth of monsters, of children, or of beasts who had two heads, or of infants who had some feature resembling those of the brute creation. These were all dreadful prodigies, which filled the people with inexpressible astonishment, and the whole Roman empire with an extreme perplexity; and whatever unhappy event followed upon these, was sure to be either caused or predicted by them.

Yet nothing is more easy than to account for these productions; which have no relation to any events that may happen to follow them. The appearance of two suns has frequently happened in England, as well as in other places, and is only caused by the clouds being placed in such a situation, as to reflect the image of that luminary; nocturnal fires, inflamed spears, fighting armies, were no more than what we call the aurora borealis, northern lights, or inflamed vapours floating in the air: showers of stones, of ashes, or of fire, were no other than the effects of the eruptions of some volcano at a considerable distance; showers of milk were only caused by some quality in the air condensing, and giving a whitish colour to the water; and those of blood are now well known to be only the red spots left upon the earth, on stones and the leaves of trees, by the butterflies which hatch in hot or stormy weather (4).

III. OF MAGIC.

MAGIC, or the pretended art of producing, by the assistance of words and ceremonies, such events as are above the natural power of man, was of several kinds, and chiefly consisted in invoking the good and benevolent, or the wicked and mischievous spirits. The first, which was called Theurgia, was adopted by the wisest of the Pagan world, who esteemed this as much as they despised the latter, which they called Goetia. Theurgia was, by the philosophers, accounted

(4) This has been fully proved by M. Reymur, in his history of insects.

counted a divine art, which only served to raise the mind to higher perfection, and to exalt the soul to a greater degree of purity; and they, who by means of this kind of magic, were imagined to arrive at what was called intuition, wherein they enjoyed an intimate intercourse with the deity, were believed to be invested with their powers; so that it was imagined, that nothing was impossible for them to perform.

All who made profession of this kind of magic aspired to this state of perfection. The priest, who was of this order, was to be a man of unblemished morals, and all who joined with him were bound to a strict purity of life; they were to abstain from women, and from animal food; and were forbid to defile themselves by the touch of a dead body. Nothing was to be forgot in their rites and ceremonies; the least omission or mistake, rendered all their art ineffectual; so that this was a constant excuse for their not performing all that was required of them, though as their sole employment (after having arrived to a certain degree of perfection, by fasting, prayer, and the other methods of purification) was the study of universal nature; they might gain such an insight into physical causes, as might enable them to perform actions, that might fill the ignorant vulgar with amazement. And it is hardly to be doubted, but that this was all the knowledge that many of them ever aspired after. In this sort of magic, Hermes, Trismegistus and Zoroaster excelled; and indeed it gained great reputation amongst the Egyptians, Chaldeans, Persians, and Indians. In times of ignorance, a piece of clock-work, or some curious machine, was sufficient to entitle the inventor to the works of magic; and some have even asserted, that the Egyptian magic, that has been rendered so famous by the writings of the ancients, consisted only in discoveries drawn from the mathematics and natural philosophy, since those Greek philosophers who travelled into Egypt in order to obtain a knowledge of their sciences, returned with only a knowledge of nature and religion, and some rational ideas of their ancient symbols.

But it can hardly be doubted, but that magic in its grossest and most ridiculous sense was practised in Egypt, at least amongst some of the vulgar, long before Pythagoras or Empedocles travelled into that country.

The

The Egyptians had been very early accustomed to vary the signification of their symbols, by adding to them several plants, ears of corn, or blades of grass, to express the different employments of husbandry; but understanding no longer their meaning, nor the words that had been made use of on these occasions, which were equally unintelligible, the vulgar might mistake these for so many mysterious practices observed by their fathers; and hence they might conceive the notion, that a conjunction of plants, even without being made use of as a remedy, might be of efficacy to preserve or procure health. " Of these, says the " Abbe Pluche, they made a collection, as an art by " which they pretended to procure the blessings, and " provide against the evils of life." By the assistance of these, men even attempted to hurt their enemies, and indeed the knowledge of poisonous or useful simples might, on particular occasions, give sufficient weight to their empty curses or invocations. But these magic incantations, so contrary to humanity, were detested and punished by almost all nations, nor could they be tolerated in any.

Pliny, after mentioning an herb, the throwing of which into an army, it was said, was sufficient to put it to the rout, asks, where was this herb when Rome was so distressed by the Cimbri and Teutones? Why did not the Persians make use of it when Lucullus cut their troops in pieces?

But amongst all the incantations of magic, the most solemn, as well as the most frequent, was that of calling up the spirits of the dead; this indeed was the quintessence of their art; and the reader cannot be displeased to find this mystery unravelled.

An affection for the body of a person, who in his life-time was beloved, induced the first nations to inter the dead in a decent manner; and to add to this melancholy instance of their esteem, those wishes which had a particular regard to their new state of existence, the place of burial, conformable to the custom of characterizing all beloved places, or those distinguished by a memorable event, was pointed out by a large stone or pillar raised upon it. To this place families, and when the concern was general, multitudes repaired every year, where, upon this stone, were made libations of wine, oil, honey, and flour; and here they sacrificed and eat in common,

having

having firſt made a trench, in which they burnt the entrails of the victim, and into which the libation and the blood was made to flow. They began with thanking God for having given them life, and providing their neceſſary food; and then praiſed him for the good examples they had been favoured with. From theſe melancholy rites were baniſhed all licentiouſneſs and levity; and while other cuſtoms changed, theſe continued the ſame. They roaſted the fleſh of the victim they had offered, and eat it in common, diſcourſing on the virtues of him they came to lament.

All other feaſts were diſtinguiſhed by names ſuitable to the ceremonies that attended them. Theſe funeral meetings were ſimply called the Manes, that is, the aſſembly. Thus the manes and the dead were words that became ſynonymous. In theſe meetings, they imagined that they renewed their alliance with the deceaſed, who, they ſuppoſed, had ſtill a regard for the concerns of their country and family, and who, as affectionate ſpirits, could do no leſs than inform them of whatever was neceſſary for them to know. Thus the funerals of the dead were at laſt converted into methods of divination, and an innocent inſtitution into one of the groſſeſt pieces of folly and ſuperſtition.

But they did not ſtop here; they grew ſo extravagantly credulous, as to believe that the phantom drank the libations that had been poured forth, while the relations were feaſting on the reſt of the ſacrifice round the pit; and from hence became apprehenſive leſt the reſt of the dead ſhould promiſcuouſly throng about this ſpot to get a ſhare in the repaſt they were ſuppoſed to be ſo fond of, and leave nothing for the dear ſpirit for whom the feaſt was intended. They then made two pits or ditches, into one of which they put wine, honey, water, and flour, to employ the generality of the dead; and in the other they poured the blood of the victim; when ſitting down on the brink, they kept off, by the ſight of their ſwords, the crowd of dead who had no concern in their affairs, while they called him by name, whom they had a mind to chear and conſult, and deſired him to draw near (5).

The

(5) Homer gives the ſame account of theſe ceremonies, when Ulyſſes raiſes the ſoul of Tireſias; and the ſame uſages are found in the poem of Silius Italicus. And to theſe ceremonies the ſcriptures frequently allude, when the Iſraelites are forbid to aſſemble upon high places.

The questions made by the living were very intelligible; but the answers of the dead were not so easily understood, and therefore the priests and magicians made it their business to explain them. They retired into deep caves, where the darkness and silence resembled the state of death, and there fasted and lay upon the skins of the beasts they had sacrificed, and then gave for answer the dream which most affected them; or opened certain books appointed for that purpose, and gave the first sentence that offered. At other times the priest, or any person who came to consult, took care, at his going out of the cave, to listen to the first words he should hear, and these were to be his answer. And though they had no relation to the business in hand, they were turned so many ways, and their sense so violently wrested, that they made them signify almost any thing they pleased. At other times they had recourse to a number of tickets, on which were some words or verses, and these being thrown into an urn, the first that was taken out was delivered to the family.

IV. OF AUGURY.

THE superstitious fondness of mankind, for searching into futurity, has given rise to a vast variety of follies, all equally weak and extravagant. The Romans, in particular, found out almost innumerable ways of divination, all nature had a voice, and the most senseless beings, and most trifling accidents, became presages of future events. This introduced ceremonies, founded on a mistaken knowledge of antiquity, that were the most childish and ridiculous, and which yet were performed with an air of solemnity.

Birds, on account of their swiftness in flying, were sometimes considered by the Egyptians as the symbols of the winds; and figures of particular species of fowl, were set up to denote the time when the near approach of a periodical wind was expected. From hence, before they undertook any thing of consequence, as sowing, planting, or putting out to sea, it was usual for them to say (6), *Let us consult the birds*, meaning

(6) Abbé Pluche's History of the Heavens, vol. I. p. 241.

meaning the signs fixed up to give them the necessary informations they then stood in need of. By doing this, they knew how to regulate their conduct; and it frequently happened, that when this precaution was omitted, they had reason to reproach themselves for their neglect. From hence, mankind mistaking their meaning, and retaining the phrase, *Let us consult the birds,* and perhaps hearing old stories repeated of the advantages such and such persons had received, by consulting them in a critical moment, when the periodical wind would have ruined their affairs, they began to conceive an opinion, that the fowls which skim through the air were so many messengers sent from the gods, to inform them of future events, and to warn them against any disasterous undertaking. From hence they took notice of their flight, and from their different manner of flying prognosticated good or bad omens. The birds were instantly grown wonderous wise, and an owl, who hates the light, could not pass by the window of a sick person in the night, where he was offended by the light of a lamp or a candle, but his hooting must be considered as prophesying, that the life of the poor man was nearly at an end.

The place where these auguries were taken, amongst the Romans, was commonly upon an eminence; they were prohibited after the month of August, because that was the time for the moulting of birds; nor were they permitted on the wane of the moon, nor at any time in the afternoon, or when the air was the least disturbed by winds or clouds.

When all the previous ceremonies were performed, the augur, cloathed in his robe, and holding his augural staff in his right-hand, sat down at the door of his tent, looked round him, then marked out the divisions of the heavens with his staff, drew a line from east to west, and another from north to south, and then offered up his sacrifice. A short prayer, the form of which may be sufficiently seen, in that offered to Jupiter, at the election of Numa Pompilius, which was as follows: " O father Jupiter, if it by they will, " that this Numa Pompilius, on whose head I have " laid my hand, should be king of Rome, grant that " there be clear and unerring signs, within the bounds " I have described." The prayer being thus ended, the priest turned to the right and left, and to whatever

ever point the birds directed their flight, in order to determine from thence, whether the god approved or rejected the choice.

The veneration which the Romans entertained for this ceremonial of their religion, made them attend the result of the augury with the most profound silence, and the affair was no sooner determined, than the augur reported his decision, by saying, *The birds approve,* or *the birds disapprove it.* However, notwithstanding the augury might be favourable, the enterprise was sometimes deferred, till they fancied it confirmed by a new sign.

But of all the signs which happened in the air, the most infallible was that of thunder and lightning, especially if it happened to be fair weather. If it came on the right-hand it was a bad omen, but if on the left a good one; because, according to Donatus, all appearances on that side were supposed to proceed from the right hand of the gods.

Let us now take a view of the sacred chickens; for an examination into the manner of their taking the corn that was offered them, was the most common method of taking the augury. And indeed the Romans had such faith in the mysteries contained in their manner of feeding, that they hardly ever undertook any important affair without first advising with them. Generals sent for them to the field, and consulted them before they ventured to engage the enemy; and if the omen was unfavourable, they immediately desisted from their enterprize. The sacred chickens were kept in a coop or pen, and entrusted to the care of a person, who, on account of his office, was called Pullarius. The augur, after having commanded silence, ordered the pen to be opened, and threw upon the ground a handful of corn. If the chickens instantly leaped out of the pen, and pecked up the corn with such eagerness as to let some of it fall from their beaks, the augury was called Tripudium, or Tripudium Solistimum, from its striking the earth, and was esteemed a most auspicious omen; but if they did not immediately run to the corn, if they flew away, if they walked by it without minding it, or if they scattered it abroad with their wings, it portended danger and ill success. Thus the fate of the greatest undertaking, and even the fall of cities and kingdoms, was thought to depend on the appetite of a few chickens.

Observations

Obfervations were alfo taken from the chattering, finging, or hooting of crows, pies, owls, &c. and from the running of beafts, as heifers, affes, rams, hares, wolves, foxes, weefels, and mice, when they appeared in uncommon places, croffed the way, or run to the right or left, &c. They alfo pretended to draw a good or bad omen from the moft common and trifling actions or occurrences of life, as fneezing, ftumbling, ftarting, the numbnefs of the little finger, the tingling of the ear, the fpilling of falt upon the table, or wine upon one's cloaths, the accidental meeting of a bitch with whelp, &c. It was alfo the bufinefs of the augur to interpret dreams, oracles, and prodigies.

The college of augurs, at firft inftituted at Rome by Romulus, was only compofed of three perfons, taken from the three tribes, into which all the inhabitants of the city were divided; but feveral others were afterwards added, and at laft, according to a regulation of Scylla, this college confifted of fifteen perfons, all of the firft diftinction, the eldeft of whom was called the mafter of the college: "It was a "priefthood for life, of a character indelible, which "no crime or forfeiture could efface; it was necef- "fary that every candidate fhould be nominated to "the people by two augurs, who gave a folemn tef- "timony upon oath, of his dignity and fitnefs for "that office (7)." The greateft precautions were indeed taken in this election; for as they were invefted with fuch extraordinary privileges, none were qualified but perfons of a blamelefs life, and free from all perfonal defects. The fenate could affemble in no place but what they had confecrated. They frequently occafioned the difplacing of magiftrates, and the deferring of public affemblies. "But the fenate, "at laft, confidering that fuch an unlimited power "was capable of authorifing a number of abufes, "decreed that they fhould not have it in their power "to adjourn any affembly that had been legally con- "vened (8)."

Nothing can be more aftonifhing, than to find fo wife a people as the Romans addicted to fuch childifh fooleries. Scipio, Auguftus, and many others, have, without any fatal confequences, defpifed the chickens
and

(7) Middleton's Life of Cicero.
(8) Banier's Mythology, vol. I. p. 400.

and the other arts of divination; but when the generals miscarried in any enterprize, the people laid the whole blame on the heedlessness with which they had been consulted; and if he had entirely neglected consulting them, all the blame was thrown upon him who had preferred his own forecast to that of the fowls; while those who made these kinds of predictions a subject of raillery, were accounted impious and prophane. Thus they construed, as a punishment from the gods, the defeat of Claudius Pulcher, who, when the sacred chickens refused to eat what was set before them, ordered them to be thrown into the sea: *If they won't eat,* said he, *they shall drink.*

V. OF THE AUSPICES.

IN the most early ages of the world, a sense of piety, and a regard to decency, had introduced a custom of never sacrificing to him, who gave them all their blessings, any but the soundest, the most fat and beautiful victims. They were examined with the closest and most exact attention. This ceremonial, which doubtless sprang at first from gratitude, and some natural ideas of fitness and propriety, at last degenerated into trifling niceties and superstitious ceremonies. And it having been once imagined, that nothing was to be expected from the gods, when the victim was imperfect, the idea of perfection was united with abundance of trivial circumstances. The entrails were examined with peculiar care, and if the whole was without blemish, their duties were fulfilled; and under an assurance that they had engaged the gods to be on their side, they engaged in war, and in the most hazardous undertakings, with such a confidence of success, as had the greatest tendency to procure it.

All the motions of the victim that was led to the altar became so many prophecies. If he advanced with an easy air in a straight line, and without offering resistance; if he made no extraordinary bellowing when he received the blow; if he did not get loose from the person that led him to the slaughter, it was a prognostic of an easy and flowing success.

The victim was knocked down, but before its belly was ripped open, one of the lobes of the liver was allotted to thofe who offered the facrifice, and the other to the enemies of the ftate. That which was neither blemifhed nor withered, of a bright red, and neither larger nor fmaller than it ought to be, prognofticated great profperity to thofe for whom it was fet apart; that which was livid, fmall, or corrupted, prefaged the moft fatal mifchiefs.

The next thing to be confidered was the heart, which was alfo examined with the utmoft care, as was the fpleen, the gall, and the lungs; and if any of thefe were let fall, if they fmelt rank, or were bloated, livid or withered, it prefaged nothing but misfortunes.

After they had finifhed their examination of the entrails, the fire was kindled, and from this alfo they drew feveral prefages. If the flame was clear, if it mounted up without dividing, and went not out till the victim was entirely confumed, this was a proof that the facrifice was accepted; but if they found it difficult to kindle the fire, if the flame divided, if it played around, inftead of taking hold of the victim, if it burnt ill, or went out, it was a bad omen.

At Rome, the aufpices were always chofen from the beft families, and as their employment was of the fame nature as the augurs, they were as much honoured. It was a very common thing indeed to fee their predictions verified by the event, efpecially in their wars; nor is this at all wonderful, the prediction never lulled them into fecurity, or prevented their taking every neceffary precaution; but, on the contrary, the affurance of victory infpired that intrepidity and high courage, which in the common foldiers was the principal thing neceffary to the attainment of it. But, if, after the appearance of a complete favour from the gods, whom they had addreffed, their affairs happened to mifcarry, the blame was laid on fome other deity. Juno or Minerva had been neglected. They facrificed to them, recovered their fpirits, and behaved with greater precaution.

However, the bufinefs of the aufpices was not reftrained to the altars and facrifices, they had an equal right to explain all other portents. The fenate frequently confulted them on the moft extraordinary prodigies.

" The

"The college of the auspices (9), as well as those of the other religious orders, had their particular registers and records, such as the memorials of thunder and lightning, the (1) Tuscan histories, &c."

VI. OF ORACLES.

OF all the nations upon earth, Greece was the most famous for oracles, and some of their wisest men have endeavoured to vindicate them upon solid principles, and refined reasonings. Xenophon expatiates on the necessity of consulting the gods by augurs and oracles. He represents man as naturally ignorant of what is advantageous or destructive to himself; that he is so far from being able to penetrate into the future, that the present itself escapes him; that his designs may be frustrated by the slightest objects; that the deity alone, to whom all ages are present, can impart to him the infallible knowledge of futurity; that no other being can give success to his enterprizes, and that it is highly reasonable to believe that he will guide and protect those who adore him with a pure affection, who call upon him, and consult him with a sincere and humble resignation. How surprising it is that such refined and noble principles should be brought to defend the most puerile and absurd opinions! For what arguments can vindicate

(9) Kennet's Roman Antiq. lib. II. c. 4.
(1) Romulus, who founded the institution of the auspices, borrowed it from the Tuscans, to whom the senate afterwards sent twelve of the sons of the principal nobility to be instructed in these mysteries, and the other ceremonies of their religion. The origin of this art amongst the people of Tuscany, is related by Cicero, in the following manner: "A peasant (says he) ploughing in the field, his ploughshare running pretty deep in the earth, turned up a clod, from whence sprung a child, who taught him and the other Tuscans the art of divination." See Cicero de Div. l. 2. This fable undoubtedly means no more, than that this child, said to spring from a clod of earth, was a youth of a very mean and obscure birth, and that from him the Tuscans learnt this method of divination. But it is not known whether he was the author of it, or whether he learnt it of the Greeks or other nations.

vindicate their presuming to interrogate the most High, and oblige him to give answers concerning every idle imagination and unjust enterprize?

Oracles were thought by the Greeks to proceed in a more immediate manner from God than the other arts of divination; and on this account scarce any peace was concluded, any war engaged in, any new laws enacted, or any new form of government instituted without consulting oracles. And therefore Minos, to give his laws a proper weight with the people, ascribed to them a divine sanction, and pretended to receive from Jupiter instructions how to new model his government. And Lycurgus made frequent visits to the Delphian oracle, that the people might entertain a belief, that he received from Apollo the platform which he afterwards communicated to the Spartans. These pious frauds were an effectual means of establishing the authority of laws, and engaging the people to a compliance with the will of the law-giver. Persons thus inspired were frequently thought worthy of the highest trust; so that they were sometimes advanced to regal power, from persuasion, "that as they were admitted to the coun-"sels of the gods, they were best able to provide for "the safety and welfare of man (2)."

This high veneration for the priests of the oracles, being the strongest confirmation, that their credit was thoroughly established, they suffered none to consult the gods but those who brought sacrifices and rich presents to them; whence few, besides the great, were admitted. This proceeding served at once to enrich the priests, and to raise the character of the oracles amongst the populace, who are always apt to despise what they are too familiarly acquainted with; nor were the rich, or even the greatest prince admitted, except at those particular times when the god was in a disposition to be consulted.

One of the most ancient oracles, of which we have received any particular account, was that of Jupiter at Dodona, a city said to be built by Deucalion, after that famous deluge which bears his name, and which destroyed the greatest part of Greece. It was situated in Epirus, and here was the first temple that ever was seen in Greece. According to Herodotus, both this and the oracle of Jupiter Hammon had the same

(2) Potter's Antiquities of Greece, vol. I. p. 263.

same original, and both owed their inftitution to the Egyptians. The rife of this oracle is indeed wrapped up in fable. Two black pigeons, fay they, flying from Thebes, in Egypt, one of them fettled in Lybia, and the other flew as far as the foreft of Dodona, a province in Epirus, where fitting in an oak, fhe informed the inhabitants of the country, that it was the will of Jupiter that an oracle fhould be founded in that place. Herodotus gives two accounts of the rife of this oracle, one of which clears up the myftery of this fable. He tells us, that he was informed by the priefts of Jupiter, at Thebes, in Egypt, that fome Phœnician merchants carried off two prieftefses of Thebes, that one was carried into Greece, and the other into Lybia. She who was carried into Greece, took up her refidence in the foreft of Dodona, and there at the foot of an oak, erected a fmall chapel in honour of Jupiter, whofe prieftefs fhe had been at Thebes (3).

We learn from Servius (4), that the will of heaven was here explained by an old woman, who pretended to find out a meaning to explain the murmurs of a brook that flowed from the foot of the oak. After this, another method was taken, attended with more formalities; brazen kettles were fufpended in the air, with a ftatue of the fame metal, with a whip in his hand (5): this figure, when moved by the wind, ftruck againft the kettle that was next it, which alfo caufing all the other kettles to ftrike againft each other, raifed a clattering din, which continued for fome time, and from thefe founds fhe formed her predictions.

Both thefe ways were equally abfurd, for as in each the anfwer depended folely on the invention of the prieftefs, fhe alone was the oracle. Suidas informs

---

(3) The Abbe Sallier takes this fable to be built upon the double meaning of the word πελείας, which in Attica, and feveral other parts of Greece, fignifies pigeons, while in the dialect of Epirus, it meant old women. See Mem. Acad. Belles Lettres, vol. V. p. 35.

(4) Servius in 3. Æn. 5, 466.

(5) As this was evidently a figure of Ofiris, which was on particular occafions reprefented with a whip in his hand, it is an additional proof that this oracle was deriv'd from Egypt.

forms us, that the anfwer was given by an oak in this grove, as Homer alfo has delivered (6); and as it was generally believed to proceed from the trunk, it is eafy to conceive how this was performed: for the prieftefs had nothing more to do than to hide herfelf in the hollow of an old oak, and from thence to give the pretended fenfe of the oracle, which fhe might the more eafily do, as the diftance the fuppliant was obliged to keep, was an effectual means to prevent the cheat from being difcovered.

There is one remarkable circumftance relating to this oracle yet remaining, and that is, that while all the other nations received their anfwer from a woman, the Bœotians alone received it from a man, and the reafon given for it is as follows: During the war between the Thracians and Bœotians, the latter fent deputies to confult this oracle of Dodona, when the prieftefs gave them this anfwer, of which fhe doubtlefs did not forefee the confequence: *If you would meet with fuccefs, you muft be guilty of fome impious action.* The deputies, no doubt furprized, and perhaps exafperated, by imagining that the prieftefs prevaricated with them in order to pleafe the Pelafgi, from whom fhe was defcended, and who were in a ftrict alliance with the Thracians, refolved to fulfil the decree of the oracle; and therefore feizing the prieftefs, burnt her alive, alledging, that this action was juftifiable in whatever light it was confidered, that if fhe intended to deceive them, it was fit fhe fhould be punifhed for the deceit; or, if fhe was fincere, they had only literally fulfilled the fenfe of the oracle. The two remaining prieftefles, (for, according to Strabo, the oracle at that time had ufually three)' highly exafperated at this cruelty, caufed them to be feized, and as they were to be their judges, the deputies pleaded the illegality of their being tried by women. The juftice of this plea was admitted by the people, who allowed two priefts to try them in conjunction with the prieftefles; on which, being acquitted by the former, and condemned by the latter, the votes being equal, they were releafed. For this reafon the Bœotians, for the future, received their anfwers from the priefts.

The

(6) Τὸν δὲς Δωδώνην φάτο Βήμεναι, ὄφρα θεοῖο
Ἐκ δρυὸς ὑψικόμοιο Διὸς βουλὴν ἐπακούσῃ.

Hom. Od. 19.

The oracle of Jupiter Hammon, in Lybia, we have already said, was derived from Egypt, and is of the same antiquity as the former of Dodona, and, though surrounded by a large tract of burning sands, was extremely famous. This oracle gave his answers not by words, but by a sign. What was called the image of the god, was carried about in a gilded barge on the shoulders of his priests, who moved whithersoever they pretended the divine impulse directed them. This appears to have been nothing more than the mariners compass (7), the use of which was not entirely unknown to that age, though so long kept a secret from the Europeans. It was adorned with precious stones, and the barge with many silver goblets hanging on either side; and these processions were accompanied with a troop of matrons and virgins singing hymns in honour of Jupiter. These priests refused the bribes offered them by Lysander, who wanted their assistance to help him to change the succession to the throne of Sparta. However, they were not so scrupulous when Alexander, either to gratify his vanity, or to screen the reputation of his mother, took that painful march through the deserts of Lybia, in order to obtain the honour of being called the son of Jupiter; a priest stood ready to receive him, and saluted him with the title of *son of the king of gods.*

The oracle of Apollo at Delphos, was one of the most famous in all antiquity. This city stood upon a declivity about the middle of mount Parnassus: it was built on a small extent of even ground, and surrounded with precipices, that fortified it without the help of art (8). Diodorus Siculus relates (9) a tradition of a very whimsical nature, which was said to give rise to this oracle. There was a hole in one of the vallies, at the foot of Parnassus, the mouth of which was very strait: the goats that were feeding at no great distance, coming near it, began to skip and frisk about in such a manner, that the goat-herd, being struck with surprize, came up to the place, and leaning over it, was seized with such an enthusiastic

_____

(7) *Umbilico similis, smaragdo & gemmis congmentatus. Hunc navigio aurato gestant sacerdotes.* Q. CURTIUS, l. 4. c. 7.
(8) Strabo, lib. xiv. p. 427, 428.
(9) Diod. 4. 1.

astic impulse, or temporary madness, as prompted him to utter some extravagant expressions, which passed for prophecies. The report of this extraordinary event drew thither the neighbouring people, who, on approaching the hole, were seized with the same transports. Surprised at so astonishing a prodigy, the cavity was no longer approached without reverence. The exhalation was concluded to have something divine in it; they imagined it proceeded from some friendly deity, and from that time bestowed a particular worship on the divinity of the place, and regarded what was delivered in those fits of madness as predictions; and here they afterwards built the city and temple of Delphos.

This oracle, it was pretended, had been possessed by several successive deities, and at last by Apollo, who raised its reputation to the greatest height. It was resorted to by persons of all stations, by which it obtained immense riches, which exposed it to be frequently plundered. At first it is said the god inspired all indifferently who approached the cavern; but some having in this fit of madness thrown themselves into the gulf, they thought fit to choose a priestess, and to set over the hole a tripos, or three-legged stool, whence she might without danger catch the exhalations: and this priestess was called Pythia; from the serpent Python, slain by Apollo. For a long time none but virgins possessed this honour, till a young Thessalian, called Echecrates, falling in love with the priestess, who was at that time very beautiful, ravished her; when, to prevent any abuses of the like kind for the future, the citizens made a law to prohibit any woman being chosen under fifty years old. At first they had only one priestess, but afterwards they had two or three.

The oracles were not delivered every day, but the sacrifices were repeated till the god was pleased to deliver them, which frequently happened only one day in the year. Alexander coming here in one of these intervals, after many intreaties to engage the priestess to mount the tripod, which were all to no purpose, the prince growing impatient at her refusal, drew her by force from her cell, and was leading her to the sanctuary, when saying, *My son thou art invincible*, he cried out, that he was satisfied, and needed no other answer.

Nothing

Nothing was wanting to keep up the air of mystery, in order to preserve its reputation, and to procure it veneration. The neglecting the smallest punctilio was sufficient to make them renew the sacrifices that were to precede the response of Apollo. The priestess herself was obliged to prepare for the discharge of her duty, by fasting three days, bathing in the fountain of Castalia, drinking a certain quantity of the water, and chewing some leaves of laurel gathered near the fountain. After these preparations the temple was made to shake, which passed for the signal given by Apollo, to inform them of his arrival, and then the priests led her into the sanctuary and placed her on the tripod, when beginning to be agitated by the divine vapour, her hair stood an end, her looks became wild, her mouth began to foam, and a fit of trembling seized her whole body. In this condition she seemed to struggle to get loose from the priests, who pretended to hold her by force, while her shrieks and howlings, which resounded through the temple, filled the deluded by-standers with a kind of sacred horror. At last, being no longer able to resist the impulses of the god, she submitted, and at certain intervals uttered some unconnected words, which were carefully picked up by the priests, who put them in connection, and gave them to the poets, who were also present to put them into a kind of verse, which was frequently stiff, unharmonious, and always obscure; this occasioned that piece of raillery, that Apollo, the prince of the muses, was the worst of the poets. One of the priestesses, who was called Phemonoë, is said to have pronounced her oracles in verse: in latter times they were contented with delivering them in prose, and this, in the opinion of Plutarch, was one of the reasons of the declension of this oracle.

Crœsus intending to make trial of the several oracles of Greece, as well as that of Lybia, commanded the respective ambassadors to consult them all on a stated day, and to bring the responses in writing. The question proposed was, "What is Crœsus, the "son of Alyattes, king of Lydia, now doing?" The rest of the oracles failed; but the Delphian answered truly, that "He was boiling a lamb and a "tortoise together in a brazen pot. This gained his confidence and a profusion of the richest offerings.

In

In return, the oracle, on the next enquiry, informed him, that "By making war upon the Perfians, he fhould deftroy a great empire." The event is well known. This vain confidence loft him both his crown and liberty (1).

Trophonius, who, according to fome authors, was no more than a robber, or at moft a hero, had an oracle in Bœotia, which acquired great reputation. Paufanias, who had confulted it, and gone through all its formalities, has given a very particular defcription of it, and from him we fhall extract a fhort hiftory of this oracle.

The facred grove of Trophonius, fays this author, (2), is at a fmall diftance from Lebadea, one of the fineft cities in Greece; and in this grove is the temple of Trophonius, with his ftatue, the workmanfhip of Praxiteles. Thofe who apply to this oracle muft perform certain ceremonies before they are permitted to go down into the cave where the refponfe is given. Some days muft be fpent in a chapel dedicated to Fortune and the Good Genii, where the purification confifts in abftinence from all things unlawful, and in making ufe of the cold bath. He muft facrifice to Trophonius and all his family, to Jupiter, to Saturn, and to Ceres, firhamed Europa, who was believed to have been the nurfe of Trophonius. The diviners confulted the entrails of every victim, to difcover if it was agreeable to Trophonius that the perfon fhould defcend into the cave. If the omens were favourable, he was led that night to the river Hercyna, where two boys anointed his body with oil Then he was conducted as far as the fource of the river, where he was obliged to drink two forts of water, that of Lethe, to efface from his mind all profane thoughts, and that of Mnemofyne, to enable him to retain whatever he was to fee in the facred cave; he was then prefented to the ftatue of Trophonius, to which he was to addrefs a fhort prayer; he then was cloathed in a linen tunic adorned with facred fillets; and at laft was conducted in a folemn manner to the oracle, which was inclofed within a ftone wall on the top of a mountain.

(1) Herodot. in Clio.
(2) Paufan. lib. ix. p. 602, 604.

In this inclosure was a cave formed like an oven, the mouth of which was narrow, and the descent to it not by steps, but by a short ladder: on going down there appeared another cave, the entrance to which was very strait. The suppliant, who was obliged to take a certain composition of honey in each hand, without which he could not be admitted, prostrated himself on the ground, and then putting his feet into the mouth of the cave, his whole body was forcibly drawn in.

Here some had the knowledge of futurity by vision; and others by an audible voice. They then got out of the cave in the same manner as they went in, with their feet foremost, and prostrate on the earth. The suppliant going up the ladder was conducted to the chair of Mnemosyne, the goddess of memory, in which being seated, he was questioned on what he had heard and seen; and from thence he was brought into the chapel of the Good Genii, where having staid till he had recovered from his affright and terror, he was obliged to write in a book all that he had seen or heard, which the priests took upon them to interpret. There never was but one man, says Pausanias, who lost his life in this cave, and that was a spy who had been sent by Demetrius, to see whether in that holy place there was any thing worth plundering. The body of this man was afterwards found at a great distance; and indeed it is not unlikely, that this design being discovered, he was assassinated by the priests, who might carry out his body by some secret passage, at which they went in and out without being perceived.

The oracle of the Branchidæ, in the neighbourhood of Miletus, was very ancient, and in great esteem. Xerxes returning from Greece, prevailed on its priests to deliver up its treasures to him, and then burnt the temple, when to secure them against the vengeance of the Greeks, he granted them an establishment in the most distant part of Asia. After the defeat of Darius by Alexander, this conqueror destroyed the city where these priests had settled, of which their descendants were then in actual possession; and thus punished the children for the perfidy of their fathers.

The oracle of Apollo at Claros, a town of Ionia, in Asia Minor, was very famous, and frequently consulted.

fulted. Claros was said to be founded by (3) Manto, the daughter of Tirosias, some years before the taking of Troy. The answers of this oracle, says Tacitus (4), were not given by a woman, but by a man, chose out of certain families, and generally from Miletus. It was sufficient to let him know the number and names of those who came to consult him; after which he retired into a cave, and having drank of the waters of a spring that ran within it, delivered answers in verse upon what the people had in their thoughts, tho' he was frequently ignorant, and unacquainted with the nature and rules of poetry. " It is said (our author " adds) that he foretold the sudden death of Ger- " manicus, but in dark and ambiguous terms."

Pausanias mentions an oracle of Mercury, in Achaia, of a very singular kind. After a variety of ceremonies, which it is needless here to repeat, they whispered in the ear of the god, and told him, what they were desirous of knowing; then stopping their ears with their hands, they left the temple, and the first words they heard after they were out of it, was the answer of the god.

But it would be an endless task to pretend to enumerate all the oracles, which were so numerous, that Van Dale gives a list of near three hundred, most of which were in Greece.

But no part of Greece had so many oracles as Bœotia, which were there numerous, from its abounding in mountains and caverns; for, as Mr. Fontenelle observes, nothing was more convenient for the priests than these caves, which not only inspired the people with a sort of religious horror, but afforded the priests an opportunity of forming secret passages, of concealing themselves in hollow statues, and of making use of all the machines and all the arts necessary to keep up the delusion of the people, and to increase the reputation of the oracles.

Nothing

---

(3) Manto has been greatly extolled for her prophetic spirit; and fabulous history informs us, that lamenting the miseries of her country, she dissolved away in tears, and that these formed a fountain, the water of which communicated the gift of prophecy to those who drank it, but being at the same time unwholesome, it brought on diseases, and shortened life.

(4) Tacit. Annal. l. 2. c. 54.

APPENDIX.

Nothing is more remarkable than the different manners by which the sense of the oracles was conveyed: besides the methods already mentioned, in some the oracle was given from the bottom of the statue, to which one of the priests might convey himself by a subterranean passage; in others by dreams; in others again by lots, in the manner of dice, containing certain characters or words, which were to be explained by tables made for that purpose. In some temples the enquirer threw them himself, and in others they were dropped from a box; and from hence arose the proverbial phrase, *The lot is fallen*. Childish as this method of deciding the success of events by a throw of dice may appear, yet it was always preceded by sacrifices and other ceremonies.

In others the question was proposed by a letter, sealed up, and given to the priest, or left upon the altar, while the person sent with it was obliged to lie all night in the temple, and these letters were to be sent back unopened with the answer. Here this wonderful art consisted in the priests knowing how to open a letter without injuring the seal, an art still practised, on particular occasions, in all the general post-offices in Europe. A governor of Cilicia, whom the Epicureans endeavoured to inspire with a contempt for the oracles, sent a spy to that of Mopsus at Mallos, with a letter well sealed up; as this man was lying in the temple, a person appeared to him and uttered the word *Black*. This answer he carried to the governor, which filled him with astonishment, though it appeared ridiculous to the Epicureans, to whom he communicated it, when to convince them of the injustice of the raillery on the oracle, he broke open the letter, and shewed them that he had wrote these words, *Shall I sacrifice to thee a white ox or a black?* The emperor Trajan made a like experiment on the god at Heliopolis, by sending him a letter sealed up, to which he requested an answer. The oracle commanded a blank paper, well folded and sealed, to be given to the emperor, who, upon his receiving it, was struck with admiration at seeing an answer so correspondent to his own letter, in which he had wrote nothing.

The general characteristic of oracles, says the justly admired Rollin (5), were ambiguity, obscurity, and
convertability;

(5) Ancient Hist. vol. 5. p. 25.

convertability; so that one answer would agree with several different and even opposite events; and this was generally the case when the event was in the least dubious. Trajan, convinced of the divinity of the oracle, by the blank letter above mentioned, sent a second note, wherein he desired to know, whether he should return to Rome after the conclusion of the war which he had then in view; the oracle answered this letter by sending to him a vine broke in pieces. The prediction of the oracle was certainly fulfilled; for the emperor dying in the war, his body, or, if you please, his bones, represented by the broken vine, were carried to Rome. But it would have been equally accomplished had the Romans conquered the Parthians, or the Parthians the Romans; and whatever had been the event, it might have been constructed into the meaning of the oracle. Under such ambiguities they eluded all difficulties, and were hardly ever in the wrong. In this all their art, and all their superior knowledge consisted; for when the question was plain, the answer was commonly so too. A man requesting a cure for the gout, was answered by the oracle, that he should drink nothing but cold water. Another desiring to know by what means he might become rich, was answered by the god, that he had no more to do but to make himself master of all between Sicyon and Corinth (6).

VII. OF ALTARS, OPEN TEMPLES, SACRED GROVES, AND SACRIFICES.

ALTARS and sacrifices mutually imply each other, and were immediately consequent to the fall of man: though the original altars were simple, being composed of earth or turf, or unhewn stones. There is great probability that the cloathing of our first parents consisted of the skins of beasts sacrificed by Adam in the interval between his offence and expulsion from paradise. Cain and Abel, Noah and the patriarchs, pursued the practice. Even those who forsook the living God, yet continued this early method of worship. These idolaters at first imitated the simple manner in which they had been raised by Noah. But the

(6) Banier, vol. I.

the form and materials infensibly changed; there were some square, others long, round, or triangular. Each feaſt obtained a peculiar ceremonial, and an altar of a particular form. Sometimes they were of common ſtone, ſometimes of marble, wood, or braſs. The altar was ſurrounded with carvings in bas relief, and the corners ornamented with heads of various animals. Some reached no higher than to the knee, others were reared as high as the waiſt, whilſt others were much higher. Some again were ſolid, others hollow, to receive the libations and the blood of the victims. Others were portable, reſembling a trevet, of a magnificent form, to hold the offering from the fire, into which they threw frankincenſe, to overpower the diſagreeable ſmell of the blood and burning fat. In ſhort, what had been approved on ſome important occaſion, paſſed into a cuſtom, and became a law.

Where the altars were placed, there was ſaid to be in the early ages of the world an houſe or temple of JEHOVAH, which was moſtly upon eminences, and always uncovered. Where they could be had, upright ſtones were erected near them. This in ſcripture is called *ſetting up a pillar*; nor was it done without a particular form of conſecration. The behaviour of the patriarch Jacob, to which we refer the reader (7), will explain the whole.

It is ſaid of Moſes likewiſe *That he roſe up early in the morning, and builded an altar under the hill, and twelve pillars, &c.* (8). The entire work of theſe ſacred eminencies was ſurrounded at a convenient diſtance, by a mound or trench thrown up, in order to prevent the profane intruſion of the people (9).

At other times the walls were incloſed by groves of oak (1); whence this tree is ſaid to be ſacred to Jove. The heathens, when they left the object, yet continued this uſage alſo of the original worſhip; which indeed was ſo linked to idolatry, that it became neceſſary for Moſes to forbid the Hebrews planting groves about their altars, to prevent their falling into
the

(7) Gen. xxviii. 18, 19, 20, 21, 22, and xxxv. 7, 14, 15.
(8) Exod. xxiv. 4. *Thecketh, inferius, deorſum*, on the declivity of the hill.
(9) Exod. xix. 12, 23.
(1) Gen. xxi. 33. xii. 6. 7, xxxv. 4. xiii. 18. Deut. xi. 30. Judges ix. 6, &c.

the practices of the nations round about them. Thefe groves were hung with garlands and chaplets of flowers, and with a variety of offerings in fo lavifh a manner, as almoft entirely to exclude the light of the fun. They were confidered as the peculiar refidence of the deity. No wonder therefore, that it was deemed the moft inexpiable facrilege to cut them down (2).

The high antiquity and univerfality of facrificing, befpeak it a divine inftitution. The utter impoffibility that there fhould be any virtue or efficacy in the thing itfelf, fhews plainly that it muft have been looked upon as vicarious, and having refpect to fomewhat truly meritorious, and which thofe that brought the facrifice were at firft fufficiently acquainted with the nature of. For it is not to be prefumed upon what grounds men could be induced to think of expiating their fins, or procuring the divine favour by facrificial oblations. It is much more reafonable to conclude it a divine appointment. All nations have ufed it. They who were fo happy as to walk with God, were inftructed in it from age to age. And they who rejected him, ftill facrificed. But they invented new rites; and at length, miftaking and perverting the original intent and meaning, offered even human victims! It is indeed moft furprifing to obferve, that almoft all nations, from the ufe of beaftial, have advanced to human facrifices; and many of them, from the fame miftake and perverfion, even to the facrifice of their own children!

This moft cruel cuftom, amongft the Carthagenians, of offering children to Saturn (3), occafioned an embaffy being fent to them from the Romans, in order to perfuade them to abolifh it. And in the reign of Tiberius, the priefts of Saturn were crucified for prefuming

(2) Lucan mentioning the trees which Cæfar ordered to be felled, to make his warlike engines, defcribes the confternation of the foldiers, who refufed to obey his orders, till taking an axe, he cut down one of them himfelf. Struck with a religious reverence for the fanctity of the grove, they imagined that if they prefumptuoufly attempted to cut down any of its trees, the axe would have recoiled upon themfelves. They however believed it lawful to prune and clear them, and to fell thofe trees which they imagined attracted the thunder.

(3) Thefe facrifices were practifed annually by the Carthaginians, who firft offered the fons of the principal citizens; but afterwards privately brought up children for that purpofe.

presuming to sacrifice children to him; and Amasis, king of Egypt, made a law, that only the figures of men should be sacrificed instead of themselves. Plutarch informs us, that at the time of a plague, the Spartans were ordered by an oracle to sacrifice a virgin; but the lot having fallen upon a young maid whose name was Helene, an eagle carried away the sacrificing knife, and laying it on the head of an heifer, it was sacrificed in her stead. The same author informs us, that Pelopidus the Athenian general dreaming the night before an engagement, that he should sacrifice a virgin to the manes of the daughters of Scedasus, who had been ravished and murdered, he was filled with horror at the inhumanity of such a sacrifice, which he could not help thinking odious to the gods; but seeing a mare, by the advice of Theocritus the soothsayer, he sacrificed it, and gained the victory.

The ceremonies used at sacrifices were extremely different, and to every deity a distinct victim was allotted (4); but whatever victims were offered, the greatest care was to be taken in the choice of them; for the very same blemishes that excluded them being offered by the Jews, rendered them also imperfect among the Pagans.

The priest having prepared himself by continence, during the preceding night, and by ablution, before the procession went a herald crying *hoc age*, to give the people notice that they were to give their sole attention to what they were about; then followed the players on several instruments, who between the intervals of playing, exhorted the people in the same manner. The priest, and sometimes the sacrificers, went before cloathed in white, and the priest, besides being dressed in the vestments belonging to his office, was sure to be crowned with a chaplet of the leaves of the tree sacred to the god for whom the sacrifice was appointed; the victim had his horns gilt, and was also crowned with a chaplet of the same leaves, and adorned with ribbands and fillets. In Greece when

the

---

(4). Lucian informs, that " The victims were also different " according to the quality and circumstance of the persons who " offered them. The husbandman, says he, sacrifices an ox; " the shepherd, a lamb; the goat herd, a goat. There are " some who offer only cakes, or incense; and he that has " nothing, sacrifices by kissing his right hand." De Sacr.

the prieſt approached the altar, he cried, *Who is here?* To which the ſpectators anſwered, *Many good people* (5). The prieſt then ſaid, *Be gone all ye profane*, which the Romans expreſſed by ſaying, *Procul eſte profani.*

The victim arriving at the altar, the prieſt laid one hand upon the altar, and began with a prayer to all the gods, beginning with Janus, and ending with Veſta, during which the ſtricteſt ſilence was obſerved. Then the ſacrifice began, by throwing upon the head of the victim corn, frankincenſe, flour, and ſalt, laying upon it cakes and fruit (6), and this they called immolitio, or the immolition. Then the prieſt took the wine, which having firſt taſted, he gave it to the by-ſtanders to do ſo too (7), and then poured it out, or ſprinkled the beaſt with it between the horns. After this the prieſt plucked off ſome of the rough hairs from the forehead of the victim, threw them into the fire, and then turning to the eaſt, drew a crooked line with his knife along the back, from the forehead to the tail, and then ordered the ſervants (8) to ſlay the victim, which they had no ſooner done than he was opened, and the duty of the aruſpex began, which was no ſooner over, than the carcaſe was cut in quarters, and then into ſmaller pieces, and, according to Pauſanias (9), and Apollonius Rodius (1), the thighs were covered with fat, and ſacrificed as the part allotted to the god (2); after which they regaled themſelves upon the reſt, and celebrated this religious feaſt with dancing, muſic, and hymns ſung in honour of the gods.

Upon ſignal victories, or in the midſt of ſome public calamity, they ſometimes offered in one ſacrifice a hundred bulls, which was called an hecatomb: but ſometimes the ſame name was given to the ſacrifice of an hundred ſheep, hogs, or other animals. 'Tis ſaid that Pythagoras offered up an hecatomb for having found

(5) Πολλοι χ'αγαθοι.
(6) All theſe were not uſed for every ſacrifice.
(7) This was called libatio.
(8) Theſe inferior officers, whoſe buſineſs it was to kill, to embowel, to flea, and to waſh the victim, were called *Victimarii, Popæ, Agonis, Cultrarii.*
(9) Lib. 5. p. 192.
(1) In Att. p. 42.
(2) In the holocauſts, the whole victim was burnt, and nothing left for the feaſt.

found out the demonstration of the forty-seventh proposition in the first book of Euclid.

VIII. OF THE PRIESTS, PRIESTESSES, &c. OF THE GREEKS AND ROMANS.

IN the early ages of the world the chiefs of families composed the priesthood; and afterwards, when public priests were appointed, kings, as fathers and masters of that large family which composed the body politic, frequently offered sacrifices; and not only kings, but princes and captains of armies. Instances of this kind are frequently to be met with in Homer.

When the ancients chose a priest, the strictest enquiry was made into the life, the manners, and even the bodily external perfections of the person to be chosen. They were generally allowed to marry once, but were not always forbid second marriages.

The Greeks and Romans had several orders of priests; but as Greece was divided into many independent states, there naturally arose different hierarchies. In several cities of Greece the Government of religon was intrusted to women, in others it was conferred on the men; while again, in others, both in concert had a share in the management of it. The priestesses of Argos were very famous. At Athens a priestess presided over the worship of Minerva; there was also a priestess for Pallas, at Clazomenæ; for Ceres, at Catanea, &c. The Hierophantæ were very famous priests of Athens, and both they and their wives, who were called Hierophantidæ, were set apart for the worship of Ceres and Hecate; as were the Orgiophantæ, and the women stiled Orgiastæ, appointed to preside over the orgies of Bacchus, &c. Besides the priestess of Apollo, at Delphos, who was by way of eminence called Pythia (3), there belonged to this oracle

---

(3) Thus the priestess of Pallas, at Clazomenæ, was called Hesychia, and that of Bacchus, Thyas; and in Crete, that of Cybele, Melissa. Among the Athenians, the inferior ministers were stiled Parasiti, a word that did not at that time carry with it any mark of reproach; for it is mentioned in an inscription at Athens, that of two bulls offered in sacrifices.

oracle five princes of the priests, and several prophets, who pronounced the sense of the oracle. There were also chief priests one of whom presided over a city, and sometimes over a whole province; sometimes he was invested with this dignity for life, and, at other times, only for five years. Besides these, there were chief priestesses, who were the superintendants of the priestesses, and were chosen from the noblest families; but the most celebrated of these was the Pythia.

The priests of Rome enjoyed several very considerable privileges; they were exempted from going to war, and excused from all burthensome offices in the state. They had commonly a branch of laurel and a torch carried before them, and were allowed to ride in a chariot to the capitol. Romulus instituted sixty priests, who were to be at least fifty years of age, free from all personal defects, and distinguished both by their birth and the rectitude of their morals.

The Pontifex Maximus, or the high-priest, was esteemed the judge and arbitrator of all divine and human affairs, and his authority was so great, and his office so much revered, " that all the emperors, af-
" ter the example of Julius Cæsar and Augustus, ei-
". ther actually took upon them the office, or at least
" used the name (4)." He was not allowed to go out of Italy, though this was dispensed with in favour of Julius Cæsar; whenever he attended a funeral, a veil was put between him and the funeral bed; for it was thought a kind of profanation for him to see a dead body.

The Rex Sacrorum (5), according to Dyonysius of Halicarnassus (6), was instituted after the expulsion of the Roman kings, to perpetuate the memory of the great services some of them had done the state. On this account, the augurs and Pontifices were directed to choose out a fit person, who should devote himself to the care of religious worship, and the ceremonies

fices, the one should be reserved for the games, and the other distributed among the priests and parasites. These parasites had a place among the chief magistrates, and the principal part of their employment was to choose the wheat appointed for their sacrifices. Banier's Mythology, Vol. 1. p. 283.

(4) Kennet's Rom. Antiq.
- (5) He was also stiled Rex Sacrificulus.
(6) Lib. 1.

monies of religion, without ever interfering in civil affairs: but left the name of king, which was become odious to the people, fhould raife their jealoufy, it was at the fame time appointed, that he fhould be fubject to the high priefts. His wife had the title of Regina Sacrorum.

The Flamines, according to Livy (7), were appointed by Numa Pompilius, to difcharge thofe religious offices, which he imagined properly belonged to the kings. At firft there were but three (8), which were chofen by the people, and their election confirmed by the high prieft. They were afterwards increafed to fifteen, three of whom were chofen from among the fenators, and were called Flamines Majores; and the other twelve, chofen from the Plebeans, were ftiled Flamines Minores.

The Feciales were alfo inftituted by Numa, and confifted of twenty perfons, chofen out of the moft diftinguifhed families. Thefe were properly the heralds of the republic, who, whenever it was injured, were fent to demand fatisfaction, which, if they could not obtain, they called the gods to witnefs between them and the enemy, and denounced war. They had the power of ratifying and confirming alliances, and were the arbitrators of all the differences between the republic and other nations; fo that the Romans could not lawfully take up arms, till the Feciales had declared that war was moft expedient.

The Pater Patratus derived his name from a circumftance neceffary to his enjoying the title; and in order that he might be more ftrongly interefted in the fate of his country, he was to have both a father and a fon living at the fame time. He was chofen by the college of Feciales out of their own body, to treat with the enemy on the fubject of war and peace.

The Epulones were minifters appointed to prepare the facred banquets at the folemn games, and had the privilege

(7) Liv. lib. 1
(8) The Flamendiafis of Jupiter, the Martialis of Mars, and the Quirinalis of Quirinus. The firft facred to Jupiter was a perfon of a very high diftinction, though he was obliged to fubmit to burthenfome regulations and fuperftitious obfervances: his wife was a prieftefs, and had the title of Flaminica; and afo enjoyed the fame privileges, and was under the fame reftrictions as her hufband. Aulus Gellius, Noct. Att. l. 10. c. 15.

privilege of wearing a robe like the pontiffs, bordered with purple. These ministers were originally three in number, to which two were afterwards added, and then two more, till in the pontificate of Julius Cæsar they were increased to ten. The most considerable of the privileges granted to the Epulones, was one which they enjoyed in common with the other ministers, their not being obliged to make their daughters vestals (9).

Besides these were the Salii, or priests of Mars; the Phæbades of Apollo; the Bassarides of Bacchus; the Luperci of Pan, and several others who presided over the worship of particular deities, each of which had a particular college, and constituted a distinct community.

OF THE TEMPLES OF THE PAGANS.

OAKEN groves, with a circular opening in the midst, or upright stones placed in the same order, inclosing an altar, were the original temples. The first covered one was that of Babel, and in all probability it was the only one of the kind, till Moses, by erecting the tabernacle, might give the Egyptians the first thought of building also a house for their gods. Had temples been built in Egypt at the time when Moses resided there, it can hardly be conceived but that he would have mentioned them; and that this moving temple might serve as a model for the rest, is the more probable, as there is a near resemblance between the Sanctum Sanctorum and the holy places in the Pagan temple. In that of Moses, God was consulted, and none suffered to enter but the priests: this exactly agrees with the holy places in the Heathen temples, where the oracle was delivered.

It was the opinion of Lucian, that the first temples were built by the Egyptians, and that from them the custom was conveyed to the people of the neighbouring countries; and from Egypt and Phœnicia it passed into Greece, and from Greece to Rome.

They all began with little chapels, which were generally erected by private persons, and these were soon succeeded by regular buildings, and the most magnificent

(9) Aulus Gellius, lib. 1. c. 12.

ficent structures, when even the grandeur and beauty of the buildings heightened the veneration that was entertained for them. They had often porticos, and always an ascent of steps, while some of them were surrounded by galleries supported by rows of pillars. The first part in entering these temples was the porch, in which was placed the holy water for the expiation of those that entered into the temple. The next was the nave (1), or body of the temple, and then the holy place (2), into which none but the priests were allowed to enter. Sometimes there was behind the buildings another part, called the back temple.

The inside was frequently adorned with paintings, gildings, and the richest offerings, among which were the trophies and spoils of war. But the principal ornaments were the statues of the gods, and those of persons distinguished by great and noble actions, which were sometimes of gold, silver, ivory, ebony, and other precious materials.

The veneration for these buildings was carried by the Romans and other nations to the most superstitious excess. Before the erecting one of these noble edifices, the Aruspices chose the place, and fixed the time for beginning the work; for here every thing was of importance. They began when the air was serene, and the sky clear and unclouded; on the limits of the building were placed fillets and garlands, and the soldiers whose names were thought auspicious, entered the enclosure with bows in their hands; then followed the vestal virgins, attended by such boys and girls who had the happiness to have their fathers and mothers living, and these assisted the vestals in sprinkling all the ground with clear water; then followed a solemn sacrifice, and prayers to the gods, to prosper the building they were going to erect for their habitation; and this being over, the priest touched the stone that was to be first laid, and bound it with a fillet, after which the magistrates, and persons of the greatest distinction, assisted the people, with the utmost joy and alacrity, in removing the stone, which was extremely large, fixed it for a foundation, throwing in with it several small gold coins, and other pieces of money.

When

---

(1) Ναὸς.
(2) Called Penetralis, Sacrarium, Adytum.

When these buildings were finished, they were consecrated with abundance of ceremony, and so great was the veneration felt by the people for the temples, that they frequently, as a mark of humiliation, clambered up to them on their knees; and so holy was the place, that it was thought criminal for a man to spit or blow his nose in it. The women prostrated themselves in them, and swept the pavements with their hair. They became sanctuaries for debtors and criminals; and on all holidays were constantly decked with branches of laurel, olive, and ivy.

One of the first temples built in Egypt, was that of Vulcan, at Memphis, erected by Menes: At first it had the primitive simplicity of all other ancient buildings, and without statues (3); but the successors of this prince strove to excel each other in embellishing this work with stately porches and statues of a monstrous size. There were indeed a great number of temples in Egypt, but the most extraordinary thing of this kind was a chapel hewn out of a single stone, which by order of Amasis was cut out of the quarries in upper Egypt, and with incredible difficulty carried as far as Sais, where it was designed to have been set up in the temple of Minerva, but was left at the gate. Herodotus mentions this work with marks of astonishment: " What I admire more, says he, than at the
" other works of Amasis, is his causing a house to
" be brought from Eliphantina, a house hewn out of
" a single stone; which two thousand men were
" unable to remove thither in less than three years.
" This house was thirty-one feet in front, twenty-
" one feet in breadth, and twelve in height; and on
" the inside twenty-seven feet in length, and seven
" feet and a half high."

The temple of Diana at Ephesus (4), has been always admired as one of the noblest pieces of architecture that the world has ever produced. It was four hundred

---

(3) According to the best historians, there were no statues in the ancient temples of Egypt. But this is not at all strange, since Plutarch, who has his authority from Varro, says, " That the Romans were a hundred and seventy years " without statues; Numa prohibited them by a law; and " Tertullian lets us know, that even in his time there were " several temples that had no statues."

(4) This temple was accounted one of the wonders of the world.

hundred and twenty-five feet long, two hundred feet broad, and supported by a hundred and twenty-seven columns of marble sixty feet high, twenty-seven of which were beautifully carved. This temple, which was 200 years in building, was burnt by Eroftratus, with no other view than to perpetuate his memory; however, it was rebuilt, and the last temple was not inferior, either in riches or beauty, to the former, being adorned with the works of the most famous statuaries of Greece.

The temple of Ceres and Proserpine was built in the Doric order, and was of so wide an extent as to be able to contain thirty-thousand men; for there were frequently that number at the celebration of the mysteries of the two goddesses. At first this temple had no columns on the outside; but Philo afterwards added to it a magnificent portico.

The temple of Jupiter Olympius, as well as the admirable statue of Jupiter placed in it, were raised from the spoils which the Elians took at the sacking of Pisa (5). This temple was of the Doric order, the most ancient, as well as the most suitable to grand undertakings; and on the outside was surrounded with columns, which formed a noble peryftile. The length of the temple was two hundred and thirty feet, its breadth ninety-five, and its height, from the area to the roof, two hundred and thirty. From the middle of the roof hung a gilded victory, under which was a golden shield, on which was represented Medusa's head; and round the temple, above the columns, hung twenty-one gilt bucklers, which Mummius consecrated to Jupiter after the sacking of Corinth. Upon the pediment in the front was represented, with exquisite art, the chariot race between Pelops and Oenomaus; and, on the back pediment, the battle of the Centaurs with the Lapithæ at the marriage of Pirithous; and the brass gates were adorned with the labours of Hercules. In the inside, two ranges of tall and stately columns supported two galleries, under which was the way that led to the throne of Jupiter.

The statue of the god and his throne were the master-pieces of the great Phidias, and the most magnificent and highest finished in all antiquity. The statue, which was of a prodigious size, was of gold and ivory, so artfully blended as to fill all beholders
with

(5) Pausanias in Iliac, p. 303, & seq.

with aftonifhment. The god wore upon his head an olive crown, in which the leaf of the olive was imitated in the niceft perfection. In his right-hand he held the figure of victory, formed likewife of gold and ivory; and in his left a golden fceptre, on the top of which was an eagle. The fhoes and mantle of the god were of gold, and on the mantle were engraven a variety of flowers and animals. The throne fparkled with gold and precious ftones, while the different materials, and the affemblage of animals and other ornaments, formed a delightful variety. At the four corners of the throne, were four Victories, that feemed joining hands for a dance; and at the feet of Jupiter were two others. On the forefide, the feet of the throne were adorned with fphinxes plucking the tender infants from the bofoms of the Theban mothers, and underneath were Apollo and Diana flaying the children of Niobe with their arrows, &c. At the top of the throne, above the head of Jupiter, were the graces and hours. The pedeftal which fupported the pile, was equally adorned with the reft: it was covered with gold; on the one fide, Phidias had engraven Phœbus guiding his chariot; on the other, Jupiter and Juno, Mercury, Vefta, and the graces: here Venus appeared as rifing from the fea, and Cupid receiving her, while Pitho, or the goddefs of perfuafion, feemed prefenting her with a crown: there appeared Apollo and Diana, Minerva and Hercules. At the foot of the pedeftal were Neptune and Amphitrite, with Diana, who appeared mounted on horfeback. In fhort, a woollen veil dyed in purple, and curioufly embroidered, hung down from the top to the bottom. A large balluftrade painted and adorned with figures encompaffed the whole work; there, with inimitable art, was painted the Atlas bearing the heavens upon his fhoulders, and Hercules ftooping to eafe him of his load; the combat of Hercules with the Nemean lion; Ajax offering violence to Caffandra; Prometheus in chains, and a variety of other pieces of fabulous hiftory.

This temple was paved with the fineft marble, adorned with a prodigious number of ftatues, and with the prefents which feveral princes had confecrated to the God.

Though the temple of Apollo at Delphos, was greatly inferior in point of magnificence to the former, yet

yet the immense presents sent to it from every quarter, rendered it infinitely more rich. The principal value of the former arose from its containing the works of Phidias, and his master-piece was really invaluable; but what this temple wanted, in not containing the productions of so curious an artist, was amply made up by a profusion of treasure, which arose from the offerings of those who went to consult the oracle. The first temple which was built being burnt, the Amphictyones, or general council of Greece, took upon themselves the care of rebuilding it; and for that purpose agreed with an architect for three hundred talents, which amounts to forty-five thousand pounds, and this sum was to be raised by the cities of Greece; collections were also made in foreign countries. Amasis, king of Egypt, and the Grecian inhabitants of that country, contributed considerable sums for that service. The Alomæonedes, one of the most powerful families in Athens, had the charge of conducting the building, which they rendered more magnificent, by making, at their own expence, considerable additions that had not been proposed in the model.

After the temple of Delphos was finished, Gyges, king of Lydia; and Crœsus, one of his successors, enriched it with an incredible number of the most valuable presents; and, after their example, many other princes, cities, and private persons bestowed upon it a vast number of tripods, tables, vessels, shields, crowns, and statues of gold and silver of inconceivable value. Herodotus informs (6), that the presents of gold made by Crœsus alone to this temple, amounted to more than two hundred and fifty talents, or 33,500l. sterling; and it is probable that those of silver were not of less value. And Diodorus Siculus (7) adding these to those of the other princes, computes them at ten thousand talents, or about 1,300,000l. (8).

Plutarch informs us (9), that amongst the statues of gold, which Crœsus placed in the temple of Delphos,
was

(6) Her. lib. 1. c. 50, 51.
(7) Diod. lib. 16. p. 453.
(8) It is impossible to form any tolerable idea of these sums without bringing also into the account the comparative scarcity of gold at that time, which rendered its real value vastly greater than what it bears at present. The mines of Mexico and Peru have destroyed all comparison.
(9) Plut. de Pyth. Orac. p. 401.

was one of a female baker, of which this was the occasion: Allyatus, the father of Crœsus, having married a second wife, by whom he had children; she formed the design of securing the crown to her own issue, by putting a period to the life of her son-in-law; and with this view engaged a female baker to put poison into a loaf, that was to be served up at the table of the young prince. The woman, struck with horror at the thought of her bearing so great a share in the guilt of the queen, let Crœsus into the secret; on which the loaf was served to the queen's own children, and their death secured his succession to the throne, which when he ascended, from a sense of gratitude to his benefactress, he erected this statue to her memory in the temple of Delphos; an honour that, our author says, she had a better title to, than many of the boasted conquerors or heroes, who rose to fame only by murders and devastation.

Italy was no less famous for a multiplicity of temples than Greece; but none of them were more noble, or more remarkable for the singularity of their form, than the Pantheon, commonly called the Rotunda, originally consecrated to all the gods, as it is now to all the saints. It is generally believed to have been built at the expence of Agrippa, son-in-law to Augustus. This noble fabric is entirely round, and without windows, receiving a sufficient degree of light from an opening admirably contrived in the center of the dome. It was richly adorned with the statues of all the gods and goddesses set in niches. But the portico, composed of sixteen columns of granate marble, each of one single stone, is more beautiful and more surprising than the temple itself, since these columns are five feet in diameter, and thirty-seven feet high, without mentioning the bases and chapiters. The emperor Constantius the Third stripped it of the plates of gilt brass that covered the roof, and of the beams, which were of the same metal. Of the copper-plates of the portico, Pope Urban the Eighth afterwards formed the canopy of St. Peter; and even of the nails, which fastened them, cast the great piece of artillery, which is still to be seen in the castle of St. Angelo.

But of the Roman temples the Capitol was the principal; with an account of which we shall therefore conclude. In the last Sabine war Tarquinius Priscus

Priscus vowed a temple to Jupiter, Juno and Minerva The event of the war corresponded with his wishes, and the Auspices unanimously fixed upon the Tarpeian mountain for the destined structure. But little more seems to have been done towards it, besides this designation, till the reign of Tarquinius Superbus, a prince of loftiness and spirit conforming to his name, who set about it in earnest; having laid out the design with such amplitude and magnificence as might suit the king of gods and men, the glory of the rising empire, and the majesty of the situation. The Volscian spoils were dedicated to this service. An incredible sum was expended upon the foundations only, which were quadrilateral, and near upon two hundred feet every way: the length exceeding the breadth not quite fifteen feet. When the foundations were clearing, a human head was found, with the lineaments of the face entire, and the blood yet fresh and flowing, which was interpreted as an omen of future empire. This head was said to have belonged to one Ollus, or Tolus, whence the structure received its compound name. Though possibly it might be as well to deduce the name from *Caput* only; and that too upon another account, because it was the commanding part, the head and citadel of Rome, and the chief place of its religious worship. The edifice was not finished till after the expulsion of the kings; the completion of it being a work, says Livy, reserved for the days of liberty. It stood the space of 425 years, to the consulate of Scipio and Norbanus, when it was consumed by fire; but it was rebuilt by Sylla, whose name was inscribed in letters of gold upon the fastigium or pediment of it. In the midst were formed three cells or temples separated by thin partitions, in which stood the golden images of the deities to whom it had been devoted. Those of Juno and Minerva were on each side of Jupiter; for it was not usual for him to be worshipped without the company of his wife and daughter. The three temples were covered by one eagle with his wings expanded. This wonderful structure seems to have been of the Doric order, in imitation of those raised to the same deity in Greece, and abounded with curious engravings and every plaistic ornament, particularly the Fastigium. The spacious entrances, or thresholds, were composed of brass. The lofty folding-doors, which were of the
same

fame metal, moſt elegantly emboſſed, grated harſh thunder upon brazen hinges, and were afterwards entirely overlaid with plates of gold. The taſſellated pavements ſtruck the eye with an aſtoniſhing aſſemblage of rich colours from the variegated marble. The beams were ſolid brafs; and the ſplendour of the fretted roof was dazzling; where (1)

———— The glitt'ring flame
Play'd on the temple's gold and awful height,
And ſhed around its trembling rays of light.

Without, the covering was of plates of brafs, faſhioned like tiles; which being gilt with gold, reflected the ſun-beams with exceſſive luſtre. The front to the ſouth was encompaſſed with a triple row of lofty marble columns beautifully poliſhed, brought from the temple of Olympian Jove at Athens, by order of Sylla: all the other ſides by a double row. The aſcent was by an hundred ſteps that gently roſe, which made the paſſage to it extremely grand and ſtriking.

But this Capitol was likewiſe burnt in the civil war between Vitellius and Veſpaſian, and reſtored by the latter, with ſome addition of height: it quickly after underwent the ſame fate, and was raiſed again by Domitian with more ſtrength and magnificence than before; who arrogated the whole honour of the ſtructure to himſelf. The poets were miſtaken, when they promiſed to this laſt fabric an eternal duration, for not many years intervened before it was fired by lightening, and a great part of it confumed. The left-hand of the golden image of Jupiter was melted. Afterwards, under Arcadius and Honorius, the plunder of it was begun by Stilicho; who ſtripped the valves or folding-doors of the thick plated gold which covered them: in one part of which was found a grating inſcription, declaring them *reſerved for an unfortunate Prince*. Genſeric, king of the Vandals, carried with him into Africa moſt of its remaining ornaments, among which one-half of the gilded tiles of brafs; and the great part of it was deſtroyed by Totilas the Goth. Theodoric indeed made ſome attempts to repair the Capitol, the Amphitheatre, and others of the more ſplendid buildings of the city; but in vain, the prevailing light of Chriſtianity left them for the moſt part uſeleſs and deſerted.

OF

(1) *Flammis nitore ſuo templorum verberat aurum,*
Et tremulum ſumma ſpargit in æde jubar. OVID FAST. l. 9.

Of the USEFULNESS of FABLE.

By Mr. ROLLIN, Profeſſor of Eloquence in the Royal College at Paris, and Member of the Royal Academy of Inſcriptions and Belles Lettres.

WHAT I have already obſerved (ſays this learned author) concerning the origin of fables, which owe their birth to fiction, error, and falſhood, to the alteration of hiſtorical facts, and the corruption of man's heart, may give reaſon to aſk, whether it is proper to inſtruct Chriſtian children in all the fooliſh inventions, abſurd and idle dreams, with which Paganiſm has filled the books of antiquity.

This ſtudy, when applied to with all the precautions and wiſdom, which religion demands and inſpires, may be very uſeful to youth.

Firſt, it teaches them what they owe to Jeſus Chriſt, their Redeemer, who has delivered them from the power of darkneſs, to bring them into the admirable light of the Goſpel. Before him what were even the wiſeſt and beſt of men, thoſe celebrated philoſophers, thoſe great politicians, thoſe famous legiſlators of Greece, thoſe grave ſenators of Rome; in a word, all the beſt governed and wiſeſt nations of the world? Fable informs us, they were blind worſhippers of the devil, who bent their knees before gold, ſilver, and marble; who offered incenſe to ſtatues, that were deaf and dumb; who acknowledged, as Gods, animals, reptiles, and plants; who were not aſhamed to adore an adulterous Mars, a proſtituted Venus, and an inceſtuous Juno, a Jupiter polluted with all manner of crimes, and for that reaſon moſt worthy of the firſt place among the Gods.

What great impurities, what monſtrous abominations were admitted into their ceremonies, their ſolemnities, and myſteries? The temples of their gods were ſchools of licentiouſneſs, their pictures invitations to ſin, their groves places of proſtitution, their ſacrifices a frightful mixture of ſuperſtition and cruelty.

In this condition were all mankind, except the people of the Jews, for near four thouſand years. In this ſtate were our fathers, and we ſhould have likewiſe been, if the light of the Goſpel had not diſperſed our darkneſs. Every ſtory in fabulous hiſtory, every circumſtance

circumstance of the lives of the Gods, should fill us at once with confusion, admiration and gratitude, and seem to cry out to us aloud in the words of St. Paul to the Ephesians: *Remember, and forget not, that being sprung from Gentiles, ye were strangers from the covenants of promise, having no hope, and without God in the world.*

A second advantage of fable is that in discovering to us the absurd ceremonies and impious maxims of Paganism, it ought to inspire us with new respect for the august majesty of the Christian religion, and the sanctity of its morals. We learn from ecclesiastical history, that an holy bishop, in order to eradicate entirely all dispositions to idolatry out of the minds of the faithful, brought to light and publickly exposed all that was found in the inside of a temple he caused to be demolished, the bones of men, the members of children sacrificed to devils, and several other footsteps of the sacrilegious worship, which the Pagans paid to their deities. The study of fable should produce a like effect in the mind of every sensible person, and it is this use the holy fathers and all the apologists of Christianity have made of it.

It is impossible to understand the books which have been written upon this subject, without having some knowledge of fabulous history. St. Augustin's great work, entitled, *De Civitate Dei*, which has done so much honour to the church, is at the same time both a proof of what I lay down, and a perfect model of the manner how we ought to sanctify profane studies. The same may be said of the other fathers, who have gone upon the same plan from the beginning of Christianity. Theophilus of Antioch, Tatian, Arnobius, Lactantius, Theodoret, Eusebius of Cæsarea, and especially St. Clement of Alexandria, whose *Stromata* are not to be understood by any one that is not versed in this part of ancient learning. Whereas the knowledge of fable makes the knowledge of them extremely easy, which we ought to look upon as no small advantage.

It is also very useful (and particularly to youth, for whom I write) for the understanding both of Greek, Latin, French, and English authors; in reading of which they must be often at a stand, without some acquaintance with fable. I don't speak only of the poets, to whom we know it is a kind of natural language; it is also frequently made use of by orators,

and

and sometimes, by an happy application, supplies them with very lively and eloquent turns: Such, for instance, amongst a great many others, is the following passage in Tully's oration concerning Mithridates, king of Pontus. The orator takes notice, that this prince flying before the Romans, after the loss of a battle, found means to escape out of the hands of his covetous conquerors, by scattering upon the road, from time to time, a part of his treasures and spoils. In like manner, says he, as it is told of Medea, that when she was pursued by her father, in the same country, she scattered the members of her brother Absyrtus, whom she had cut to pieces, along the way, that his care in gathering up the dispersed members, and his grief at the sight of so sad a spectacle, might retard his pursuit. The resemblance is exact, except that, as Tully remarks, Æeta, the father of Medea, was stopped in his course by sorrow, and the Romans by joy.

There are different species of books exposed to the view of the whole world, such as pictures, prints, tapestry, and statues. These are so many riddles to those who are ignorant of fabulous history, from whence their explication is frequently to be taken. These matters are likewise frequently brought into discourse, and it is not, in my opinion, over agreeable to sit mute, and seem stupid in company, for want of being instructed, whilst young, in a matter so easy to be learnt.

ONE ONLY SUPREME GOD, OMNIPOTENT, AND THE AUTHOR OF FATE.

NOTWITHSTANDING the monstrous multiplicity of Homer's Gods, he plainly acknowledges one first being, a superior God, upon whom all the other Gods depended. Jupiter speaks and acts every where as absolute, and infinitely superior to all the other Gods in power and authority, as able by a word to cast them all out of heaven, and plunge them into the depths of Tartarus, as having executed his vengeance upon some of them; whilst all of them own his superiority and independence. One single passage will suffice to shew the idea which the ancients conceived of Jupiter.

" Aurora

"Aurora now, fair daughter of the dawn,
"Sprinkled with rofy light the dewy lawn;
"When Jove conven'd the fenate of the fkies,
"Where high Olympus' cloudy tops arife;
"The Sire of Gods his awful filence broke,
"The heav'ns attentive trembled as he fpoke:
  "Celeftial ftates, immortal Gods, give ear!
"Hear our decree, and reverence what you hear;
"The fix'd decree, which not all heav'n can move,
"Thou, Fate! fulfil it; and ye powers approve!
"What God but enters yon' forbidden field,
"Who yields affiftance, or but wills to yield;
"Back to the fkies with fhame he fhall be driv'n,
"Gafh'd with difhoneft wounds, the fcorn of heav'n;
"Or far, oh! far from fteep Olympus thrown,
"Low in the dark Tartarean gulph fhall groan,
"With burning chains fix'd to the brazen floors,
"And lock'd by hell's inexorable doors;
"As deep beneath th' infernal centre hurl'd,
"As from that centre to th' ætherial world.
"Let him, who tempts me, dread thefe dire abodes;
"And know, th' Almighty is the God of Gods!
"League all your forces then, ye pow'rs above,
"Join all, and try th' omnipotence of Jove:
"Let down our golden, everlafting chain, [main:
"Whofe ftrong embrace holds heaven and earth and
"Strive all, of mortal and immortal birth,
"To drag by this the Thund'rer down to earth:
"Ye ftrive in vain! If I but ftretch this hand,
"I heave the Gods, the ocean, and the land,
"I fix the chain to great Olympus height,
"And the vaft world hangs trembling in my fight.
"For fuch I reign, unbounded, and above,
"And fuch are men and Gods compared to Jove.
  "Th' Almighty fpoke, nor durft the pow'rs reply,
"A rev'rend horror filenc'd all the fky:
"Trembling they ftood before their fov'reign's look.

POPE.

A FURTHER ILLUSTRATION

OF THE

DII MAJORES of the ROMANS;

PARTICULARLY ADAPTED TO THE CLASSICS.

IN the works of the poets, painters, and statuaries, the greatest characteristic of Jupiter is majesty. The ablest of the last was Phidias of Athens, and the Jupiter Olympius was his master-piece. Being asked from what pattern he framed so divine a figure, he answered, from the archetype which he found in Homer (A. l. 528, 29, 30), which Mr. Pope has thus translated,

> He spoke, and awful bends his sable brows;
> Shakes his ambrosial curls and gives the nod,
> The stamp of Fate and sanction of the God:
> High heav'n with trembling the dread signal took,
> And all Olympus to the center shook.

It is observed, that all the personal strokes in this description relate to the hair, the eye-brows, and the beard (before spoken of). And to these the best heads of Jupiter owe most of their dignity. However mean our opinion may be of these appurtenances, and of the last particularly, yet all over the east a full beard still conveys the idea of majesty, as it did then amongst the Greeks; as their busts of Jupiter and the medals of their kings testify. But Rome, long before she lost her liberty, had parted with this natural ornament; insomuch that a beard was only worn by persons under disgrace or misfortune. Virgil therefore, in his imitation of this passage (Æn. 9. l. 104, 5, 6), has preserved only the nod, with its stupendous effect; but neglected the hair, the eyebrows, and the beard, those chief pieces of imagery, whence the artist took the idea of a countenance proper for the king of gods and men.

His

His statue in the Verospi palace at Rome, though one of the best extant, does by no means come up to the idea which the ancient poets have impressed of him. Yet the dignity of his look, the fullness of the hair about his face, the venerable beard, the sceptre in his left hand, and the fulmen in his right, easily bespeak the deity represented.

But the ancient sceptres were not short and adorned, like the modern; but as long, at least, as the bearer. Originally they were no other than walking-sticks. That of Latinus was a young tree stript of its branches. Æn. xii.

The fulmen had three different meanings, as differently represented. One way it is a conical wreath of flames, like the bolt. This was held down in the hand, and shewed Jupiter to be mild and calm. Another way it is the same figure, with two transverse darts of lightning, and sometimes with wings on each side, to denote rapidity. This represented him as executing vengeance. The *thundering legion* bore this upon their shields, which spread over all the field; as is seen in the Antonine pillar. The epithets of *trifidum* and *trisculum* (three-forked) are given to this. The third way is a handful of flames, which Jupiter holds up, when exacting punishment in a more extraordinary manner. But it was neither the sceptre nor the fulmen of Jupiter, but that air of majesty which the artists endeavoured to express in his countenance, which chiefly indicated the superiority of Jupiter on all occasions. The last kind are the *iracunda fulmina* of Horace.

On a gem at Florence, the mild Jupiter appears with a mixture of dignity and ease; that serene majesty which Virgil gives him, when receiving Venus with such paternal tenderness in the first Æneid.

But the statues of the terrible Jupiter differ in every particular from those of the mild. The last were generally of white marble, the other of black. The mild sat with an air of tranquillity. The terrible stood, and was more or less disturbed, with an angry or clouded countenance, and the hair so discomposed as to fall half way down the forehead. Yet he is never represented so angry but that he still retains his majesty.

On medals and gems the thundering Jupiter holds up the three-forked fulmen, standing in a chariot hurried on by four horses. And the poets describe the noise of his thunder, as caused by the rattling of his chariot and horses over the arch of heaven. Thus Horace, (Od. l. 1. 34.) according to Mr. Francis,

> For lo! that awful heav'nly fire,
> Who frequent cleaves the clouds with fire,
> Parent of day, immortal Jove,
> Late through the floating fields of air,
> The face of heav'n serene and fair,
> His thundering steeds and winged chariot drove!

Juno had various characters among the Romans. The Juno Matrona is covered like a Roman matron, with a long robe from head to foot. By this name Horace speaks of her in the battle of the giants; though at other times she is indifferently called by this, or that of the Juno Romana. So *gens togata* signified the Roman people.

But the Juno Regina, and the Juno Moneta, are always in a more splendid and magnificent habit. In the first Æneid, Virgil speaks of the Carthaginian Juno; in the second of the Juno Argiva, who was worshipped under that name even in Italy.

The Mild Juno appears on a Greek medal, with a gentle and good-natured countenance, standing in a chariot drawn by peacocks. Here she appears almost naked. So Homer gives her the epithet of λευκώλενος, with white elbows or arms. But he is never imitated in this by the Roman poets. She is represented by all of them as an imperious and jealous wife, oftener scolding than caressing. It is wonderful that she should be thus generally exposed in a disagreeable light, when considered on all hands as the patroness of marriage.

Pallas or Minerva is a beauty, but of a severer kind, having none of the graces or softnesses of Venus. Dignity, firmness, and composure, with a kind of masculine sternness, form the distinguishing character of her face; which has therefore been often mistaken for that of Alexander the Great. Her dress and attributes are well adapted to her character. Her head is armed with an helmet, and the plume nods dreadfully in the air. Her right hand holds a spear, and her left a shield, with the head of the dying Medusa thereon. The same figure is seen upon her

her breast-plate, and is sometimes most beautiful, and sometimes quite the reverse. The Strozzi-Medusa at Rome has indeed a dead look, but with it a beauty which death itself cannot extinguish. The poets describe both the beauties and horrors of Medusa's face, and her serpents, particularly two, whose tails are entwined under her chin, and their heads reared over her forehead. (Ovid Met. iv. 793.) Minerva herself has sometimes serpents about her bosom and shoulders.

The poets and artists agree. They give to the aspect of Minerva much beauty, but more terror. With all her grace, she is entitled the virago, and the stern goddess. They speak of a threatening turn in her eyes. Virgil ascribes a fiery motion to those of the Palladium (the tutelary Minerva). As making her appearance first in Africa, she has much of the Moor in her complexion; and her light-coloured eye shews it more strongly. From this colour of her eyes she is called by Homer γλαυκωπις, or grey-eyed; though it is strange that no poet of the Augustan age has copied this epithet.

Jupiter, Juno, and Minerva, are frequently joined together by the Roman authors, as well as in ancient inscriptions and in the works of the artists. They were considered as the guardians of the empire, and invoked by name, while the rest were referred to in general. Hence Cicero addresses—"Thee, O greatest "Jupiter!—and thee, O royal Juno!—and thee, "Minerva!—and ye, the other immortal gods and "goddesses!" The same distinction is in Livy. They are frequently seen together on gems and medals; and sometimes (as in a medal of Antoninus) they are represented by their attributes only; as Minerva, by the owl; Jupiter, by the eagle; and Juno, by the peacock.

Neptune is generally represented standing with a long trident in his right hand, (Ovid Met. vi. l. 77.)

> The god of ocean, figur'd standing, here
> With his long trident strikes the ragged rock.

This was his peculiar sceptre; and the same poet says, that with the stroke of it, the waters were let loose for the general deluge, (Met. 1.)

Then.

Then with his mace the monarch ſtruck the gound,
With inward trembling earth receiv'd the wound,
And riſing ſtreams a ready paſſage found.

But this was laid aſide when he was to appeaſe the ſtorm, (Met. 1. l. 331.)

> The ſea-god lays aſide his trident mace,
> And ſmooths the waves.

His aſpect is always majeſtic, ſerene and placid in good figures, whatever occaſion may be given for anger and diſturbance, (Virgil Æn. 1. l. 130, 1.)

> Much mov'd and ſeeing from his wat'ry bed,
> Above the waves he rear'd his placid head.

He is deſcribed by the poets as paſſing over the ſurface of the waters, in his chariot drawn ſwiftly by ſea-horſes, (Virgil Æn. 1. l. 159, 60.)

> His ſteeds he turns, upborne in open air,
> And giving to his eaſy car the reins,
> With rapid flight he ſkims the liquid plains.

Venus is figured with the prettieſt face that can be conceived. She has all the taking airs, wantonneſſes, and graces, which the poets and artiſts could confer upon her. Her ſhape the moſt bewitching; all ſoft and full of tenderneſs. Her complexion ſo exquiſite, that it required the utmoſt ſkill of Apelles to expreſs it. Her eyes were occaſionally wanton, quick, lan-guiſhing, or petulant. Her face and air were correſ-pondent. Sometimes a treacherous ſmile is evident on her face. But in whatſoever circumſtances ſhe is repreſented, all about her is graceful and charming. And this is no where more conſpicuous than in the Venus of Medici. If in this figure ſhe is not really modeſt, ſhe at leaſt counterfeits modeſty extremely well, according to Ovid, (De Art. Amand. l. 2. v. 613, 14.)

> Where Venus 'ſelf, with half-averted face,
> With her left hand o'erſhades the ſecret place.

With regard to ſhape and proportion, this ſtatue will ever be the ſtandard of female beauty and ſoftneſs. Some few have ſuſpected the head, but without ſuffi-cient reaſon, to have been the work of another artiſt; while others have diſcovered beauties, which ſeem only to have been the work of their own fancies.

They

They say that three different paffions are expreffed in it; that at your firſt approach, averſion appears in her look. Move a ſtep or two, and you perceive compliance in it. One ſtep more (ſay they) to the right, turns it into a little inſulting ſmile, as if ſhe had made ſure of you.

Befides the infulting ſmile with which ſhe appears in ſome figures, ſhe is repreſented ſmiling in others, and in a moſt perſuaſive attitude. Such was the Erycina ridens of Horace, and the Venus Appias in the forum ; and ſuch was the deſign on the medal of Aurelius, in which Venus is entreating Mars. This laſt was inſcribed to the Veneri Victrici, as ſure of carrying her point. In a ſtatue at Florence, ſhe holds one of her hands round the neck of Mars, and the other on his breaſt enforcing her requeſt. Virgil deſcribes her in theſe circumſtances urging her petition to the demurring Vulcan, (Æn. viii. l. 387, 8.)

———She ſpoke, and threw
Her arms around him with reſiſtleſs grace,
And footh'd him, doubting, with a ſoft embrace.

She is alſo frequently repreſented as the genius of indolence, reclined on a bed in a languiſhing poſture, and generally attended by Cupids, the miniſters of her commands. She thus appears in one of the fineſt-coloured pictures in the Barnardini Palace at Rome. The air of the head rivals Guido, as the colouring does Titian.

Yet in the poets of the third age, as Flaccus and Statius, ſhe appears in a quite contrary character, as the furious Venus, or the goddeſs of jealouſy. The laſt of theſe poets has a Venus improba. If this be not the ſame with the furious, it can only ſuit the vicious or abandoned Venus.

Mars is never repreſented without his attributes, the helmet and ſpear. He does not even quit theſe when going on his amours. His moſt celebrated one, next to that with Venus, was with Rhea Sylvia, the mother of Romulus and Remus. In a relievo belonging to the Bellini Family at Rome, having deſcended, he moves towards Rhea, who lies aſleep. On the reverſe of the medal of Antoninus, he is ſuſpended in the air, juſt over the Veſtal Virgin. There is a paſſage in Juvenal, on this occaſion, which ſhews the uſefulneſs of antiques for the explanation of the poets (Juv. Sat. 11.)

> Or elfe a helmet for himfelf he made,
> Where various warlike figures were inlaid:
> The Roman wolf fuckling the twins was there,
> And Mars himfelf armed with his fhield and fpear,
> Hov'ring above his creft, did dreadful fhow,
> As threat'ning death to each refifting foe,
>
> DRYDEN.

Juvenal here defcribes the fimplicity of the old Roman foldiers, and the figures that were generally engraven on their helmets. The firft was the wolf giving fuck to Romulus and Remus. The fecond, which is comprehended in the two laft verfes, is not fo intelligible. The commentators are extremely at a lofs to know what is meant by the *Pendentifque Dei*, as it is in the original. Some fancy it to exprefs only the great embofíment of the figure; others, that it hung off the helmet in *alto relievo*, as in the foregoing tranflation. Lubin thinks him faid to be hanging, becaufe the fhield which bore him, hung on the left fhoulder. One old interpreter thinks, that by hanging, is only meant a pofture of bending forward to ftrike the enemy. Several learned men imagine a fault in the tranfcriber, and that it fhould be *pendentis*; but upon no authority. Mr. Addifon has certainly hit upon the true meaning. The Roman foldiers (fays he), who were not a little proud of their founder and the military genius of the republic, ufed to bear on their helmets the firft hiftory of Romulus, who was begot by Mars and fuckled by a wolf. The figure of the god was made, as if defcending on the prieftefs. The occafion required that his body fhould be naked. (Ovid. de Faft. 1. 3.)

> Then too, our mighty Sire, thou waft difarmed,
> When thy rapt foul the lovely prieftefs charm'd
> That Rome's high founder bore—

though on other occafions he is drawn as Horace defcribes him,

> Begirt with adamantine coat of mail.

The fculptor, however to diftinguifh him, has given him his attributes, a fpear in one hand, and a fhield in the other. As he was reprefented defcending, his figure appeared fufpended in the air over the Veftal Virgin, in which fenfe the word *pendentis* is extremely proper and poetical. The fame figures are alfo on another

another medal of Antoninus Pius, ſtamped in compliment to that emperor for his excellent government, whom the ſenate regarded as a ſecond founder. The ſtory alluded to, is thus related by Ovid (de Faſt. lib. 3. eleg. 1.)

As the fair Veſtal to the fountain came,,
(Let none be ſtartled at a Veſtal's name)
Tir'd with the walk, ſhe laid her down to reſt,
And to the winds expos'd her glowing breaſt
To take the freſhneſs of the morning air,
And gather'd in a knot her flowing hair:
While thus ſhe reſted on her arm reclin'd,
The hoary willows waving with the wind,
And feather'd quires that warbled in the ſhade,
And purling ſtreams that through the meadow ſtray'd,
In drowſy murmurs lull'd the gentle maid.
The god of war beheld the virgin lie,
The god beheld her with a lover's eye;
And by ſo tempting an occaſion preſs'd,
The beauteous maid, whom he beheld, poſſeſs'd:
Conceiving as ſhe ſlept, her fruitful womb
Swell'd with the founder of immortal Rome.
ADDISON.

Vulcan, the god of fire, is never otherwiſe deſcribed than as a mere immortal blackſmith. But the poets have given him the additional diſgrace of Lameneſs, (Horat. Od. 1. 4.)

While Vulcan's glowing breath inſpires
The toilſome forge, and blows up all its fires.

He is black, and hardened from his cuſtomary labour, with a fiery red face; thence called *ardens Vulcanus*. He is ever the ſubject of pity or ridicule; the grand cuckold of heaven; and his lameneſs ſerved only to divert the gods. (Ovid. de Art. Amand. lib. 2. v. 567, 8, 9, 10.

How oft woul'd Vulcan's too laſcivious bride
His large ſplay-feet and callous hands deride,
And hobbling, while his abſence this allows,
Ape, before Mars, the limping of her ſpouſe!
'Twas pretty all; whate'er ſhe did became;
Such winning grace adorn'd the lovely dame.

Veſta had no ſtatue. Ovid indeed ſpeaks of her images in one place (Faſt. lib. 3. v. 45, 6); but in the courſe

course of the same work corrects himself (Fast. lib. 6. v. 295 and seq.)

> Long thought I, Vesta had her statues too,
> But in her temple no such form I view;
> Fire unextinguish'd there indeed is known,
> But Vesta and the fire no image own.

The figures which are supposed to be hers, having nothing which would not be as proper for a Vestal Virgin. Even those on medals, which have her name, may only mean one of the Vestals her representatives. And indeed there is one inscribed with the name of Vesta, wherein the figure is in the act of sacrificing, which is applicable to the priestess, but by no means to the goddess.

Apollo is always to be distinguished in his statues and heads by the beauty of the face, in which there is an air of divinity not to be conceived without the help of the artist. He is more comely than Mercury, but not so effeminate as Bacchus, who rivals him in beauty. His features are quite regular, his limbs exactly proportioned, and there is as much softness as is consistent with strength. He is ever young and beardless. His long and beautiful hair falls in easy waves down his shoulders, and sometimes over his breast. A grace results from the whole, which it were a vain talk to describe to any person who has not seen the *Apollo Belvidera*. (Tibull. lib. 2. eleg. 3. v. 11. 12.)

> Admetus' herds the fair Apollo fed;
> Nor harp, nor unshorn locks avail'd him then.

In the statue just mentioned, the noblest in the world, he is represented as the *Apollo Venator*. His hair is gathered a little above his forehead. His robe, fastened with a gem over his breast, falls loosely down his back, and is thrown over his arm. His feet are covered with fine buskins: the rest of his body is naked; and he has a bow in his hand, as if he had just discharged an arrow.

The Musical Apollo is sometimes naked, with the hair gathered over the forehead, his lyre in one hand, and his plectrum in the other. Sometimes he is dressed in a long robe, with his hair flowing at full length, and crowned with laurel.

Diana, the goddess of the chace, is commonly represented as running, with her vest flying back, though girt

girt around her. Her stature is tall and her face, though very handsome, is somewhat manly. Her legs are naked, well-shaped and strong. Her feet are sometimes clad in buskins, and sometimes bare. A quiver adorns her shoulder, and she has in her right-hand a spear or bow. These statues were frequent in woods. The story of Actæon is to be seen on a gem in Maffei's Collection.

Ceres has her head crowned either with corn or poppies, and her robes fall down to her feet. Her beauty seems to have been of the brunette kind; and her dress was adapted to her complection. But her breasts are in most figures represented very large. Virgil describes her as regarding the husbandman from heaven, and blessing his work. (Georg. lib. 1. v. 95. 6.)

> Nor from high heav'n amid the starry train
> The yellow Ceres him beholds in vain.

In this character she appears in a picture in the Vatican manuscript.

Mercury, as the messenger of Jupiter, is young, airy, and light; all proper for swiftness. His limbs are finely turned, and he is inferior in beauty to none of the gods, except Apollo and Bacchus. (Horat. Carm. lib. 1. ode 2. v. 41 and seq.)

> Or thou, fair Maia's winged son, appear,
> And mortal shape, in prime of manhood, bear;
> Declar'd the guardian of th' imperial state,
> Divine avenger of great Cæsar's fate.

The attributes by which he is distinguished, are the petasus, or winged cap; the talaria, or wings for his feet; and the caduceus, or wand, entwined by two serpents, His harp, or long sword, is added to these, with a particular hook to the latter. He is thus represented in the Vatican manuscript, with his vest floating behind him in the air, to denote his swiftness.

We have already given a full account of this deity, in the chapter of Mercury; so that nothing material can be here added. We shall therefore take leave of the reader by presenting him with the translation of an ode, probably written for the celebration of his feast, in which his ingenuity and office are fully described. (Horat. Carm. lib. 1. ode 10.)

> Thou God of Wit, from Atlas sprung,
> Who by persuasive pow'r of tongue,

And graceful exercise, refin'd
The savage race of human kind;
Thou winged messenger of Jove,
And all th' immortal pow'rs above;
Thou parent of the bending lyre,
Thy praise shall all its sounds inspire;
Artful and cunning to conceal
Whate'er in playful theft you steal;
When from the god, who gilds the pole,
Ev'n yet a boy, his herds you stole,
With angry look the threat'ning pow'r
Bad thee thy fraudful prey restore;
But of his quiver too beguil'd,
Pleas'd with the theft, Apollo smil'd.
Thou wast the wealthy Priam's guide,
When safe from stern Atrides' pride,
Through hostile camps, which round him spread
Their watchful fires, his way he sped.
Unspotted spirits you consign
To blissfull seats and joys divine,
And powerful with your golden wand
The light unbodied crowd command.
Thus grateful does thy office prove
To gods below, and gods above.

INDEX.

INDEX.

A

	Page
ABAS turned by Ceres into a newt, or water-lizard	114

Achelous, who assumed all shapes, conquered by Hercules 135
   An explication of this fable *ibid*
Acheron sent to hell, and transformed into a river 48
Achilles, his birth and education, 153. Is concealed, to prevent his going to Troy, and is discovered by Ulysses, *ibid*. Divine honours paid him 154
Acrisius shuts up Danae in a brazen tower, 33. Causes Danae and her son Perseus to be put into a chest, and cast into the sea, 144. Receives an accidental hurt, which causes his death *ibid*
Actæon turned into a stag, and devoured by his own dogs, 82. The literal sense of the fable *ibid*
Adonis beloved by Venus, 92. Killed by a wild boar, and turned by that goddess into the flower anemone *ibid*
Æacus, who, his history 53
Ægeus throws himself from a rock, and is drowned in the sea, which afterwards was called the Ægean sea 151
Ægis, Jupiter's shield, why called by this name 30
Ægina, corrupted by Jupiter under the appearance of fire 32
Aglaia, one of the graces 79
Æolus, god of the winds, his history 157
Æsculapius, the god of physic, his birth and skill 69. His coming to Italy in the form of a serpent, 70. Killed by Jupiter, *ibid*. The origin of the fable, 71. The manner in which he was represented *ibid*
Æta, the father of Medea, deprived of the golden fleece 148
Aglaia, one of the graces, and the wife of Vulcan 79
Alchymy, or the transmutation of metals, &c. founded only on the names given to the planets 230
Alcides, one of the names of Hercules 137
Alcithoe, for deriding the priestesses of Bacchus, transformed into a bat 121
Alcmena, deceived by Jupiter under the form of her husband Amphytrion 32
Alecto, one of the furies 56
Alpheus, in love with Diana 83

Altars,

INDEX.

Altars, sacred groves, and sacrifices, 253. Of the simplicity of the most early ages, and the introduction of altars, 254. The original of sacred groves, *ibid.* Of the ancient sacrifices, *ibid.* Of human victims, 255. The ceremonies used at sacrifices, and the manner in which they were performed   256, 257
Althæa causes the death of her son   83
Amalthæa, the goat that nursed Jupiter   90
Amathus the women of changed into oxen   93
Amazons, defeated by Hercules   132
Ambarvalia, festivals in honour of Ceres, how performed 117
Amphion, said to raise the walls of Thebes by the harmony of his lyre   156
Amphitrite, Neptune's wife   41
Emycus, son of Neptune, killed by Pollux   142
Ancile, a brass buckler, said to be sent from heaven   110
Andromeda, exposed to a sea monster, delivered by Perseus 144
Anteus, a giant squeezed to death by Hercules   134
Antiope, debauched by Jupiter in the form of a satyr   32
Apollo, his birth and adventures, 60. The principal places where he was worshipped, 64. The origin of the fable of Apollo, 66. In what manner he was represented, 68. His offspring, 69. His oracle at Delphos described   65
Arachne pretending to excel Minerva in weaving, is turned into a spider, 106. The origin of this fable   108
Ariadne gives Theseus a clue, by which he gets out of the labyrinth; but he ungratefully leaves her; she is found by Bacchus, who takes her, 121. Her crown turned into a constellation   *ibid*
Argonauts, Jason's companions, who attended him in his expedition to fetch the golden fleece, 147. The origin of the fable of the Argonauts expedition   149
Argus, who had an hundred eyes, ordered to watch Io, but is killed by Mercury, when Juno turns him into a peacock, 34. This fable explained   *ibid*
Arion, a skilful musician, being robbed and thrown into the sea, is carried to land on the back of a dolphin   156
Aristæus, his history   75
Auruspices, or foretelling future events, by inspecting the entrails of victims, 241. From whence these superstitious observances were derived, *ibid.* The manner in which the entrails were examined, and what were the rules of judging   *ibid*
Ascalaphus, telling that Proserpine had eaten some grains of a pomegranate, is transformed into a toad   45
Asterio, carried away by Jupiter in the shape of an eagle   32
Astrea returns to heaven, and is changed into the constellation Virgo   187

Astrology,

INDEX.

Aſtrology, its origin, 227. The names of the Zodiac, and thoſe of the planets, imagined to be indications of their ſeveral offices, and to produce good and evil, according to their names, 228. The ſigns ſuppoſed to preſide over all parts of the human body 230
Atalanta and Hippomenes turned into lions 93
Atlas, his deſcent and offspring, 7. His exploits, 8. Perſeus, by ſhewing him Meduſa's head, turns him into a mountain, 9. The origin of the fable of Atlas *ibid*
Atropos, one of the deſtinies 49
Atys, beloved by Cybele, is murdered by his father's order, 26. Turned into a pine-tree *ibid*
Augeas's ſtable, containing three thouſand oxen, cleanſed by Hercules in a day, and himſelf ſlain for his perfidy 131
Augury, or forming a judgment of futurity by the flight of birds, 236. From whence it aroſe, 237. The manner in which the ceremony was performed, and what were the rules of judging, *ibid*. Of the ſacred chickens, and the other methods of divination, 238. Of the college of augurs, and the qualifications neceſſary to render a perſon capable of being choſe into the office 239
Aurora, her deſcent, 5. Carries Cephalus and Tithonus into heaven, *ibid*. Her deſcription 6

B

Bacchanalia and Brumalia, feſtivals in honour of Bacchus 123
Bacchus, his education and exploits, 119. His names, 122. His principal feſtivals, 123. How repreſented by the poets and painters, *ibid*. The true origin of this fabulous deity, 124. His attendants 125
Battus, turned into a touch-ſtone 88
Belides, their crime and puniſhment in Tartarus 57
Bellerophon, his hiſtory, 145. The origin of the fable *ibid*
Bellona, the goddeſs of war, deſcribed 113
Boar of Erimanthus taken by Hercules 130
Bolina, to ſave herſelf from Apollo, throws herſelf into the ſea 64
Bona Dea, one of the titles of Cybele 25
Boreas, the North wind, his hiſtory and offspring 158
Branchidæ, oracle of 250
Britomartis, being entangled in her own nets, is ſaved by Diana 82
Bull, one that breathed fire, taken by Hercules 131
Buſiris, a cruel tyrant taken by Hercules, and ſacrificed to Neptune 134

C.

Cabiri, three great deities introduced from Egypt into Samotbracia 181

Cacus,

INDEX.

Cacus, the son of Vulcan, a notorious robber, killed by Hercules 103
Cadmus, his history, 154. He and his wife Hermione turned to serpents, 155. This fable explained ibid
Cælus, the son of Gaia or Terra 2
Cæculus, son of Vulcan 103
Cænis, transformed into a man 42
Califto, debauched by Jupiter under the form of Diana; turned into a bear, and made a constellation 31
Calliope, one of the Muses presiding over rhetoric 77
Calumny an altar erected to her, 193. A picture of this goddess drawn by Appelles described ibid
Capitol at Rome described 267
Castalia turned into a fountain 64
Castor and Pollux, their birth and actions, 141. Their sharing immortality between them, and being made the constellation Gemini 143
Cecrops turned into apes 15
Celeus, killed by Ceres 114
Cephalus, beloved by Aurora. 5. Kills his wife Procris without design 6
Cerberus described, 52. Dragged out of hell by Hercules, 133. The origin of the fables related of this monster 59
Ceres, her birth, 113. Her adventures while in search of her daughter Proserpine, 114. Her several names, and a description of the manner in which sacrifices were offered to her, 115. The origin of the fables, and of the mysterious rites of Ceres, 116. The manner in which she was represented by the poets and painters, 118. The temple of Ceres and Proserpine 264
Chaos, according to Hesiod, the father of the gods, 1. Why represented as a god ibid
Charon, his office and character, 51. The origin of this fabulous character 60
Charybdis, turned into a whirlpool 164
Chenchrius, killed by Diana, and transformed into a fountain 84
Chimæra, destroyed by Bellerophon 146
Chione, deprived of speech by Diana 83
Circe, a famous sorceress, banished for killing her husband, 76. falls in love with Glaucus, and turns her rival Scylla into a sea monster, ibid. Turns the companions of Ulysses into swine, ibid. The origin of this fable ibid
Cissus, transformed by Bacchus into the plant ivy 121
Clemency, altars and images erected to this virtue 191
Clio, one of the Muses, presiding over history 78
Clotho, one of the destinies 49
Clytie, changed into a sun-flower 64
Clytoris, deflowered by Jupiter in the shape of an ant 33

INDEX.

Cocytus one of the infernal rivers   49
Compitalia, a festival in honour of the Lares   173
Concordia, or concord, a goddess   189
Cupid, two of this name mentioned by the poets, 97. The manner in which Cupid is represented by the poets and painters, *ibid*. The origin of this little god derived from the Egyptian Horus   98
Cybele, or Vesta the elder, her history, and the description of her image, 25. Her priests, sacrifices, &c.   27
Cyclops described, 104. Their employment, *ibid*. Killed by Apollo   61
Cycnus, a savage prince, vanquished by Hercules   134
Cycnus, turned into a swan   61
Cynthia, one of the names of Diana   84
Cyparissus, turned into a cypress-tree   62
Cypria and Cytherea, names given to Venus   92
Cytheron, rejecting Tisiphone's love, is turned into a mountain   55

D.

Danae, seduced by Jupiter in the form of a golden shower   32
Daphne turned into a laurel   63
Dejanira, the wife of Hercules, the innocent cause of his death   136
Death, the daughter of Nox or Night   52
Deities inferior, attending mankind from their birth to their decease   182
Delius, one of the names of Apollo   64
Delphos, the temple and oracle of Apollo there   65
Destinies or Fates, their names and offices. The mythology of these characters   50
Deucalion, restores the race of mankind destroyed by the deluge, 13. Other fables of the same kind   243
Diana, her adventures, 85. Her several names, and the different characters under which she was worshipped, 86. The origin of the fable relating to this goddess, 87. Her temple at Ephesus described   263
Diomede, the tyrant of Thrace, vanquished by Hercules, and given as a prey to his own horses, who breathed fire, and were fed with human flesh   131
Dissertation on the theology of the heathens   194
Dryades, the nymphs of the forests and woods   168

E.

Echo, has a daughter by Pan; but he slighting her, she pined away till she had nothinng left but her voice   166
Egyptians, some remarks on the ceremonies used at their funerals, 59. Temples first built by the Egyptians   263

Eleusinian

Eleusinian rites 116
Elysian fields described, 58. The origin of the fables relating to them 59, 60
Endymion, beloved by Diana, 85. The origin of this fable *ibid*
Epimetheus, opens Pandora's box 11
Epulones, their office 260
Erato, one of the Muses presiding over elegiac poetry and dancing 78
Erichthonius, the son of Vulcan, the first inventor of chariots 103
Erimanthian boar seized by Hercules 130
Erisicthon, punished by Ceres with perpetual hunger, and sells his daughter under different shapes to supply his wants 114
Eumenides, or the Furies, described, 56, 57. The fable of the Furies explained 55
Euphrosyne, one of the Graces 79
Europa, debauched by Jupiter in the shape of a white bull, 154
Eurydice, her story 73
Eurystheus commands Hercules to perform his labours 129
Euterpe, the muse of tragedy 78

F.

Fame, how represented 188
Fauns, rural gods 127, 167
Faunus, a rural god, from whence sprung the Fauns 127, 167
Faustitas, or Public Felicity, many temples consecrated to her, 191. How represented *ibid*
Feciales, their office 260
Feronia, the goddess of woods and orchards 168
Fides, or Faith, the manner in which her sacrifices were performed 190
Flamines, their office 260
Flora, goddess of flowers 171
Floralia, feasts in honour of Flora *ibid*
Fortuna, or Fortune, worshipped as a goddess, 187. Her various names, *ibid*. How represented 188
Furies, their office, characters and persons described, 55. The fable of the Furies explained *ibid*

G.

Galanthis changed into a weasel 129
Gallus, or Alectryon, transformed into a cock 101
Ganymede, carried by Jupiter into heaven, and made his cup-bearer. 141
Genii, or Dæmons, attendant spirits, 175. The sacrifices and offerings made them *ibid*

Geryon,

INDEX.

Geryon, king of Spain, who had three bodies, killed by Hercules　132
Giants, their war with Jupiter, and defeat, 20. An explication of this fable　21, 22
Glaucus, a fisherman, made a sea god　162
Golden Age described　19
Golden Fleece, an account of the ram that bore it, 149. Its being guarded by a dragon and bulls breathing fire, *ibid.* And of its being carried away by Jason　*ibid*
Good Genius, a temple erected to him　192
Good Sense, an altar erected to him　191
Gorgons described　163
Graces, three attendants on the Muses, 79. Their origin, *ibid.* How represented　80
Grææ, sisters to the Gorgons, described　163
Groves, from whence they were considered as sacred　254

H.

Hamadryades, nymphs who animated some tree　168
Harpies, their names, and a description of them; with the mythology of their characters　50
Harpocrates, the god of silence, his origin　191
Health, her temple　192
Hebe, her birth and history, 140. Her temples　*ibid*
Hecate, one of the names given to Diana, 86. Her figure as goddess of the infernal regions, *ibid.* The origin of this goddess, and of her different names and characters　87
Helena, carried away by Theseus　151
Helle, when on the point of being sacrificed, is carried through the air on the ram that bore the golden fleece; but falling, is drowned in that sea, which, from her, is called the Hellespont　147
Hercules, his birth, 128. His labours, 129, 130, 131, 132, 133, 134, 135. His death, 136. The origin of these fables　139
Hermaphroditus and Salmacis, formed into one person called an Hermaphrodite　89
Hermes, one of Mercury's names　88
Hermione, the wife of Cadmus, turned into a serpent　155
Hesione, exposed to a sea monster, and delivered by Hercules　134
Hesperides, their garden guarded by a dragon with an hundred heads; Hercules kills the dragon, and takes away the golden fruit, 133. An explication of the fable of the Hesperides　139
Hesperus, the son of Atlas, transformed into the morning star　8
Hind, with brazen feet and golden horns, taken by Hercules　130

Hippolitus

INDEX.

Hippolitus rejects the solicitations of Phædra, flies to escape the effects of her revenge, and is killed by a fall from his chariot   151
Hippomenes and Atalanta turned into lions   193
Honour, her temple   189
Hope worshipped, 190. How represented   *ibid*
Horæ, or the Hours, their descent, and how employed   98
Horn of plenty, its origin   29
Hyacinthus, killed by Apollo, and changed into a flower   61
Hyades, lamenting the loss of their brother Hyas, are turned into stars   8
Hydra, a monstrous serpent, killed by Hercules   130
Hymen, his birth, and the manner in which he was represented, 98. His origin an Egyptian Horus   *ibid*
Hyperion, the son of Cælus and Terra, assassinated   4

J & I

Janus, his history, 23. His image described, 24. The meaning of the fable of Janus   25
Japetus, the father of Epimetheus and Prometheus   10
Jason, his birth and education, 146. Undertakes a voyage to fetch the golden fleece, which he gains by the assistance of Medea, 148. The actions of this sorceress, who follows him to Greece, *ibid*. Jason's leaving her, and her revenge   149
Idalia, one of the names of Venus   91
Idmon, the son of Apollo, killed by a wild boar   74
Idolatry, its original   198
Illustration of the Dii Majores of the Romans   275
Infernal regions described   48
Inferior deities, attending mankind from their birth to their decease   182
Inferior rural deities   186
Ino and Melicertes turned into Marine deities, and take the names of Leucothea and Palemon   161
Io, her story   34
Iolaus, at the intercession of Hercules, restored to youth, after his death, returns to earth to revenge the insults offered to the Heraclidæ   137
Iris, the messenger of Juno   38
Isis, an Egyptian goddess, whose worship was introduced at Rome   176
Itys murdered by Progne, and turned into a pheasant   111
Juno, her birth and name, 37. The manner in which she was represented   39
Jupiter, his birth and education, 29. His war with the giants, 30. His other exploits, 31. His intrigues, *ibid*. An explication of the fables related of Jupiter, 35. The manner in which he was represented, 36. His oracle at Dodona

dona described, 246. And that of Jupiter Ammon in
Lybia, 247. The temple of Jupiter Olympius, &c. 264
Ixion, his crime and punishment in Tartarus 56, 57

L.

Lachesis, one of the destinies 49
Lares, domestic gods, their descent, 173. The manner in
which they were represented *ibid*
Latona, the mother of Apollo and Diana, turns the clowns
of Lycia into frogs, for refusing to let her drink 60
Leda, debauched by Jupiter in the shape of a swan, 32.
Brings forth two eggs 141
Lethe, the river of forgetfulness 58
Leucippus stabbed 63
Leucothoe turned into the tree that bears frankincense 64
Liberty, altars and temples consecrated to her 191
Limniades, nymphs who frequented lakes 168
Linceus kills Castor, and is himself killed by Pollux 142
Linus punished with death, for presuming to sing with
Apollo 62
Linus, son of Apollo, his story, 74. The origin of the
fable, 75
Lucina, one of the names of Juno and of Diana 38, 85
Luna, or the Moon, one of Diana's names 84
Lupercalia, a feast celebrated in honour of Pan 166
Lycaon, for his impiety and inhumanity, turned into a wolf 31
Lycas, being hurled into the air by Hercules, falls into the ri-
ver Thermopolis, where he is transformed into a rock 136
Lycian clowns, turned into frogs, for muddying the water,
when Ceres wanted to drink 115
Lycurgus having affronted Bacchus, is deprived of his rea-
son 121

M.

Mænades, the priestesses and nymphs of Bacchus 126
Macris, the nurse of Bacchus 119
Magic, of two kinds, 232. Its origin, 234. Of calling up the
spirits of the dead *ibid*
Magna Pales, one of the names of Cybele. 27
Mars, how produced, 109. His different names, 110. His
intrigue with Venus, 101. His offspring, 111. The origin
of the fables relating to this god, 112. The manner in
which he has been represented by poets, painters, and
statuaries *ibid*
Marsyas, pretending to equal Apollo in music, is flead alive,
and afterwards changed into a river 62
Medea, a sorceress, assists Jason in obtaining the golden fleece,
148. Her exploits *ibid*

O 3 Medusa,

INDEX.

Medusa, her hair turned to snakes by Minerva, 106. All that looked at her turned into stones, *ibid*. Her head cut off by Perseus 144
Megæra, one of the furies 56
Melantho, surprised by Neptune as she was riding on a Dolphin 42
Meleager, his story, 82. His sisters turned into hen turkies 83
Melpomene, one of the Muses, who presided over lyric and epic poetry 78
Mentha, changed into mint 39
Mercury, his birth, thefts, and his other exploits, 87. His various offices, 88. The real origin of this fabulous deity, 89. His oracle in Achaia 251
Mercy, altars and temples erected to this virtue 191
Metra transforms herself into various shapes, and is as often sold by her father 42
Midas, for giving an unjust sentence against Apollo, is rewarded with asses' ears, 62. Bacchus grants his wish that whatever he touched might be changed into gold 121
Minerva, her several names, 105. Her character and exploits, 106. Her temples, statues, &c. 107. The origin of this goddess, and of the fables related of her, *ibid*. How represented by the poets and sculptors 109
Minos, one of the judges of hell, his history 53
Minotaur, a monster who lived on human flesh, killed by Theseus, 150. This fable explained 152
Mænades tear Orpheus in pieces 74
Momus censures the actions of the gods 158, 159
Morpheus, the god of sleep, described 159
Muses, their birth and distinct provinces, 77. Their origin 79
Mythology of the heathens, 211. Of fiction in general, *ibid*. By what means allegories became objects of faith, illustrated by some observations on the ceremonies with which the Egyptians buried their dead, 212. A prayer used by the Egyptians at their funerals, 213. Many of the heathen fables derived from the fictions of the poets, a concern for the honour of the ladies, and a similitude of names, 214. The sentiments of the Pagans in relation to the origin of the world, compared with those given us by Moses, 217. Of the golden age, as described by the philosophers and poets, 219. Of the fall of man, as described by Pythagoras, Plato, and several Indian and Chinese authors, 220. Of good or bad dæmons, *ibid*. Of the fables of the Titans and Giants, *ibid*. Traditions relating to the universal deluge, 222. The heathen fables filled with noble sentiments, 225. Of the morals of the Greek and Roman philosophers, *ibid*. In what Pagan idolatry consisted 223

N. Naiades,

N.

Naiades, nymphs of brooks and rivers 168
Napeæ, the tutelar guardians of vallies and flowery meads *ibid*
Næmean lion killed by Hercules 129
Nemefis, one of the goddeffes of juftice, how reprefented 187
Neptune, his defcent, 40. His remarkable actions, 41. The mythological fenfe of this fable, 43. The manner in which he was painted *ibid*
Nereus, a fea god 160
Nereids, fea nymphs, the fifty daughters of Nereus 161
Neffus, the centaur, killed by Hercules with a poifoned arrow 136
Niobe's children flain by Apollo, and herfelf ftupified with grief for the lofs of her children, is turned into a ftone, 63. The origin of this fable *ibid*
Nox, and her progeny 52
Nyfus, after having loft his purple lock of hair, and his kingdom, is transformed into a hawk 164

O.

Oceanus, the fon of Cælus and Terra 4
Omphale, queen of Lydia, gains fuch an afcendant over Hercules, as to make him fit among her women and fpin, 135
Ops, one of the names of Cybele 25
Oreades, nymphs who prefide over mountains 168
Orion, his furprifing birth and adventures, 159. Killed by Diana, and made a conftellation 160
Orpheus, his ftory, 73. The origin of this fable 74
Of Oracles, 242. That much of the happinefs of life is owing to our ignorance of futurity, *ibid*. On the firft rife of oracles, and the ufe made of them by the greateft legiflators, 243. Of the oracle of Jupiter at Dodona, *ibid*. A remarkable circumftance relating to this oracle, 245. Of the oracle of Jupiter Ammon in Lybia, 246. Of the oracle of Apollo at Delphos, a tradition concerning the rife of it, and the manner in which its anfwers were delivered, 247. Of the oracle of the Triphonius, 249. Of the oracles of the Branchidæ, 250. Of Apollo at Claros, and that of Mercury in Achaia, 251. Some obfervations on the different ways by which the fenfe of the oracles were conveyed 252
Orgia, feftivals in honour of Bacchus 123
Orus, an Egyptian deity 177
Ofiris, an Egyptian deity 176

P.

Palemon and Ino, changed into marine deities 162
Pales, the goddefs of fhepherds 169

Palilia,

INDEX.

Palilia, feasts in honour of Pales *ibid*
Palladium, a statue of Minerva, said to fall down from heaven 107
Pallas, one of the names of Minerva 105
Pan, the chief of all the rural gods, 165. His amours, *ibid*. His festivals, and the manner in which he s described by poets and painters 169
Pater Patratus, his office 260
Pandora, the first woman, 11. Her box, and the evils that spread from thence amongst mankind *ibid*
Parcæ, or Destinies, their office, and the mythology of their characters 49
Paris decides the dispute between the three goddesses, and gives the golden apple to Venus 93
Parthenis, one of the names of Minerva 105
Peace, an altar erected to her, 189. How represented *ibid*
Pecunia, or Money, a goddess 192
Pegasus, or flying horse, how produced, 80. The origin of the fable *ibid*
Penates, domestic deities, 174. Three ranks of them *ibid*
Pentheus, torn in pieces by his own mother and sisters 121
Perseus, his descent, 143. The gifts he received from the gods, 144. Cuts off Medusa's head, *ibid*. Turns Atlas into a mountain, 9. Delivers Andromeda, founds an academy, dies, and is placed among the stars, 144. An explanation of the fable of Perseus and Andromeda 146
Phœbe and Talayra carried away by Castor and Pollux 142
Phœbus, one of the names of Apollo 64
Phædra, attempts to debauch her son Hippolitus; her suit is rejected, and she lays violent hands on herself 151
Phaeton obtains leave of his father Apollo to drive the chariot of the sun for one day; but losing the reins, is struck down by Jupiter, 72. His sisters turned into poplar-trees, *ibid*. The origin of this fable *ibid*
Philomela turned into a nightingale 111
Phineus, tormented by the harpies, for revealing the mysteries of Jupiter 50
Phlegethon, one of the infernal rivers 49
Phlegyas burns the temple of Apollo, is punished in Tartarus 56
Phorcus, or Phorcys, one of the sons of Neptune, being vanquished by Atlas, who threw him into the sea, is changed into a sea-god 163
Phryxus rejects the advances of Ino, and escapes the effects of her revenge, by being carried through the air on the ram that bore the golden fleece 147
Picus turned into a wood-pecker 76

Piety,

INDEX.

Piety, or filial affection, what it was that occasioned a chapel being erected to this virtue   190
Planets, the names given them, became indications of their several offices, 228. Why they were supposed to produce metals   230
Pleiades, the daughters of Atlas, taken up into heaven, where they form the constellation that bears their name   8
Pluto, his descent, 44. Steals away Proserpine, 45. The manner in which he is represented by the painters and poets, 46. The mythology of the fable   *ibid*
Plutus and Pecunia deified by the Romans   192
Pollux and Castor, their birth and exploits, share immortality between them, and are made the constellation Gemini, 143. A temple erected to them   *ibid*
Polyhymnia, one of the Muses, who presided over harmony of voice and gesture   78
Polyphemus, a monstrous giant with but one eye   104
Pomona, the goddess of fruit-trees, courted and married by Vertumnus   172
Pontifex Maximus, or the high-priest, his office   259
Priapus, the tutelar deity of vine-yards and gardens. The several names given him, and his image described   170
Priests and priestesses of the Greeks and Romans, 258. Of the Pontifex Maximus, or the high-priest, 259. Of the Rex Sacrorum, *ibid*. Of the Flamines, 260. Of the Feciales, *ibid*. Of the Pater Patratus, *ibid*. Of the Epulones   *ibid*
Procris makes Cephalus a present of an unerring dart   6
Procrustes killed by Theseus   150
Prodigies, the superstition of the Romans in relation to them, and how they may be accounted for   231
Progne turned into a swallow   111
Prometheus makes a man of clay, and animates him with fire stolen from heaven, 10. His punishment, 11. Delivered by Hercules, *ibid*. This fable explained   12
Propœtides turned into stones   95
Proserpine carried away by Pluto, 45. Her various names, 47. The mythological sense of the fable   48
Proteus, the son of Neptune, one that could transform himself into any shape   162
Pyrene turned into a fountain   85
Pudicitia, or Chastity, honoured at Rome under two names 190
Pygmalion falls in love with a statue of his own making, which Venus, at his request turns into a woman   95
Pyrrha, the wife of Deucalion   93
Python, a monstrous serpent, slain by Apollo; and the origin of the fable   63

Rhadamanthus,

INDEX.

R.

Rhadamanthus, one of the judges of hell 53
Rex Sacrorum, his office 259
Rhea, one of the names of Cybele 25

S.

Sacrifices originally extremely simple, 254. Of human victims, 255. The ceremonies used at sacrifices, and the manner in which they were performed 256
Salmoneus punished in Tartarus, for imitating thunder, &c. 57
Salus, or Health, her temple, 192. How represented ibid
Saturn devours his male children, 14. Taken prisoner by Titan, but set at liberty by Jupiter, who afterwards dethrones him, 15. The fable of Saturn explained, 14, 15, 16, 17. Festivals in honour of Saturn, ibid. His amours ibid
Satyrs, the attendants of Bacchus, described, 127. Their original ibid
Sciron killed by Theseus 150
Scylla, the daughter of Phorcus, turned by Circe into a monster, throws herself into the sea, and is changed into a rock 163
Scylla, the daughter of Nysus, betrays her father, by cutting off a purple lock of hair, and is turned into a lark 164
Semele destroyed by Jupiter's embraces 33
Silence, worshipped by the Romans, 192. The origin of this supposed deity ibid
Silenus, the companion of Bacchus, described, 125. The origin of this fabulous character 127
Silver age described 36
Sisiphus, his punishment in Tartarus 57
Stable of Augeas cleaned by Hercules 132
Stymphalides, monstrous birds destroyed by Hercules 131
Styx, a river of hell 49
Sylvanus, a rural deity 126
Sylvani, who 167
Syrens, described, 81. The origin of the fable ibid
Syrinx flies from Pan, and is changed into a tuft of reeds 165

T.

Tantalus, his crime and punishment in Tartarus 57
Tartarus described, 54. The fabulous persons punished there, 56. The origin of these fables 57
Temples first built by the Egyptians, 261. The ceremonies used by the Romans before they began to build a temple, 262. Of the temple of Vulcan at Memphis, and an extraordinary chapel hewn out of one stone, 263. Of the temple of Diana at Ephesus, ibid. Of the temple of Ceres and Proserpine, 264. A particular description of the temple of Jupiter Olympus. Of his statue and his throne, ibid.

Of

INDEX.

Of the temple of Apollo at Delphos, and the immense treasures it contained, 267. Of the temple in Italy, *ibid.* Particularly the Pantheon, *ibid.* The capitol 268
Thalia, the muse of comedy 78
Thalia, one of the graces 79
Thamyris, contending with the Muses, is punished with blindness and cast into hell *ibid*
Themis, her birth and actions 186
Theology of the heathens, a dissertation upon it, 194 The first nations of the world had very exalted sentiments of the deity, *ibid.* Emblems of the deity become the cause of idolatry, 197. The reason of the names given to the signs of the Zodiac, 203. Egypt the grand mart of idolatry *ibid.* That the ancient eastern nations had a reserved meaning in all their fables, 205. On the deification of great and eminent men, 208. That the Greeks took their gods from the Egyptians, and the Romans from the Greeks *ibid*
Tereus, after marrying Progne, falls in love with her sister Philomela: her barbarous treatment; for which Tereus is turned into a lapwing 111
Terminalia, a Roman festival 171
Terminus, the god who presides over landmarks 170
Terra, the mother and wife of Cælus 2, 3
Tethys, the wife and sister of Oceanus 4
Theia, the daughter of Cælus and Terra, marries Hyperion, 4. Disappears in a storm of thunder and lightning *ibid*
Theophane, changed into an ewe by Neptune, who debauches her under the form of a ram 42
Theseus, his birth and exploits 150
Thetis, the mother of Achilles 153
Tiresias, deprived of sight by Minerva, but receives the gift of prophecy 106
Tisiphone, one of the furies, being rejected by Cythæron, kills him by throwing one of her snakes at him 55
Titans make war on Jupiter, and are subdued 20
Tithonus marries Aurora, and obtains immortality; but g owing decrepid with age, is turned into a grashopper 56
Tityus, his punishment in Tartarus 56
Triptolemus, fed by Ceres, and sent by her in a chariot to instruct mankind in the benefit of tillage 114
Triton, the son of Neptune, described 161
Trophonius, his oracle described 249
Truth, how represented 191
Tyndaridæ, who 141
Typhon, or Typhæus, one of the giants who made war against Jupiter, 21. His figure described *ibid*
Tyrrhenian merchants changed by Bacchus into dolphins 119

Venus,

INDEX.

V & U.

Venus, how produced, 90. Her various names, 91. Her actions, 92. The distinction of two Venuses, 94. An explanation of these fables, *ibid*. How represented, 95. Her attendants *ibid*

Vertumnalia, feasts in honour of Vertumnus 172

Vertumnus and Pomona, their story, 172. Vertumnus thought by some to be an emblem of the year *ibid*

Vesta the elder, her history, 25. The manner in which she is represented *ibid*

Vesta the younger, the goddess of fire, 27. Her chastity, 28. Vestal Virgins *ibid*

Victory, a goddess, how represented, 192

Virginia, the daughter of Aulus, dedicates a chapel to Pudicitia Plebeia 191

Virtue and Honour, temples erected to them 189

Vulcan, his employment, and the curious works he performed, 99. His various names, 100. Discovers Mars with his wife Venus, by means of a net, and exposes them to the ridicule of the gods, 101. The manner in which he was represented, *ibid*. The origin of these fables, *ibid*. His offspring, 102. His temple as Memphis described 263

Ulysses discovers Achilles, notwithstanding his being disguised, and takes him with him to the siege of Troy, 153. Is preserved from Circe's enchantments, 76. Blinds the giant Polyphemus 104

Urania, the divine muse 78

Uranus, the offspring of Gaia or Terra 2

X.

Xisuthrus, saved from the deluge, a Chaldæan tradition 222

Z.

Zephyrus blows Apollo's quoit against Hyacinthus's head, and kills him 61

Zodiac, its invention, and the reason of the names given to the signs 203, 204

FINIS.